LEE GEOK BOI

ASIAN
Noodles

mc Marshall Cavendish
Cuisine

To my daughters Shakuntala and Savitri, my son-in-law Tom, and my grandsons Arjuna and Rama.

Long may they enjoy many meals of home-cooked Asian noodles.

Designer: Bernard Go Kwang Meng
Photographer: Kiyoshi Yoshizawa, Jambu Studio

First published as Classic Asian Noodles
Copyright © 2007 Marshall Cavendish International (Asia) Private Limited

This new edition 2015

Published by Marshall Cavendish Cuisine
An imprint of Marshall Cavendish International

Other Marshall Cavendish Offices:
Marshall Cavendish Corporation. 99 White Plains Road, Tarrytown NY 10591-9001, USA • Marshall Cavendish International (Thailand) Co Ltd. 253 Asoke, 12th Floor, Sukhumvit 21 Road, Klongtoey Nua, Wattana, Bangkok 10110, Thailand • Marshall Cavendish (Malaysia) Sdn Bhd, Times Subang, Lot 46, Subang Hi-Tech Industrial Park, Batu Tiga, 40000 Shah Alam, Selangor Darul Ehsan, Malaysia

Marshall Cavendish is a trademark of Times Publishing Limited

National Library Board Singapore Cataloguing in Publication Data

Lee, Geok Boi, author.
Asian noodles / Lee Geok Boi. – Singapore : Marshall Cavendish Cuisine, ©2007.

Originally published 2007: Classic Asian noodles.
pages cm
ISBN : 978-981-45-6151-8 (paperback)

1. Noodles. 2. Cooking, Asian. I. Title

TX809.N65
641.822 – dc23   OCN892517145

Printed in Singapore by Craft Print International Ltd

Contents

Introduction

Although the history of noodles is somewhat shrouded in mystery, the Chinese were believed to have been eating noodles by A.D. 100, and China certainly has a larger variety of noodles than any other culture. Legend even has it that Venetian traveller Marco Polo returned from his epic sojourn in China with noodle-makers and made a noodle-eating nation out of Italy. This theory is disputed, but it remains undisputed that close contact with the Chinese, at first through trade and subsequently through migration, was what brought noodles to South East Asia. Archaeological digs in Singapore have uncovered large quantities of ceramic shards that some historians believe are from food containers, and these have been traced to kilns in southern China. In addition to trade in foodstuffs, Chinese migration to South East Asia and elsewhere also contributed to the spread of noodles. Today, thanks to global trade and the Japanese invention of instant noodles, there is almost nowhere in the world where we do not find noodles of some kind.

Singapore could possibly be called the noodle capital of the world, given the abundant variety of noodles and noodle dishes found here. No one in this city is more than 5 minutes away from a bowl of noodles albeit instant noodles. Freshly-prepared noodles are usually just a short walk away to the nearest food centre or coffee shop. Wet markets, supermarkets and provision shops carry an ever-increasing variety of fresh and dried noodles and the different fixings for noodle dishes. One reason is the predominance of southern Chinese in the population, creating an early demand for commercial noodle production, one of Singapore's earliest industries. Noodles are believed to have been the poor man's food in China up until the 16th century. Certainly in 19th century Singapore, millions of cheap bowls of noodles would have been downed by the thousands of manual labourers and the working classes in the growing city. Up to the 1970s, itinerant noodle hawkers prowled the city and suburbs before they came to be located permanently in sheltered hawker centres and food centres, then air-conditioned food courts in the 1990s. The multi-ethnic composition of Singapore's population is another reason for the wide range of noodle dishes found here. Burmese, Chinese from China, Indians, Indonesians, Japanese, Koreans, Malays, Thais and Vietnamese, among others, have all added their touch to Singapore's spread of noodle dishes. Demand and competition have brought new kinds of noodles and noodle dishes into the market. Innovative cooks invent new noodles such as Hong Kong's milk noodles. A relative newcomer are noodles made from soybean flour which gives these noodles a higher protein content than any other kind of noodles. Also fairly new are narrow flat mung bean noodles which once used to come only in thin strands.

In Asia, noodles can be divided into rice noodles, wheat noodles and noodles made from various starches, the best known being mung bean or cellophane noodles made from mung bean starch. Rice and wheat noodles come fresh and dried. However, not all fresh noodles are available in dried form and there are dried noodles that are not found fresh.

Outside of Asia, finding the right kind of noodles for a particular recipe will be a bit of a challenge. Labelling is confused and confusing. Names for noodles as well as their appearance change when they are exported. It is not unusual to see rice vermicelli that looks rather like mung bean noodles or vice versa, packaged with an unhelpful label. Different exporting countries make noodles with varying combinations of flours and starches, giving a different texture and appearance to the noodles, as well as different handling properties. A more accurate guide to the type of noodle is to read the ingredients label, although labelling is not always accurate. Only experience with that particular brand will yield the necessary knowledge about handling and flavour. While the recipes in this book indicate the noodles typically used in Asia, substitutions with another noodle preferably made of the same starch will give an equally tasty dish. In fact, some noodle stalls in Singapore give customers a choice of noodles to a standard preparation.

Asian noodle dishes are always one-dish meals as they invariably include vegetables and meat or seafood. Noodles are eaten most commonly for lunch, but they are also enjoyed for breakfast and as a snack throughout the day, and even for dinner. In some Asian communities, noodles take on symbolic significance when eaten during festivals such as the Lunar New Year. The long noodles are associated with longevity and are thus rarely cut up for that reason.

These recipes are meant to serve between four and six adults. So if you are planning to feed a larger party, remember to increase the quantities or try out a few different recipes. Noodle dishes are versatile and can easily be stretched to accommodate more guests.

The recipes are arranged according to the type of noodles required to recreate the authentic flavour as found in hawker stalls and in homes in Asia. Thus, for example, the section on rice noodles is categorised into rice vermicelli, broad rice noodles and mouse-tail noodles. Within these categories, the recipes are further organised into "dressed and fried noodles" or "soup noodles". Dressed and fried noodles are dishes with little or no gravy or at most a thick sauce. Soup noodles are those that need to be served in a bowl because of the liquid soup or gravy poured over the noodles. If followed fairly closely, these recipes will allow you to enjoy the authentic flavours of many of Asia's classic noodle dishes. Noodles have always been my favourite food. In my family, I became known as the "Noodle Queen," always preferring noodles to rice. I learnt to fry noodles in my teens before I learnt to cook rice and I have never lost my taste for or fascination with noodles. Since my first attempt at frying rice noodles, I have been collecting noodle recipes and trying them out for more than four decades. Wherever my travels take me, I will always be checking out the markets and supermarkets for noodles and ingredients for preparing noodle dishes. This book of Asian noodles is the result of this lifelong passion for noodles. Enjoy!

Lee Geok Boi

Making Noodles

The art of Chinese noodle-making lies in getting those long strands, but if we are not purist and content just to get a tasty dish of fresh noodles in a place where fresh Asian noodles are not easily found, a cook with a bag of flour, a rolling pin and a long, sharp knife can turn out tasty homemade noodles. Wheat flour noodles are the easiest to make at home, especially if you already have a pasta extruder with a linguine or vermicelli plate. But even without one, wheat flour noodles can be hand-rolled and cut, the way it is traditionally done in many parts of Asia. The Northern Chinese make noodles by pulling a soft wheat flour dough into long, thin strands, an art that some Chinese noodle restaurants put on display for customers. Wheat noodles can also be made by pinching the dough into small pieces, the way buckwheat noodles were once made in Japan.

Rice noodles, on the other hand, are made neither by rolling, pulling nor pinching. Broad-cut rice noodles are made from a batter steamed into sheets which are then cut into strips of varying widths. In the case of rice vermicelli, the semi-cooked rice flour dough is extruded directly into a steamer or first onto a piece of banana leaf or similar, and the nest of rice flour strands steamed. For this, you need a hand-held extruder with extruder plates of different sizes for the different kinds of rice vermicelli. The piece of home kitchen equipment that does this job perfectly is a South Indian string-hopper maker found in many South Indian and Sri Lankan homes. Produced in India, this extruder is used not only for rice vermicelli but also for *muruku*, a crispy South Indian snack that some will insist is really a kind of deep-fried noodle.

An essential piece of equipment for rolling out the dough when making wheat noodles is a long rolling pin. Chinese rolling pins come without handles and in different lengths for noodle-making. A good substitute would be a French rolling pin which has a tapered convex centre portion but no handles. To cut the noodles, you need a long knife. A bread knife

will not do as this knife calls for a sawing motion, which is what you must not do when cutting noodles. Noodles have to be cut in one single stroke albeit a slow stroke. The tip of the knife is positioned at one end of the piece of folded dough, with the knife held at an angle that ensures that the noodle strip is evenly sized. The knife is then pressed down into the dough with a slight roll at the bottom so that the strand is cut right through. The cut strand is then pushed away from the sheet with the knife and dusted with cornflour. You pick up speed with practice.

Another essential in Chinese noodle-making is alkali salts which give Chinese noodles their bite. The alkali salts called "*kee*" in Hokkien may be potassium bicarbonate ($KHCO_3$) or sodium bicarbonate ($NaHCO_3$) which is more commonly known as bicarbonate of soda or baking soda. Commercial noodle-makers may also combine the two alkalis. While sodium bicarbonate comes white in colour, potassium bicarbonate is sold as either orange or yellow-coloured crystals which

have to be pounded to a powder. Asian stores around the world may carry these salts dissolved in water and variously labelled "potassium water", "lye" or "alkali water". The alkali salts give wheat noodles their characteristic yellowish tint as well as their "springiness".

Fresh uncooked noodles can be stored in the refrigerator for up to a week. Wheat noodles should be dusted liberally with cornflour—not wheat flour—to prevent them from sticking together. (Wheat flour gets absorbed into the noodles unlike cornflour.) Broad rice noodles are already oily when prepared, but oiling the cut noodles further is an added precaution against sticking. Rice vermicelli may be stacked together when cool and will not stick together. In general, bag noodles into serving portions if possible, as the noodles harden in the refrigerator and break up when pulled apart into serving sizes. To soften, leave the noodles at room temperature, reheat briefly or blanch in warm water if required immediately.

Fresh Rice Vermicelli or String-Hoppers MIFEN OR IDYAPAM

Thin rice vermicelli, also known as *idyapam* in Tamil, is often freshly made in South Indian and Sri Lankan homes. If you have a string-hopper extruder (page 9), rice vermicelli is not difficult to make.

MAKES ABOUT 600 G (1 LB 5¹⁄₃ OZ)

1 tsp salt

750 ml (24 fl oz / 3 cups) boiling water

500 g (1 lb 1¹⁄₂ oz) rice flour

Muslin cloth or banana leaf

Cooking oil for greasing

1. Put the salt and water into a large pot and bring to the boil. Using a wooden spoon, quickly stir rice flour into boiling water to form a thick paste. Turn off heat. Shape paste into a lump, cover with a clean kitchen towel and set aside to cool.

2. When cool enough to handle, knead to get a smooth dough that is not sticky to the touch. Add more rice flour if necessary. Cover dough with plastic wrap to prevent it from drying out while preparing the steamer.

TO MAKE RICE VERMICELLI

1. Spread a piece of muslin cloth large enough to cover the steamer plate and with a bit of extra cloth at the side for lifting noodles out of the hot steamer. Alternatively, oil the steamer plate.

2. Fit the desired extruder plate into the mould and fill with dough. Turn the handle to extrude the dough in strands onto the piece of muslin. The strands should fit comfortably into the steamer without scrunching. The noodles may be extruded in circles into nests or as long strands that fill the steamer plate.

3. Alternatively, extrude the dough onto a greased banana leaf, forming the strands into a circle of about 10-cm in diameter. Slip the nest of strands onto the prepared steamer plate.

4. Steam for 3 minutes for fine strands, a little longer for coarse ones, until noodles change colour.

5. If using a muslin cloth, lift up the cloth on either side and turn the noodles out onto a bamboo tray to cool. The noodles can be stacked when cold but not when warm. If steaming the noodles directly on the oiled steamer plate, slip a palette knife under the noodles and lift out.

TO MAKE STRING-HOPPERS

1. Cut out a piece of banana leaf into a circle of about 12-cm (5-in) in diameter, grease the leaf with oil and place on a flat surface.

2. Fit the string-hopper mould with the finest extruder plate. Fill the mould with dough and turn the handle to extrude the rice vermicelli onto the banana leaf. As you turn the handle, move the mould in a circular direction so that the strands of rice vermicelli fall in a circle of about 10-cm in diameter. With a knife, cut the strands off by running the blade against the extruder plate.

3. Holding the leaf by the edge, slip the noodles onto an oiled steamer tray. Steam for about 3 minutes or until string-hoppers change colour.

4. If there is room in the steamer for more circles of vermicelli, fill it up, but do not overlap. Take out the ones that went in first as you go along.

Fresh Broad Rice Noodles

KUAY TIAO

This noodle can be made into a sheet, in which case it becomes *chee cheong fun*,
a Cantonese dim sum treat served either stuffed or plain. If the sheet is cut into squares,
it becomes *kuay chap*, a hearty peasant noodle dish. If it is cut into strips,
it becomes *kuay tiao* (broad rice noodles). The simplest mixture is a combination of
rice flour and a stiffer starch such as tapioca or cornflour. The amount of water and cornflour
determine how thin and tender the sheet is. Less cornflour gives a more tender sheet
but the thinner and more tender the noodle, the harder it is to handle and fry.
This is why commercial *kuay tiao* is a little tougher than most of us would prefer,
while the best restaurant-made *chee cheong fun* is always tender and delicate.
The sheet hardens as it cools, so if it is to be filled, the filling should be layered,
then rolled up quickly. Steam the rice sheet on a piece of white cotton with a tight weave
such as calico so that the batter does not leak out. It should also be white so that
no dye bleeds into the rice sheet. Do not use muslin or cheesecloth as the weave is too loose.

MAKES ABOUT 200 G (7 OZ)

200 g (7 oz) rice flour

3 Tbsp tapioca starch/ cornflour

250 ml (8 fl oz / 1 cup) cold water

3 Tbsp cooking oil

1 tsp salt

600 ml (19$^1/_3$ fl oz) hot water

1. Prepare a piece of close-weave cotton large enough to cover the bottom of the steamer tray with an overhang for lifting the cloth out of the steamer.

2. Mix the two types of flour together with the cold water to a smooth mixture. Add oil and salt.

3. Stir the hot water into the cold water mixture.

4. Spread the piece of cotton smoothly at the bottom of the steamer tray making sure there are no kinks. Stir the batter well, then ladle in enough batter to cover the piece of cloth. Keep the layer as thin as you can.

5. Be sure the steamer is level so that the sheet comes out of even thickness. Cover and steam for about 3 minutes or until dough turns translucent.

6. Lift the cloth out of the steamer and cool for 1 minute before rolling up the sheet. If you are filling it with meat or prawns, layer the filling as you roll.

7. The noodles can be used straight away with a dressing or in soup. No further cooking is required. If the noodles have been stored in the refrigerator or in a cold room and have hardened, heat briefly in a microwave oven or pour hot water over them to soften the noodles if they are to be fried or dressed.

Fresh Plain Wheat Noodles

MAKES ABOUT 600 G (1 LB 5^1/$_3$ OZ)

500 g (1 lb 1^1/$_2$ oz) plain wheat flour

2 tsp salt

250 ml (8 fl oz / 1 cup) water

Cornflour for dusting

1. Sift plain flour and salt into a mixing bowl. Make a well in the centre of the flour, add water and knead to a stiff, smooth dough.

2. Divide dough into 2 balls, then place in a sealed plastic bag and leave dough to rest for 1 hour.

3. Dust a working surface with cornflour and roll out each ball of dough into a fairly thin, rectangular sheet. Dust both sides of the sheet with cornflour to prevent sticking.

4. Fan-fold each sheet of dough to the length of your longest knife. Cut into thin strips, loosening and sprinkling them with cornflour as you cut. Keep the strips neatly together and bundle into serving portions. Dust liberally with cornflour to prevent sticking.

5. Leave the noodles to dry for 1 hour before boiling.

Homemade Fresh Egg Noodles

MAKES ABOUT 600 G (1 LB 5^1/$_3$ OZ)

500 g (1 lb 1^1/$_2$ oz) plain wheat flour

2 tsp salt

2 egg yolks, lightly beaten

225 ml (7^1/$_2$ fl oz) water

Cornflour for dusting

1. Sift flour and salt into a large mixing bowl. Make a well in the centre of the flour. Add egg yolks and water to well.

2. Using your hands, mix together flour, water and egg. Knead to a smooth dough. Divide dough into 2 balls.

3. Place dough in a covered bowl or inside a sealed plastic bag and rest dough for 1 hour.

4. Dust a working surface with cornflour and roll out each ball of dough into a fairly thin, rectangular sheet. Dust both sides of each sheet with cornflour to prevent sticking.

5. Fan-fold each sheet of dough to the length of your longest knife. Cut into thin strips, loosening and sprinkling them with cornflour as you cut. Keep the strips neatly together and bundle into serving portions. Dust liberally with cornflour to prevent sticking.

6. These noodles can be dried for use on another day but should be refrigerated. Boil the noodles until nearly cooked before frying.

Fresh Cooked Wheat Noodles

HOKKIEN MEE

This particular noodle is hard to find outside of areas with large Hokkien communities.
The noodles have to be fresh and they do not keep well so they are hardly ever exported. Happily,
it is not impossible to make these noodles at home even without a noodle extruder.
Although it will take a little more time, you can cut the noodles, but use a little less water
in the dough so that it is stiffer. This will make rolling and cutting easier.

MAKES ABOUT 600 G (1 LB 5^1/$_3$ OZ)

500 g (1 lb 1^1/$_2$ oz) plain
wheat flour

2^1/$_2$ tsp alkali salts

1^1/$_2$ tsp salt

500 ml (16 fl oz / 2 cups)
water

TO MAKE EXTRUDED NOODLES

1. Sift plain flour, alkali salts and salt together into a bowl. Bring water
   to the boil in a pot. Using a wooden spoon, quickly stir flour mixture
   into boiling water to form a thick paste. Turn off heat. Form paste into
   a lump. Cover with a clean kitchen towel and set aside to cool.

2. When cool enough to handle but still warm, knead into a smooth
   dough. Cover and rest dough for 30 minutes.

3. To make noodles, bring a large pot of water to the boil. Fill extruder
   with dough and extrude noodles into boiling water in long continuous
   strands until extruder is empty.

4. When water returns to the boil, scoop noodles out and drop into
   a cold water bath or put into a colander and run cold water over
   noodles. Stir some oil into noodles to keep them separated.

5. Repeat steps 3 and 4 until dough is used up.

6. The noodles are only partially cooked and need to be blanched just
   before serving in soup. If noodles are to be fried, rinse noodles in
   some warm water to soften just before frying.

TO MAKE CUT NOODLES

1. If noodles are to be cut rather than extruded, reduce quantity of water
   for dough by 125 ml (4 fl oz / ^{1}/$_2$ cup).

2. Dust a work surface with cornflour and roll dough out into a fairly
   thin rectangular sheet. Fan-fold to the size of your longest knife.

3. Cut dough into thin strips, loosening and sprinkling them with
   cornflour as you cut.

4. Put cut noodles into boiling water and go through steps 4–6 above.

Cantonese-Style All-Egg Noodles

MAKES ABOUT 600 G (1 LB 5^1/$_3$ OZ)

500 g (1 lb 1^1/$_2$ oz) plain wheat flour

^{1}/$_2$ Tbsp alkali salts

6 eggs, about 300 g (11 oz)

Cornflour for dusting

1. Sieve plain flour and alkali salts into a mixing bowl. Make a nest in the centre of the flour.

2. Break the eggs into the nest and using your hands, gradually mix the flour into the eggs to get a stiff dough. Knead thoroughly until smooth.

3. Divide dough into 2 balls. Place in a covered bowl and rest for 1 hour.

4. Dust a working surface with cornflour and roll out each ball of dough into a fairly thin, rectangular sheet. Dust both sides of the sheet with cornflour to prevent sticking.

5. Fan-fold each sheet of dough to the length of your longest knife. Cut into thin strips, loosening and sprinkling them with cornflour as you cut. Keep the strips neatly together and bundle into serving portions. Dust liberally with cornflour to prevent sticking.

6. The uncooked noodles can be stored refrigerated for up to 1 week or frozen for up to 6 months.

Chinese-Style Egg Noodles

MAKES ABOUT 600 G (1 LB 5^1/$_3$ OZ)

500 g (1 lb 1^1/$_2$ oz) plain wheat flour

3 tsp salt

1 tsp alkali salts

125 ml (4 fl oz / ^{1}/$_2$ cup) water

3 eggs, about 220 g (8 oz)

Cornflour for dusting

1. Sift flour into a mixing bowl and make a well in the centre.

2. Dissolve salt and alkali in water.

3. Break eggs into flour well and add water mixture. Using your hands, mix eggs and water into flour and knead to form a stiff smooth dough. Divide dough into 2 balls, then leave to rest for 1 hour.

4. Dust a working surface with cornflour and roll out each ball of dough into a fairly thin, rectangular sheet. Dust both sides of each sheet with cornflour to prevent sticking.

5. Fan-fold each sheet of dough to the length of your longest knife. Cut into thin strips, loosening and sprinkling them with cornflour as you cut.

6. Bag noodles into individual servings if not using immediately.

Simple Egg Noodles

This simple recipe uses the weight of the eggs in their shells
double that of the wheat flour and ½ tsp bicarbonate of soda to every egg used.

2 tsp bicarbonate of soda

3 tsp salt

Plain wheat flour double
the weight of the eggs in
their shell

4 eggs in their shells

1. Sift the bicarbonate of soda and salt into the flour. Break the eggs into the flour and knead until the dough is smooth.

2. Divide the dough into 2 balls, cover and rest for 1 hour.

3. Dust a working surface with cornflour and roll out each ball of dough into a fairly thin, rectangular sheet. Dust both sides of the sheet with cornflour to prevent sticking.

4. Fan-fold each sheet of dough to the length of your longest knife. Cut into thin strips, loosening and sprinkling them with cornflour as you cut. Keep the strips neatly together and bundle into serving portions. Dust liberally with cornflour to prevent sticking.

5. Bag the noodles into individual portions if not using immediately.

Japanese Buckwheat Noodles

SOBA

Buckwheat flour has very little binding starch and is traditionally made with grated *yamaimo* (*dioscorea batatas, dioscorea opposita*), an Asian yam that exudes a lot of mucus. Even then, the dough is difficult to roll out and cut. It has been said that the test of a master noodle-maker is in the ability to make pure buckwheat noodles. However, pinched buckwheat noodles are not impossible to make; that was how buckwheat noodles were made once upon a time in Japan. Peel *yamaimo*, then measure the quantity needed. Buckwheat noodles may also be made with a cooked paste of buckwheat flour and wheat flour, and the paste extruded directly into boiling water.

MAKES ABOUT 600 G (1 LB 5⅓ OZ)

50 g (1¾ oz) peeled
yamaimo, grated

½ Tbsp salt

200 ml (6½ fl oz) warm
water

500 g (1 lb 1½ oz)
buckwheat flour

Cornflour for dusting

1. Grate *yamaimo* finely. Wear gloves if you are allergic to raw yam.

2. Dissolve salt in warm water.

3. Put buckwheat flour into a large mixing bowl and make a well in the centre of the flour. Add water and grated yam and knead with hands to get a crumbly mixture. Keep kneading to get a smooth dough. Place dough in a covered bowl and leave to rest for 1 hour.

4. Knead dough well, then pinch and press dough into small flat pieces. Dust with cornflour if noodles stick. Leave noodles to dry for 1 hour.

5. Boil noodles until tender but al dente.

Japanese Thick Wheat Noodles

UDON

Japanese noodle-maker Nissin markets flour for making udon. Look for it in supermarkets that carry a wide range of Japanese products. If unavailable, use plain wheat flour. Although step 3 says to avoid adding more water, in places with low humidity, unlike very humid Singapore, flour is often very dry. In this situation, a little more water will be required to get a stiff smooth dough. Add this extra water by wetting your hands as you knead flour and water together so that enough is added to form a stiff smooth dough without over-softening it.

MAKES ABOUT 600 G (1 LB 5$^1/_3$ OZ)

1 Tbsp salt

100 ml (3$^1/_3$ fl oz) warm water

500 g (1 lb 1$^1/_2$ oz) udon flour

Cornflour for dusting

1. Dissolve salt in warm water.

2. Put udon flour into a large mixing bowl, make a well in the centre of the flour and pour in salted water.

3. Stir flour into water to get a crumbly mixture, then knead mixture to get a smooth ball of dough. Resist the temptation to add any more water. The crumbly dough will get smooth as you keep kneading.

4. Place dough in a covered bowl and leave to rest for 1 hour.

5. Dust a working surface with cornflour and roll dough out into a fairly thin, rectangular sheet. Dust both sides of sheet with cornflour to prevent sticking.

6. Fan-fold dough to the length of your longest knife. Cut into 0.8-cm ($^1/_3$-in) strips, loosening and sprinkling them with cornflour as you cut to prevent sticking.

7. Cook udon using boil-discard-add method (page 20).

South Asian Wholemeal Noodles

These noodles can be rolled out and cut into long strips or squares, pinched and pressed into flat little pieces or rolled into balls. *Atta* (wholemeal wheat flour) is a standard ingredient in South Asian homes for making Indian breads such as *chapati*. The flour can also be used to make noodles which are then added to soups or cooked with *dhal* and vegetables. Alternatively, boil and dress the noodles or fry them with meat and vegetables (page 140).

2 tsp salt

250 ml (8 fl oz / 1 cup) water

500 g (1 lb 1½ oz) *atta* (wholemeal wheat flour)

1. Dissolve salt in water in a large mixing bowl. Stir in flour and knead to form a smooth, stiff dough.

2. Knead for 10 minutes, then leave dough to rest for 1 hour in a covered bowl or a sealed plastic bag.

3. Dust a working surface with wholemeal flour and roll dough out into a fairly thin, rectangular sheet. Dust both sides of sheet with wholemeal flour to prevent sticking.

4. Fan-fold dough to the length of your longest knife. Cut into thin strips about 0.2-cm ($\frac{1}{12}$-in) wide (the noodles swell during boiling), loosening and sprinkling them with wholemeal flour as you cut.

5. Cook noodles using the boil-discard-add method (page 20). It will take about 20 minutes to cook through, depending on the width and thickness of noodles.

6. Scoop noodles out into a cold water bath.

New Year Cake or Glutinous Rice Flour Cake

NIAN GAO

This noodle is a Foochow specialty. Fresh *nian gao* will be softer than the dried variety, but it will be nearly as chewy. This is a texture that some will love and others hate.

MAKES ABOUT 600 G (1 LB 5$\frac{1}{3}$ OZ)

500 g (1 lb 1$\frac{1}{2}$ oz) glutinous rice flour

290 ml (9$\frac{4}{5}$ fl oz) water

1 tsp salt

TO MAKE FRESH *NIAN GAO*

1. Mix rice flour, water and salt together to form a stiff dough. Divide into 2–3 pieces and shape each into a square, rectangle or round tube. Rest for 1 hour on a flat plate.

2. Prepare a cold water bath in a large bowl and bring a large pot of water to the boil.

3. Using a sharp knife, cut dough into pieces about 0.2-cm ($\frac{1}{8}$-in) and drop into boiling water. When cakes float, they are cooked. Scoop out into a cold water bath.

4. Keep dropping pieces of dough into boiling water. Uncooked pieces will sink while cooked ones will float.

5. When pot of water gets too starchy, discard and start with a fresh pot of water.

6. Rice flour cake made this way cannot be stored except in a bowl of water. Fry up noodles on the same day.

TO MAKE DRIED *NIAN GAO*

1. Mix flour, water and salt together.

2. Line a straight-sided cake tin that will fit into a steamer or covered wok with greaseproof paper.

3. Press dough into prepared tin and steam cake for 1 hour or until centre of cake feels mushy. Remove from steamer and leave to cool.

4. Leave rice cake in tin and refrigerate until hardened. This will take at least 2 months.

5. Slice cake into even pieces of about 0.2-cm ($\frac{1}{8}$-in) thickness and spread out to dry in the sun.

Ladakhi Handmade Bow-Tie Noodles

MAKES ABOUT 600 G (1 LB 5⅓ OZ)

500 g (1 lb 1½ oz) plain wheat flour

2 tsp salt

250 ml (8 fl oz / 1 cup) water

Cornflour for dusting

1. Sift flour and salt into a mixing bowl. Make a well in the centre of the flour, add water and knead to a stiff, smooth dough.

2. Divide dough into 2 balls. Place dough in a sealed plastic bag and rest dough for 1 hour.

3. Dust a working surface with cornflour and roll out each ball of dough into a fairly thin sheet.

4. Using a small round cookie cutter, cut out circles of dough.

5. To make a bow-tie, dab the centre of a dough circle with water, then fold two opposite edges towards the centre. Press down to hold them in place and form the shape of a "bow-tie".

6. Repeat until dough is used up. To roll together and re-use the trimmings, wet hands just a little to get a smooth dough and roll out again.

7. Spread bow-ties out on a large tray to dry out for at least 1 hour before cooking.

How to Prepare Noodles and Accompaniments

TECHNIQUES

BOILING NOODLES

The length of time required to cook noodles depends very much on the type of noodle, how fresh or dried it is and if dried, whether the noodles have been pre-soaked or not. The best test is to bite a piece of the noodle after 1 minute of cooking. You can then estimate how much longer you need to cook it. The next best thing is to know the types of noodles and their origins. For example, dried rice vermicelli from Thailand or Vietnam requires a longer boiling time compared to that from China.

When noodles are put into boiling water, they should be stirred straight away to prevent clumping or uneven cooking. Cover the pot to return the water to the boil more rapidly, but watch out for boiling over, especially if the pot is not large enough for the quantity of noodles. Once the pot has boiled up, leave it uncovered. The heat should be as high as possible so that the noodles cook rapidly.

While rice noodles call for simple boiling as described above, wheat noodles often require a more complicated method of boiling. Thick dense noodles such as dried *la mian*, thick *mee sua* and thick udon or fresh egg noodles coated with a lot of cornflour should be cooked using the boil-discard-add method, while some thin wheat noodles benefit from the two-pot method. These methods are described below.

Boil-discard-add method

The noodles are put into a pot of boiling water. After 5 minutes, half the water is discarded and replaced with fresh, cold water, then returned to the boil. This can be repeated a second or even a third time until the noodles are tender but al dente.

Two-pot method

Two pots of water are brought to the boil, the second 5 minutes after the first. The noodles are placed in the first pot for 3–5 minutes, then scooped out, rinsed in cold water and placed into the second pot of clean, boiling water. The time of boiling will depend on the thickness of the noodles. It can be 3 minutes in the first pot and a 30-second blanching in the second pot or longer, if required. The first boiling cooks the noodles and removes the starch, and the second boiling or blanching reheats the noodles.

BLANCHING

An ingredient is put briefly into boiling water, then removed. The time the ingredient is left in the water depends on the ingredient. Bean sprouts, for example, are blanched for only 10 seconds. Another method is by pouring boiling water over the ingredient placed in a colander or wire sieve.

BRUISING

A root herb such as galangal or ginger is skinned and the root smashed with the side of a cleaver or handy stone. *See also* Crushing.

CLEANING AND PREPARATION

Banana Flowers The flower bulb is cut in half and boiled in salted water for 5 minutes. Only the tender parts of the red sepals are eaten. To test for tenderness, slice the outer bracts with a knife. If it slices easily, it is tender enough to be eaten. Each floret has a tiny spine that must be removed and the floret sliced.

Bean Sprouts To prepare, rinse in several changes of cold water, removing any dark or mushy sprouts and bean skins. The tails were traditionally plucked to give a clean white sprout. Today, premium-priced cleaned sprouts without tails can be bought in some supermarkets in Singapore. This step is worth doing for noodle dishes where the sprouts are eaten raw. To keep the bean sprouts crisp, add towards the end of cooking time.

Chillies The seeds are usually removed when blending partly because they do not process well in a blender and because the bulk of the chillies is desired without so much of the heat. If using fresh chillies, rinse before seeding. If using dried chillies, seed before rinsing and soaking. Avoid touching cut chillies with bare hands. Wash hands well after processing chillies and do not touch eyes or sensitive skin. Intense chilli burns can cause swelling.

Choy Sum Rinse well to get rid of grit. If the greens are very limp, soak for a few minutes in cold water. Separate stems from leaves; place stems into the pan first as they take longer to cook.

Coriander Leaves (cilantro) Keep the roots if the coriander is being used for a Thai recipe. For other dishes, the root is discarded and the coriander leaves rinsed and swished in cold water before chopping.

Galangal The skin is peeled with a sharp knife because it is too tough for scraping. Slice and chop coarsely before processing.

Garlic Peel away the skin and discard the stem end. Raw chopped garlic stores well refrigerated. Oxidation can turn chopped garlic a greenish colour. To avoid this, cover chopped garlic with oil.

Ginger, Lesser Galangal (*kencur*), Chinese Keys (*krachai*) The thin skin is usually scraped away with a small knife.

Lemongrass Discard the hard outer sheaves and use the moist inner section. Only about 10–12 cm (4–5-in), starting from just above the woody root is used. Cut and discard the woody bulb end and the top skinnier end. Slice thinly before processing. Lemongrass has very fine hair-like fibres that do not process well. Coarsely cut lemongrass gives a spice paste with lots of fine hair-like fibres.

Mushrooms Dried mushrooms such as shiitake should be rinsed quickly in cold water, then soaked in cold or warm water until soft before slicing. The water used for soaking can be added to the dish for added flavour.

Prawns (shrimps) Rinse first, then shell. In some recipes, the tails are kept intact. In others, all the shell is removed. Keep the shells and heads for making prawn stock. Prawns are sometimes boiled before shelling. In such recipes, rinse well and place the prawns in a pot, then cover with water and bring to the boil. Prawns are cooked when they change colour.Shell when cool and return the heads and shells to the boiling water and simmer for another 5 minutes to get prawn stock.

Shallots The papery skin is peeled off with a small knife and the root end cut off and discarded. Peeling shallots or onions may cause tearing. To avoid this, soak in water and peel in the basin of water. This prevents the fumes from the shallots or onion from irritating the eyes.

Spring Onions (scallions) Trim off the roots and any yellowed leaves. Swish the spring onions in cold water, taking special care of the part where the leaves start branching out as grit tends to collect there. Spring onions are either cut into finger lengths or chopped. However, if the spring onions are particularly chunky, the white bulb end should be split in half before cutting or chopping.

Water Convolvulus (*kangkong*) Trim off the roots and about 2.5 cm (1 in) of the stem above the roots as it is tough. Rinse well in cold water. If the stem is thick, split it in half or quarter down the middle. Keep stems and leaves together and cut into short lengths.

COCONUT CREAM/MILK

Extracting Pure cream is extracted by putting fresh grated coconut into a muslin bag and squeezing out the cream. Alternatively, a little water may be mixed with the grated coconut before squeezing. The addition of water will yield more cream. Do not discard the grated coconut after extracting the cream. It can be soaked in water and squeezed again to extract coconut milk.

Cooking Coconut cream/milk can be cooked to three different stages, depending on the recipe. The first stage is a near-boil, when cooking is stopped just as the liquid starts to bubble. The second stage is a medium-boil when boiling has started and is stopped 5 minutes later. The third is hard-boil where the goal is to bring out the coconut oil. This takes about 20 minutes of boiling.

COLD WATER BATH

A bowl of, preferably, ice-cold water standing by the stove for dropping in certain types of noodles after blanching. *See* Rinsing. Shredded vegetables such as cucumber or lettuce can also be left to soak in a cold water bath for 5 minutes or so to get the shreds really crisp. However, this is a special treat as soaking cut vegetables in water robs them of water-soluble vitamins.

CRUSHING

Certain fragrant leaves such as kaffir lime leaves or curry leaves are usually crushed or crumbled up to release the oils before the leaves are added to the pot. Delicate leaves such as basil or mint are used whole or chopped just before use so as not to lose the essential oils.

DEVEINING

Prawns (shrimps) usually have a line of dirt that needs to be removed before cooking, so they do not taste gritty when cooked. Using a small, sharp knife, slit the top of the prawn and pull out the line of dirt. This process is called deveining.

DRAINING

Blanched vegetables and boiled noodles should be drained well using a colander or sieve scoop. In the case of noodles, toss and lift the noodles several times with a pair of chopsticks to get rid of as much of the boiling water as possible, and shake the colander or sieve scoop. Blanched vegetables such as bean sprouts can be tossed to get rid of water. Blanched cabbage or chrysanthemum leaves can be pressed with a spoon against the sieve scoop to squeeze out the water.

DRY-FRYING

No oil or liquid is used as the aim is essentially to toast the ingredient and take away the raw taste. Flours such as chickpea flour in Burmese cooking are often dry-fried, as are dried red chillies for Thai chilli flakes and grated coconut for salads. Seed spices such as coriander and cumin seeds are usually dry-fried before they are ground into spice paste or made into curry powder in the best homemade curry powders

FRYING NOODLES

Noodles should be fried over high heat, meaning that the cook has to work fast and have all the ingredients needed on hand. The ingredients should be cleaned, cut, measured and assembled on a plate before the start of frying. Sauce mixtures and seasoning should be measured out in handy bowls. Place the ingredients in the order in which they are required, especially if the recipe is new to you. Keep the recipe handy too.

If the noodles need to be pre-boiled, time it such that the boiled noodles can be drained and fried immediately. Boiled noodles that are left sitting will cool and clump up. To avoid this, some cooks stir oil into boiled noodles. I prefer to time the boiling to fit in with the frying. *See also* Sprinkling water.

Frying with a spatula in one hand and chopsticks in the other ensures good mixing as the noodles can be tossed up. Avoid breaking the noodles into short lengths.

FRYING SPICE PASTES

Spice pastes are fried in oil until the oil rises to the top. The paste has to be stirred constantly to cook it evenly, prevent burning and evaporate the water used to blend the spices. Some cooks grind the spice paste in a blender with the oil for frying added instead of using water. (I prefer to use water because cleaning an oily blender afterwards is more difficult.) If the spice paste has been ground with oil, just put it into the pot and fry as usual.

GARNISHING

Not all garnishes are optional. While meat, egg or seafood garnishes are optional, some such as limes, fried shallots, garlic oil and herbs are often essential to enhance the flavour of the dish. Condiments are not always optional either, as some have lime juice, vinegar or fish sauce. A little experimental tasting will reap tasty rewards.

POUNDING

The traditional South East Asian and South Asian method of mixing various ingredients into a spice paste is either to pound them in a mortar and pestle or to grind them in a *batu geling* (grinding stone). A *batu geling* consists of a piece of flat granite paired with a granite "rolling pin". The spices are ground by rolling the pin over them repeatedly. Pounding in a mortar and pestle is used for wet ingredients such as fresh chillies and shallots, while grinding in a *batu geling* is more commonly used for hard seed spices such as coriander seeds. The *batu geling* gives a finer spice paste than the mortar and pestle. Grinding with a *batu geling* is the method commonly used by South Indians and once upon a time, a good wet market in Singapore would have an Indian woman who sold spice mixes that she ground on the spot. Although the modern electric blender is replacing the *batu geling*—and mortar and pestle— in many homes in South East Asia, the mortar and pestle is still indispensable for certain South East Asian condiments, one of which is *sambal belacan*. Other South East Asian condiments such as Vietnamese *nuoc cham* or Laotian *jeo som* are also better pounded rather than blended. The two main problems with mixing these condiments in a blender are the air introduced into the condiment and, in the case of *sambal belacan*, the liquid needed to move the blades.

RINSING

Certain kinds of noodles benefit from having a stream of cold water poured over them. The rinsing gets rid of any starch clinging to the noodles which could make them gummy, and stops the cooking. However, these noodles should also be returned to a pot of clean boiling water to raise the temperature before eating. For this, use the two-pot method (page 20). Alternatively, dispense with the cold water rinse and just go for the boiling water rinse. To do this, have ready a jug of boiling water. Pour the boiling water over the noodles while shaking the sieve scoop or colander at the same time. Drain well.

SPRINKLING WATER

When stir-frying noodles, have a small container of water or stock handy before the wok is heated up. Water is sprinkled on the noodles during frying when the noodles look hard, but the other ingredients are dry and starting to burn. The liquid slows down the cooking. If necessary, cover the noodles for 1–2 minutes to cook them more evenly. Do not sprinkle too much water to avoid soggy, overcooked noodles.

SUBSTITUTING

Traditionally, certain kinds of noodles go with particular preparations and substitutions are not always possible if the original flavour is to be kept. However, there are many recipes where substitutions do not seriously affect the flavour or may even be an option. If a substitution has to be made because the required noodles are not available, substitute with noodles made of the same grain, such as dried thin rice vermicelli for fresh coarse rice vermicelli, dried egg noodles for fresh egg noodles or glass noodles for sweet potato starch noodles. The wonderful thing about noodles is that they are very forgiving, and if trying to re-create a particular ethnic flavour is not a goal, you can make do with whatever noodles you can get hold of and you will still be assured of getting a tasty result.

THICKENING

This is done in a number of ways depending on the recipe. In Chinese cooking, the thickener is usually cornflour mixed with water or stock. South East Asian noodle dishes are thickened in more varied ways. A common method is to sprinkle the assembled dish with toasted flours such as chickpea flour, crumbled crackers, crushed deep-fried noodles or ground peanuts. Gravy and soups can also be thickened with added starches such as rice flour or mashed potatoes or sweet potatoes. Ground spice pastes also serve to thicken soups and gravies besides flavouring them.

VELVETING

This is a traditional Chinese technique to keep meat and seafood moist during cooking. The sliced meat or seafood is marinated in a mixture of soy sauces, cornflour and water with an oil such as sesame oil. Stock may also replace water for more flavour. The marinated meat or seafood can sometimes be fried first, then removed and added at the end when the noodles are done.

EQUIPMENT

BLENDER

The blender has replaced the grinding stone and mortar and pestle in many modern homes in Asia. It is essential for the speedy preparation of the spice pastes used in South East Asian cooking, but the drawback is that some liquid is usually needed to grind the ingredients to a smooth paste. The amount required depends on the blender, with some needing more liquid than others. Some blenders produce a smooth fine paste, while others are more choppers than grinders. Seed spices also do not grind down finely enough in blenders. To grind seed spices, use a spice mill.

If you grind a large quantity of spice pastes, it is worthwhile dedicating a blender to the task as ridding the usually plastic bowl of strong smells of garlic or prawn (shrimp) paste is not easy.

COLANDER

If the quantity of noodles is too much to fit into a wire scoop, use a colander and drain as described under *Techniques*.

LONG CHOPSTICKS

These are very useful for stirring noodles when they are first put into boiling water, as well as for dressing and frying noodles. When frying noodles, I combine chopsticks with a spatula.

MORTAR AND PESTLE

The proliferation of the electric blender has not made the mortar and pestle redundant, as there are still some items of Asian, especially South East Asian cooking, that are best done in a mortar and pestle.

POT FOR BOILING

Noodles should be boiled in as large a pot as possible, so that there is plenty of water to dilute the starches and prevent boiling over. A good stockpot or spaghetti pot works well.

WIRE SCOOP

The traditional Chinese wire scoop for noodles has a bamboo handle with a scoop made of a yellow wire, but the holes of the wire mesh can be too large, allowing the noodles to fall through easily. An updated version with a plastic handle has a scoop of fine-meshed wire which keeps the noodles in better and allows you to hold the scoop of noodles under a running tap. It is an excellent piece of equipment for blanching vegetables and noodles. Whether you choose the traditional Chinese wire scoop or the updated one, it should fit into the pot that you use for boiling noodles. Both kinds of scoops come in various sizes.

WOK

A wok is indispensable for frying noodles, be it flat-bottomed or the traditional round-bottom wok. Woks also come non-stick and so less oil is required to prevent the noodles from sticking. However, high heat is often called for in stir-frying to achieve a particular flavour, and non-stick pans should never be subjected to high heat. Note that the coating used for non-stick pans has in recent years come under suspicion and is generating health concerns. Whatever your choice, your wok should be large enough to allow easy stirring of the quantity of noodles you would usually cook. Alternatively, have a large and a smaller wok for different needs. I use the traditional cast-iron wok as well as a smaller enamel wok, both of which causes the noodles to stick like crazy unless there is enough oil.

MEASUREMENTS

Do not be daunted by the precise measurements in the recipes. The aim was to guide someone new to these dishes to arrive at a certain flavour. Traditional measures such "a handful" or "a rice bowl" are estimates based on long experience and familiarity, but can bring about uncertain results for someone new to preparing that dish. Essentially, these measurements achieve the balance and ratio between ingredients that are necessary to produce a particular flavour. However, the really great thing about preparing noodle dishes is that unlike baking, precise measurements are not critical to the success of the recipe. You will end up with something edible, if not downright tasty, even when you are missing one or two ingredients. Nor do you have to be all that precise with the measurements. An onion extra or short will not lead to a collapse of the recipe. However, too many adjustments and substitutions will affect the final flavour.

Key flavours to keep in mind are spiciness and saltiness. A dish that is too spicy or too salty is inedible. On the other hand, if it is not salty or spicy enough, the dish lacks zing. So note that the salt level in these recipes is to my taste, which is on the low, although not rock-bottom, end of the salt scale. (It was actually a compromise between my taste buds and my blood pressure.) However, do not bump up the salt until you know the salt level of your particular brand of soy sauce or fish sauce, and whether my salt level is right for you too. The amount of spiciness is harder to control because it depends on the chillies used, and the amount of heat can vary with the season as well as the type of chillies. So, while the recipes specify the quantity of chillies, feel free to reduce, bump up or combine fiery with bland chillies. Reducing the amount of chillies will affect the volume of spice paste and therefore the thickness of the gravy. Adjust by adding a little more of other ingredients, say shallots, or use chillies that you know from experience to be very bland. The spiciness in these recipes tends to be in the medium or three-alarm range on a scale of one to five. In certain recipes where noodles need to be dressed individually, adjustments can be made to suit individual tastes and serving sizes.

In Asia, spiciness and saltiness are also adjusted with the condiments that are de rigueur with many of the dishes. The good thing about adjustable spiciness is that family members who cannot or do not want to take spicy food can also share the meal. There could be situations where you might want to use really bland chillies just to get the right colour and flavour, but accompany the dish with a condiment that has real heat for those who want it that way.

While the recipes specify fresh herbs and roots, you may be in a part of the world where the fresh ingredients are not available. If so, look for the dried variety. In some temperate countries, some South East Asian roots and herbs may appear fresh seasonally, while some come pickled in salt. When using dried herbs, remember that some types of herbs can be more strongly flavoured than the fresh stuff, so adjust the amount used. If using pickled herbs, adjust the salt level elsewhere in the recipe.

The one area where some precision in measurements is necessary is in noodle-making. Too much water creates more problems than too little. So while you may find a "thumb-size" piece of galangal too imprecise when making *mee rebus*, it really does not affect the outcome of the dish significantly, whatever the length of your thumb. But in noodle-making, it does matter if your tablespoon is the metric 15 ml or the less-than-15-ml US tablespoon. Always start with less water and increase as needed.

WEIGHTS AND MEASURES

Thumb-size refers to length rather than width. A thumb-size piece of an ingredient translates roughly to a length of 5 cm (2 in).

1 Tbsp *belacan* = 15 g ($^1/_2$ oz)
1 tsp *belacan* = 5 g ($^1/_6$ oz)
1 small bunch spring onion/coriander leaves/ Chinese celery = 15 g ($^1/_2$ oz)
2 shallots = 25 g (1 oz)
2 cloves garlic = 10 g ($^1/_3$ oz)

1 small onion = 50 g ($1^3/_4$ oz)
1 medium onion = 75 g ($2^1/_2$ oz)
1 large onion = 100 g ($3^1/_2$ oz)
1 large tomato = 150 g ($5^1/_3$ oz)
1 slice ginger or galangal is 0.2-cm ($^1/_{10}$-in) thick

LIQUID INGREDIENTS
60 ml = 2 fl oz = $^1/_4$ cup (4 Tbsp)
75 ml = $2^1/_2$ fl oz = $^1/_3$ cup
125 ml = 4 fl oz = $^1/_2$ cup
250 ml = 8 fl oz = 1 cup
500 ml = 16 fl oz = 2 cups

SERVING SIZES

Unless specified to serve one, all the recipes
serve between four and six adults, depending on
appetites. However, certain recipes, for example,
laksa and *mee siam*, do tend to generate some
leftovers partly because some will prefer more
or less gravy and garnishes. When serving these
dishes, only blanch the quantity of noodles to be
consumed immediately. That way, leftovers can
be served up later and the noodles will always
taste fresh.

The quantity of noodles calculated per person
is 150 g ($5^1/_3$ oz) for fresh noodles and 75 g
($2^1/_2$ oz) for most dried noodles. The addition of
meat, seafood and vegetables increases the final
serving size. In Asia, noodle dishes started out
as cheap meals, and the more expensive meat
and seafood were used in very tiny quantities as
garnishes. With prosperity, there is now more
meat and seafood in noodle dishes although
their proportion should ideally remain less
than half that of the noodles. Taste, too, has
something to do with this ratio between meat
and noodles. Many Asians prefer more noodles
and vegetables to meat and seafood.

Condiments, Sauces, Oils, Stocks and Garnishes

Condiments, sauces, oils, stocks and garnishes are essential in flavouring many noodle dishes. It is worthwhile doing a batch of these ingredients as many will keep well for several weeks, if not months, in the fridge or freezer. Condiments to go with Asian noodle dishes are usually served in individual dip saucers in some cases; in others, the jar of condiment is kept at the table for guests to help themselves. The recipes here are for generic ingredients that recur in more than one recipe. The finished quantities are usually more than enough for one serving.

Anatto Oil

This oil is common in Filipino noodle dishes, so if you plan to do more than the occasional Filipino noodle dish, keep some anatto oil handy. It gives the noodles a golden glow and a mild saffron-like flavour.

MAKES 180 ML (6 FL OZ / ¾ CUP)

45 g (1½ oz) anatto seeds

180 ml (6 fl oz / ¾ cup) cooking oil

1. Heat oil and anatto seeds in a small pot until hot. Remove from heat and set aside until cool. Discard seeds and store oil in a clean dry bottle.

Fried Shallots and Shallot Oil

When sliced shallots are fried in oil, the resulting fragrant oil is referred to as shallot oil.
Use the oil and shallots to dress noodles or flavour soups.
Both the oil and fried shallots can also be used to dress blanched vegetables.

MAKES 250 ML (8 FL OZ / 1 CUP)

150 g (5⅓ oz) peeled shallots

250 ml (8 fl oz / 1 cup) cooking oil

1. Slice peeled shallots thinly.

2. Heat oil in a wok and fry shallots, stirring constantly until shallots are dry and golden in colour.

3. Scoop shallots out onto a large platter lined with paper towels. When cool, bottle fried shallots and refrigerate to extend shelf life.

4. Pour cooled oil into a bottle with a screw-cap and store in the fridge to extend shelf life.

Note:

When frying shallots, lower the heat if bits of shallots start to brown too quickly while still moist and soft. For golden brown shallots, watch the heat and colour carefully. When the shallots are pale yellow, turn the heat off and continue stirring until the colour deepens. If the shallots are still too pale, turn the heat on briefly and keep stirring until the shallots are a pale yellow. The shallots will brown considerably in the residual heat. Repeat the on-off heat as necessary to get the best colour. Burnt shallots taste bitter.

Fried Garlic and Garlic Oil

Like shallot oil, garlic oil is used to dress noodles or steamed vegetables or
added to soups. Fried garlic can be sprinkled on soups as well as stir-fried vegetables during
the frying in place of raw garlic. The fried garlic and oil can be bottled together
if preferred. Note that garlic browns more quickly than shallots.
The same on-off heat technique (page 29) can be used for frying garlic.

MAKES 250 ML (8 FL OZ / 1 CUP)

150 g (5¹/₃ oz) garlic, peeled

250 ml (8 fl oz / 1 cup) cooking oil

1. Chop peeled garlic in an electric food chopper until fairly fine but not mushy.

2. Heat oil in a wok and add chopped garlic. Stir constantly until garlic begins to turn a nice shade of yellow. Lower heat if garlic is browning unevenly.

3. Remove from heat but continue stirring until garlic is a golden brown.

4. Scoop garlic onto a plate lined with paper towels if bottling fried garlic and oil separately. When cool, bottle oil and garlic in containers with a screw-cap and store in the fridge to extend shelf life.

Burmese Fried Garlic

This fried garlic is sometimes crushed into a powder and sprinkled on noodle dishes.
The thin slices of garlic can also be used whole and is tasty with salads.

MAKES 1 CUP

150 g (5¹/₃ oz) garlic, peeled

1 tsp ground turmeric

Peanut oil for frying

1. Slice garlic thinly and rub in ground turmeric.

2. Heat oil in a wok and fry garlic over low heat until crisp, taking care not to burn garlic.

Sambal Belacan

This Malay/Straits Chinese condiment is to be distinguished from *belacan* or prawn paste. *Sambal belacan* tastes best pounded in a mortar and pestle (rather than a blender). However, the chillies can be coarsely chopped in a food chopper to reduce pounding time. *Sambal belacan* keeps well in the fridge for up to a month. It can also be packed into serving sizes and kept frozen. Use firm Malaysian-style prawn paste that comes in a block, firm enough to cut, rather than the liquid variety in a jar.

150 g (5^1/$_3$ oz) fresh red chillies, seeded

45 g (1^1/$_2$ oz / 3 Tbsp) dried prawn paste (*belacan*)

1. Chop chillies coarsely in a blender.

2. Toast dried prawn paste. If toasting on a grill or in an oven-toaster, press into a thin flat piece, then toast both sides until slightly brown. Do not burn it or the *sambal* will taste bitter. Alternatively, crumble the prawn paste in a wok and dry-fry until slightly brown. Stir constantly when dry-frying.

3. Pound chopped chillies and toasted prawn paste in a mortar and pestle to a paste. Store in a clean glass jar in the fridge.

Sambal Belacan with Lime Juice

Sambal belacan with lime juice keeps well in the fridge, but a fresh condiment can also be made with frozen *sambal belacan*.

2 Tbsp *sambal belacan*

3 Tbsp lime juice

1. Mix *sambal belacan* and lime juice together. Store in a clean glass bottle in the fridge.

Fresh Red Chillies with Light Soy Sauce

This condiment should be prepared when needed. Noodle stalls in Singapore usually serve this condiment with both soup and dry noodles for added spice.

2 fresh red chillies, seeded and thinly sliced

Light soy sauce to taste

1. Place desired amount of chillies in a small dip saucer. Pour in light soy sauce to taste and serve with a noodle dish.

Pickled Green Chillies

Pickled chillies keep very well. Although aged pickled green chillies may sometimes
be a little soft, they are still tasty enough to add quick spice to certain noodle dishes.
Note that pickled jalapeno chillies keep particularly well. I once had a jar for
more than 4 years and they were still crisp!

MAKES 1 JAM JAR

250 g (9 oz) fresh green
chillies, rinsed and coarsely
sliced

A kettle of boiling water

500 ml (16 fl oz / 2 cups)
Chinese white rice vinegar

1 Tbsp sugar

1 tsp salt

1. Place cut chillies in a sieve and pour boiling water over it. Shake sieve
   to drain any excess moisture. Leave chillies to cool in sieve.

2. Spoon stone-cold chillies into a glass jar, discarding the seeds. Pour in
   rice vinegar to cover chillies. Stir in sugar and salt.

3. Cover jar and pickle chillies at least overnight before serving.

4. Pickled green chillies are usually served in individual dipping saucers
   with some light soy sauce.

Cooked Dried Red Chilli Paste

This chilli paste is basic to a number of classic South East Asian noodle dishes such as
Penang or Singapore *char kuay tiao*. The chilli paste keeps well frozen. It can be used in
place of chilli oil or flakes, or to spice up a bland curry quickly. Combine bulky but bland chillies
such as Mexican *guajillo* with super hot Thai bird's eye chillies (the dried ones). Such a combination
speeds up the seeding. Do not use smoke-dried chillies so as not to alter the flavour.

500 g (1 lb 1^1/$_2$ oz) dried
red chillies, seeded

125 ml (4 fl oz / ^{1}/$_2$ cup)
water

125 ml (4 fl oz / ^{1}/$_2$ cup)
cooking oil

^{1}/$_2$ tsp salt

1. Rinse seeded chillies well, then soak in a basin of clean water until
   soft. Drain and blend softened chillies with water to a fine paste.

2. Spoon ground chillies into a large ovenproof dish with a cover. It
   should not be more than three-quarters full, preferably less. Stir in oil
   and salt.

3. Cover dish and cook in the microwave oven on High for about
   20 minutes, taking care to stir the paste every 5 minutes. If the paste
   becomes too dry, stir in some water.

4. Cool, bottle then freeze until needed.

Raw Dried Red Chilli Paste

This ground paste is always used as part of a spice paste and never added raw to noodle dishes. A box of ground dried red chillies is handy to have in the freezer. Seed the chillies even when they are relatively bland because the seeds do not grind well.

500 g (1 lb 1½ oz) dried red chillies, seeded

125 ml (4 fl oz / ½ cup) water

1. Rinse seeded chillies well, then soak in a basin of clean water until soft. Drain and blend softened chillies with water to a fine paste. Store in the freezer and use in ground spice paste mixtures.

Dried Red Chilli Paste with Dried Prawns

Use this chilli paste for dressing noodles or as a condiment with fried noodles such as Singapore-style fried Hokkien *mee* or Penang-style Hokkien *mee* soup.

2 tsp dried prawns (shrimps), softened in some water

200 g (7 oz) dried red chillies, seeded

125 ml (4 fl oz / ½ cup) water

125 ml (4 fl oz / ½ cup) cooking oil

1. Drain and remove any bits of shell from the dried prawns.

2. Rinse seeded dried chillies and soak in water until soft. Drain and blend softened chillies, dried prawns and 125 ml (4 fl oz / ½ cup) water together until fine.

3. Place chilli paste in a covered microwave-safe container and cook in the microwave oven on High for 15 minutes. Alternatively, place chilli paste in a saucepan and cook over low heat for 25 minutes. Stir constantly when sauce thickens. If sauce is too dry, add 2–3 Tbsp water and cook for another 3 minutes. A spoonful of sauce should drop easily off the spoon without shaking.

Singapore-Style Fresh Red Chilli-Vinegar Sauce

MAKES 1½ CUPS

100 g (3½ oz) fresh red chillies, seeded

1 slice ginger

1 tsp salt

2 tsp sugar

4 Tbsp white rice vinegar

1. Process all ingredients in a blender until chillies are fine.

2. Bottle and leave the sauce to rest for a few hours before using.

Garlic Chilli Sauce

This chilli sauce can be cooked on a stove-top, but cooking in the microwave oven is easier. Use big chillies as they are easier to seed, but spice them up with a few bird's eye chillies. Rest the sauce for a few hours or overnight to allow the flavours to meld.

MAKES 2 CUPS

200 g (7 oz) fresh red chillies, seeded

100 g (3^1/$_2$ oz) garlic

125 ml (4 fl oz / ^{1}/$_2$ cup) water

2 tsp Chinese white rice vinegar

2 tsp sugar

1^1/$_2$ tsp salt

1. Process chillies, garlic and water in a blender until very fine. Transfer mixture to an ovenproof dish,

2. Mix vinegar, sugar and salt into ground chillies, then cook in the microwave oven on High for 13 minutes, stirring every few minutes. The sauce should be of a thick pouring consistency.

3. Leave sauce to cool before bottling. Store in the fridge to extend shelf life.

Thai Chilli-Vinegar Dip

MAKES ^{1}/$_4$ CUP

6 bird's eye chillies, chopped

2 Tbsp fish sauce

2 Tbsp white rice vinegar

1. Combine chillies, fish sauce and vinegar in a saucer. Serve with a noodle dish.

Chinese Salted Tientsin Cabbage

One of China's numerous pickled vegetables, this particular salted vegetable is often added to noodle soups for texture and flavour. It is sold ready-made in little packets, sometimes labelled "Salted Tientsin cabbage". When making your own, pick a sunny day, as the pickled cabbage should be sunned before storage. The salted vegetable keeps well in the fridge.

4 large leaves Tientsin cabbage

^{1}/$_2$ cup salt

1. Trim off thick stems and discard. Shred leaves and chop coarsely into short pieces.

2. Mix salt into cabbage and let stand for 1 hour, before squeezing out liquid until cabbage is dry.

3. Sun cabbage for several hours until completely dry. Bottle until needed.

4. The salted cabbage should be well-rinsed and chopped finely before adding to soup.

Chinese Chilli Oil

This is the condiment used commonly in northern China and Hong Kong to give food an extra bite. Bottled chilli oil is found in Asian stores all over the world, but if you can find any of the super-hot chillies such as habanero, *prik kee nu* or bird's eye chillies in dried form, you can make your own chilli oil. The hotter the chilli, the less oil you will need to spice up the noodles.

MAKES 1 CUP

10 dried super-hot chillies, wiped clean

250 ml (8 fl oz /1 cup) cooking oil

1. Chop chillies including seeds, taking care not to touch chillies with your bare hands. Put into a small pot.

2. Add oil and place over medium heat for 10 minutes, taking care not to burn chillies. Leave oil to cool in the pot, then bottle with or without chillies.

Hong Kong Dried Chilli Oil

This is basically ground dried chillies cooked in oil. The oil is favoured more than the ground dried chillies which are full of seeds, although the ground chillies may also be added to noodles.

MAKES 1¹/₂ CUPS

200 g (7 oz) dried red chillies, wiped clean

¹/₂ Tbsp dried prawns (shrimps)

250 ml (8 fl oz / ¹/₂ cup) cooking oil

1. Process chillies, dried prawns and oil in a blender until chillies are coarsely ground. Transfer mixture to a pot and place over medium heat for 10 minutes. Leave oil to cool, then bottle oil together with ground chillies.

Toasted Red Chilli Flakes

This is a standard condiment in Myanmar and Indochina. Ready-made toasted red chilli flakes is available, although the commercial variety tends to be full of seeds.

50 g (1³/₄ oz) dried red chillies, seeded and cut up coarsely

1. Dry-fry chillies in a wok for about 2 minutes over low heat, taking care not to burn chillies. When loose seeds at the bottom of the wok turn black, remove from heat.

2. Leave chillies to cool, then place in a spice mill and grind. The chillies should be in flakes. Alternatively, process chillies in a blender by pulsing to achieve fine flakes. Cut larger flakes with a pair of scissors. Store in a bottle.

Cambodian Spicy-Sweet Fish Sauce
TUK TREY CHU P'EM

The Cambodians do not eat as much spicy food as the Thais, so make this
dipping sauce with relatively mild chillies. The ground roasted peanuts should be
sprinkled into the dip just before serving.

3 Tbsp sugar

3 Tbsp hot water

4 Tbsp fish sauce

3 fresh mild chillies, seeded
and finely chopped

1 clove garlic, peeled and
finely chopped

4 Tbsp lime juice

75 g (2$^{1}/_{2}$ oz) roasted
peanuts, coarsely ground

1. Melt sugar in the hot water, then pour into a bottle with fish sauce,
    chillies, garlic and lime juice. Store refrigerated.

Seven-Flavour Chilli
SHICHIMI TOGARASHI

This is a mix of seven ingredients and the combination may vary, with some using more than
these seven ingredients. Instead of mandarin orange peel, you can also use orange or lemon peel.
Some combinations include hemp (cannabis) seeds and/or poppy seeds.
Reduce the amount of chilli powder if you prefer it less spicy.

1$^{1}/_{2}$ Tbsp white sesame
seeds

Mandarin orange peel

$^{3}/_{4}$ Tbsp chilli powder

1 Tbsp black sesame seeds

1 tsp ground seaweed

$^{1}/_{2}$ tsp mustard powder

$^{1}/_{2}$ tsp ground ginger

1. Dry-fry white sesame seeds over low heat until fragrant and starting
    to brown. Remove from heat but keep stirring for another 2 minutes.
    (Black sesame seeds are usually not toasted.)

2. Pound in a mortar and pestle to break up the seeds and release the
    oils.

3. Use a sharp knife to cut off the thin layer of zest from the mandarin
    orange peel. Chop very finely to get $^{1}/_{2}$ tsp.

4. Combine ingredients in a bottle. Refrigerate to extend its shelf life.

Garam Masala

In this recipe, a mix of ground spices and whole seeds is used,
as some spices are hard to reduce to powder in a home kitchen.
Toasting whole seed spices before grinding gives a superb spice fragrance.

1 Tbsp coriander seeds

2 tsp cumin

4 pods large brown cardamoms

$^1/_2$ tsp grated nutmeg

$^1/_2$ tsp ground cloves

$^1/_2$ tsp ground cinnamon

1 tsp ground black pepper

1. Dry-fry coriander and cumin seeds until fragrant.

2. Seed cardamoms, discarding shells and keeping the tiny black seeds.

3. Put grated nutmeg, cardamom seeds, toasted coriander and cumin seeds in a mortar and pound to a fine dust.

4. Mix in ground cloves, cinnamon and black pepper and bottle the blend. Store in the fridge to extend shelf life.

Straits Chinese Meat Curry Powder

This curry powder can be used in any recipe calling for curry powder. If desired,
the curry powder can be lightly toasted in the oven before bagging. Take care not to burn it.

MAKES 500 G (1 LB $1^1/_2$ OZ)

250 g (9 oz) ground coriander

50 g ($1^3/_4$ oz) ground cumin

50 g ($1^3/_4$ oz) ground fennel

150 g ($5^1/_3$ oz) chilli powder

2 Tbsp ground turmeric

1 Tbsp ground white pepper

1 tsp ground green cardamoms

1 tsp ground cinnamon

2 tsp ground cloves

1. Mix all the ingredients together in a large plastic bag. Hold the mouth of the bag close and shake the bag well to mix the ingredients.

2. Store in a resealable plastic bag in the fridge to extend shelf life.

Korean Sesame Salt

Korean and Japanese noodle dishes are often sprinkled with sesame salt or seven-flavour chilli (page 36). Bottled sesame salt is found in Asian stores, but making it at home is easy and it tastes more fragrant. Sesame salt keeps well in the fridge. Change the ratio of sesame seeds and salt to suit your taste.

60 g (2 oz) white sesame seeds

1^1/$_2$ tsp fine salt

1. Dry-fry sesame seeds over low heat until fragrant and brown. Remove from heat immediately and continue stirring for another 2 minutes.

2. Leave to cool, then pound sesame seeds with salt in a mortar and pestle to get a very coarse powder. Bottle and store in the fridge to extend shelf life.

Vietnamese Chilli Dipping Sauce
NUOC CHAM

This sour spicy dipping sauce will keep in the fridge for several days. It tastes great with any of the Vietnamese noodle dishes and can also be used as a dressing for Vietnamese salads.

MAKES ABOUT ^{1}/$_2$ CUP

3 Tbsp fresh lime juice

6 bird's eye chillies, finely pounded

2 cloves garlic, peeled and finely pounded

1 tsp sugar

2 Tbsp fish sauce

1. Place all ingredients in a small bottle with a lid. Cover and shake to mix well.

Quickie Pickled Radish, Chinese-Style

200 g (7 oz) white or green radish

125 ml (4 fl oz / ^{1}/$_2$ cup) Chinese white rice vinegar

200 g (7 oz) sugar

1 tsp salt

1. Peel radish and slice thinly or into matchsticks.

2. Bring a pot of water to the boil and blanch radish for 5 seconds. Place radish in a colander and leave to drain and cool.

3. Bring vinegar, sugar and salt to the boil until sugar dissolves. Leave to cool completely, then pour solution into a jar large enough to hold radish.

4. Squeeze water from radish, then place radish into the jar with vinegar solution. Leave to stand for 24 hours before consuming.

Korean Kimchi

Kimchi adds tang to many rich fried noodle dishes. It is traditionally made at the start of autumn, after which the jars of kimchi are buried to ferment in the cold of winter. In the tropics, kimchi should be left in the fridge. Use glass or porcelain crocks for fermentation and pick jars with covers that can pop up. The fermentation produces gases, so the jars should not be packed to the brim but only three-quarters full. Once kimchi has fermented, it can be re-packed together to save fridge space. Always handle kimchi with a clean, dry spoon to prevent spoilage.

2 kg (4 lb 6 oz) Tientsin cabbage

225 g (8 oz) salt

4 litres (128 fl oz / 16 cups) water

500 g (1 lb $1^{1}/_{2}$ oz) white radish, peeled and cut into finger-length fine strips

500 g (1 lb $1^{1}/_{2}$ oz) watercress, rinsed and coarsely chopped

100 g ($3^{1}/_{2}$ oz) spring onions (scallions), rinsed and cut into finger-lengths

100 g ($3^{1}/_{2}$ oz) green chives, rinsed and cut into finger-lengths

SPICE PASTE

50 g ($1^{3}/_{4}$ oz) prawns (shrimps), squid or oysters

$^{3}/_{4}$ cup raw dried red chilli paste (page 33)

175 g ($6^{1}/_{2}$ oz) garlic, peeled

100 g ($3^{1}/_{2}$ oz) old ginger, peeled

$^{1}/_{2}$ Tbsp salt

Water for blending

1. Rinse cabbage. Halve the stems and cut into strips 2–4-cm (1–1.5-in) wide. Cut the leaves into larger pieces. The size is not important and kimchi can also be sliced more thinly before cooking.

2. Mix salt and water in a large basin. Add cabbage and radish to soak for at least 4 hours until very limp.

3. Meanwhile, prepare spice paste. If using prawns, shell and devein before processing. Place all ingredients except salt into a blender and process to a fine paste, adding a little water if necessary. Stir salt into ground paste.

4. Put watercress into a bowl together with some salted water from soaking cabbage. Leave for at least 30 minutes. Squeeze water from watercress and set aside.

5. In a container large enough to hold everything, mix spice paste with spring onions, chives and watercress.

6. Squeeze out salted water from cabbage and radish and mix well into the spice paste mixture.

7. Pack kimchi into jars until three-quarters full.

8. Spread a thick layer of newspapers in a cool corner of the kitchen counter. Place jars of kimchi on the newspaper with lids loosely on. Wrap jars loosely with a thick layer of newspapers and let kimchi sit for 72 hours undisturbed.

9. After 72 hours, transfer jars to the fridge to complete fermentation. Do not stir or disturb the fermentation in any way.

10. The kimchi is ready for eating after a month. Kimchi keeps very well in the fridge for many months although it will continue to ferment and turn more sour with time.

Chinese Fish Balls and Fish Cakes

Fish balls and fish cakes are a common ingredient added to South East Asian noodles. The traditional method of making fish balls was to pound fish meat and salt in a mortar and pestle until the mixture turned smooth and glossy. To make your own fish balls, use a non-oily white fish. The flesh should be firm and easily scraped away from the bones. The traditional fish used in Singapore goes by a local name that translates into English as "sweet potato fish". It is a pink-yellow fish with hard bones, scales and a distinctive yellow tail, hence its name, yellow tail fusilier *(Fam. Lutjanidae caesio erthrogaster cuvier)*. Fish balls can also be made with pike-conger eel *(Fam. Muraenesicudae congresox talabonoides (Bleeker))*. Pike-conger eel has the advantage of having no scales and bones that are easily removed. The basic fish paste can also be used to make Chinese fish cakes and *kamaboko* (Japanese fish cake).

FISH BALLS (MAKES 16–20)

Fish paste

250 g (9 oz) boneless fish meat

$^3/_4$ tsp salt

3 Tbsp water

1. Combine ingredients in a blender and process for 10 minutes to get a smooth and elastic paste.

2. To make fish balls, put $^1/_2$ Tbsp salt into each of 2 small basins of water. One basin is for holding the fish balls and the other is for wetting your hands and the spoon.

3. Wet your left hand first in the salted water, then take a handful of the fish paste and squeeze and shape it into a lump that is free of air bubbles. To shape the ball, squeeze some fish paste out from the circle formed by your thumb and forefinger when your fist is clenched. The ball should be reasonably smooth and without air holes inside. Pat with the wet spoon to get a smooth ball (page 41).

4. Scoop the ball out using the spoon and drop it into the basin of salted water. If the ball is not round enough, pat or roll carefully until it is round. Repeat until you get an even number of fish balls. Rest fish balls for a couple of hours in the salted water before cooking. Uncooked fish balls keep well in the fridge for several days but change the salted water daily.

5. To cook fish balls, bring a pot of water to the boil. Drop in fish balls and when they float, the fish balls are cooked. Scoop out the fish balls and store in a covered box in the fridge if not immediately required.

FISH CAKE (MAKES 4)

1. To make fish cake, prepare the fish paste as in step 1 above. Wet both hands with salted water and form fish paste into 4 loaves. Heat oil for deep-frying and deep-fry fish cakes until golden brown. Cool and slice or cut into wedges. Use as a garnish or for frying with noodles.

Prawn Cakes

Slices of prawn cake are sometimes used as garnish, although given the higher price of prawns, it is not common. The preference is to use the prawns whole. Still, prawn cakes are very tasty and prawns are sometimes more easily available than the right kind of fish for fish cakes. Measure out the prawn meat after shelling.

MAKES 3 CAKES

200 g (7 oz) prawn meat

$^1/_2$ tsp salt

Cooking oil for frying

1. Place prawn meat and salt into a blender and process for 10 minutes to a smooth, thick paste.

2. Prepare a small basin of lightly salted water.

3. Wet both hands with salted water and form paste into 3 flat cakes. Leave prawn cakes in salted water for 1 hour.

4. Pour oil into a frying pan or wok until about 2-cm (1-in) high. Heat oil over medium heat. Pat prawn cakes dry, then lower into hot oil and fry until nicely brown and pink. Drain well and slice to serve.

Meat Balls

These meat balls can be made with either pork or beef. Fish and prawn balls can be made the same way.

MAKES ABOUT 20 BALLS

200 g (7 oz) minced pork or beef

1 tsp salt

$^1/_2$ tsp ground white pepper

1. Combine ingredients in a blender and process for 10 minutes to form a thick, smooth paste.

2. Prepare 2 basins of lightly salted water (page 40).

3. Wet both hands with salted water, then take a handful of meat paste and clench your fist, allowing meat paste to be squeezed out from between your thumb and index finger. Scoop ball of meat paste out with a wet spoon and place in basin of salted water. Repeat to get about 20 meat balls, depending on the size of the balls.

4. To cook meat balls, bring a pot of water to the boil and drop meat balls in. Boil until balls float up or about 10 minutes, depending on the size of the balls.

Boiled Prawns

This is a standard garnish in dressed, fried and soup noodles in South East Asia. It is important that the prawns used are fresh and not overcooked. The fresh prawns complete with shell, heads and tails are dropped into boiling water and taken out as soon as they turn pink. The prawns are then shelled, but the tails may be kept depending on preference. The shells and the prawn heads may be boiled for 10 minutes to get prawn stock. If the prawns are large, they should be deveined (page 22). Half the weight of prawns is in the head and shells, thus 100 g (3¹/₂ oz) prawns with head and shell will yield about 50 g (1³/₄ oz) shelled prawns, enough for just one serving.

500 g (1 lb 1¹/₂ oz) fresh prawns (shrimps) in their shells, rinsed

1. Bring a small pot of water to the boil, then drop in prawns. When prawns change colour, remove from heat. If prawns are large, simmer for another 1 minute to cook the inside.

2. Leave prawns to cool in the stock. When cool, shell prawns. Devein prawns if large.

3. Return prawn heads and shells to the stock and return to the boil for 10 minutes.

4. Discard shells and heads and freeze stock for use another time.

Chinese Red Roast Pork
CHA SHAO

Chinese-style red roast pork is a common garnish for Chinese noodle dishes.
The traditional way to prepare this dish is with a well-marbled piece of pork.
The fat keeps the meat tender and juicy. These days, fatty pork is out of favour with the health-conscious and most accept the drier texture of lean pork. Use chicken breast if desired.

500 g (1 lb 1¹/₂ oz) pork, preferably with some fat

A few drops red food colouring

2 tsp sugar or honey

1 Tbsp dark soy sauce

¹/₂ Tbsp light soy sauce

1. Cut pork into thick strips about 5 cm (2 in) across and about 2.5-cm (1-in) thick.

2. Mix all ingredients and leave to marinate for a few hours or overnight.

3. Grill pork on both sides over medium heat until done. Takes about 15 minutes each side. The time depends on the thickness of the meat.

4. Leave to cool until pork can be handled. Slice according to preference.

Burmese Dhal Crackers

This is an essential ingredient in Burmese noodle dishes. Substitute with fish or prawn crackers, if desired. These crackers may also be used in other Asian noodle dishes that call for a garnish of deep-fried noodles or rice crackers.

100 g (3$\frac{1}{2}$ oz) rice flour

2 Tbsp mung *dhal*, rinsed and soaked overnight

$\frac{1}{4}$ tsp ground turmeric

1 tsp salt

200 ml (6$\frac{1}{2}$ fl oz) water

Cooking oil for deep-frying

1. Stir together rice flour, mung *dhal*, turmeric, salt and water to a thin batter.

2. Heat oil in a wok or frying pan. The level of oil should be high enough to deep-fry the crackers.

3. When oil is hot, ladle in a scoop of batter. The batter will spread out and float up. Fry over medium heat until golden brown and *dhal* is crisp. Drain cracker on some paper towels. You can fry more than one cracker at a time if the frying pan is large enough to accommodate several floating crackers.

4. Store in an airtight container.

Pork Stock

Pork stock keeps well frozen. Frozen stock is handy for making quick noodle soups.

MAKES 4 LITRES (128 FL OZ / 16 CUPS)

2 kg (4 lb 6 oz) pork bones with some meat

6 litres (192 fl oz / 24 cups) water

1. Place pork bones and water into a large stockpot and bring to the boil. Skim off any scum that rises to the top.

2. Simmer gently for 2 hours or until stock is reduced to about 4 litres (128 fl oz / 16 cups).

3. Leave to cool slightly, then discard bones and reserve meat. Strain stock to remove any bone fragments.

4. Store in 1-litre (32-fl oz / 4-cups) freezer containers and freeze stock and meat until needed.

Prawn Stock

Save the shells and heads whenever preparing prawns. Freeze until you have at least
500 g (1 lb 1^1/$_2$ oz) to make stock. Some cooks make prawn stock by
pounding the shells and heads to a pulp before mixing in water and
straining the liquid to be boiled up for stock. This method is much easier.

MAKES 2 LITRES (64 FL OZ / 8 CUPS)

1 kg (2 lb 3 oz) prawn shells
and heads

2 litres (64 fl oz / 8 cups)
water

1. Put shells and heads into a pot with water and boil for 10 minutes.
   Cool, then strain stock. Freeze stock in 500-ml (16-fl oz / 2-cups)
   freezer containers until needed.

Fish Stock

MAKES 1 LITRE (32 FL OZ / 4 CUPS)

500 g (1 lb 1^1/$_2$ oz) fish
bones, tail pieces

1 litre (32 fl oz / 4 cups)
water

1. Combine ingredients into a pot and bring to the boil. Lower heat and
   simmer for 10 minutes. Strain stock, cool and freeze until needed.

Chicken Stock

MAKES 4 LITRES (128 FL OZ / 16 CUPS)

2 kg (4 lb 6 oz) chicken
bones and parts (back and
feet)

5 litres (160 fl oz / 20 cups)
water

1. Combine ingredients in a large stockpot. Simmer for 45 minutes.
   Leave to cool, then skim off fat.

2. Strain stock, cool and store in 1-litre (32-fl oz / 4-cups) freezer
   containers in the freezer until needed.

Beef Stock

MAKES 4 LITRES (128 FL OZ / 16 CUPS)

2 kg (4 lb 6 oz) beef bones
with some meat

6 litres (192 fl oz / 24 fl oz)
water

1. Rinse bones and place in a large stockpot with water. Bring to the boil
   and skim off any scum that floats to the top during boiling.

2. Simmer over low heat for 3 hours or until liquid is reduced to about
   4 litres (128 fl oz / 16 cups). Leave to cool, then skim off as much fat
   as possible.

3. Freeze in 1-litre (32-fl oz / 4-cups) freezer containers until needed.

Lard

Ask the butcher for the right kind of fat to make lard . Lard keeps well in the freezer.

250 g (9 oz) pork fat, cut into 1-cm (¹/₂-in) cubes

1. Heat fat in a large saucepan over low heat to extract oil. Take care that the bits of crackling do not burn . The crispy pieces of crackling are delicious with dressed or fried noodles.

Dashi

Dashi is the basic soup stock for many Japanese dishes including noodle soups. It is made with *konbu* (kelp) and shaved bonito. Dried sardines *(niboshi)* or dried anchovies *(yakiboshi)*, *ikan bilis* in Malay, can be used in place of bonito. Alternatively, prepare plain *konbu* dashi or mushroom dashi. Japanese *konbu* is available from Japanese supermarkets as well as stores patronised by Koreans and mainland Chinese. In Singapore and Hong Kong, *konbu* can also be found in wholesale dried goods markets especially those specialising in seafood. They are usually priced lower than Japanese *konbu*. Dried anchovies are also found in wet markets in most parts of South East Asia where these little dried fish are also used as a soup stock ingredient. Dashi does not freeze well and it is best to make and use the dashi up within a few days. To turn dashi into a dipping sauce or soup broth, mirin and light soy sauce are added to the dashi.

MAKES 1 LITRE (32 FL OZ / 4 CUPS)

20-cm (8-in) length *konbu* (kelp), about 10 g (¹/₃ oz)

1 litre (32 fl oz / 1 cup) water

6 g (¹/₅ oz / ¹/₃ cup loosely packed *katsuobushi* (shaved bonito)

1. Do not wash *konbu*, but wipe clean with a paper towel. With a pair of scissors, make cuts along both sides of the sheet of *konbu* but without cutting it right through. Put *konbu* and water in a saucepan and leave to soak for 5 hours.

2. Bring *konbu* and water to the boil. Just as bubbles start to appear, remove *konbu* and set aside.

3. Add shaved bonito and simmer for 1 minute. Remove from heat and strain dashi.

Rice Noodles

Rice noodles are made from rice flour, sometimes with the addition of another starch to give the noodles more bulk, but they do not all taste alike. Fresh and dried forms of the same noodle taste different, and their labels are no less confusing. Rice sticks from Thailand look different from rice sticks from China, and what is labelled "vermicelli" may not necessarily be rice sticks. It is, therefore, important to read the ingredients label to identify the flour used to distinguish the type of noodles. This is perhaps the best guide, in addition to looking closely at the appearance of the noodles. This way, if you want broad rice noodles, it does not matter if the packet is labelled as something you are unfamiliar with, so long as the main ingredient is rice flour and the noodles are wide-cut ribbons.

Rice noodles are made either by turning rice flour into a dough, then extruding and steaming the dough, or making a rice flour batter and steaming it into sheets (page 11). The noodles are then dried or used fresh. Fresh rice noodles are pre-cooked and need only be blanched in boiling water for about 20 seconds, depending on the freshness of the noodles and how long they have been refrigerated, to be ready. The longer they have been refrigerated, the drier they get and hence a longer boiling time may be needed. If the noodles come as a large, uncut sheet, steam it until it is soft and pliable before cutting into strips or squares. Do not fry cold, hard rice noodle ribbons without softening them first. The action of stir-frying will turn the noodles into a mass of broken, chunky bits. Dried rice noodles need to be soaked in cold water until pliable. If the dried noodles are to be added to soup, they can be reconstituted by boiling without pre-soaking. If the dried noodles are to be fried, the softened noodles should be allowed to dry a little before frying.

Watch the time carefully when handling rice noodles, as the time required for these noodles to become tender varies with the manufacturer. Over-soaked or-boiled rice noodles fall apart easily when cooked. On the other hand, rice noodles should not be so hard that frying time has to be extended, as this would overcook the vegetables. Time the addition of vegetables such that they remain crisp and the noodles properly tender. During frying, if the noodles are harder than desired, sprinkle in some water, cover and turn down the heat for a minute. This should be sufficient to soften the noodles to the right tenderness. Unless they are mouse-tail noodles, cooked rice noodles should be in long strands. The noodles should also be al dente.

RICE VERMICELLI

Rice vermicelli (*mifen* or *bee hoon*) comes in strands that range from very fine to coarse. Dried rice vermicelli has bigger variations in thickness, while fresh rice vermicelli is generally medium to coarse. Brown rice vermicelli has an excellent texture because brown rice is firmer than white rice. Coarse rice vermicelli features prominently in some South East Asian noodle dishes, such as *laksa* and Burmese *mohinga*. Today, a spinach-coloured rice vermicelli is also available.

BROAD RICE NOODLES

Known as *guotiao* in Chinese and *kuay tiao* in Hokkien, broad rice noodles look like Italian linguine or fettucine but tastes nothing like pasta. The noodles are usually sold fresh in South East Asia. They are also available dried. Fresh *kuay tiao* is soft, pliable and usually coated with a layer of oil to prevent the noodles from sticking. Dried broad rice noodles are never as tasty as the fresh variety because the dried form is too firm. Even the fresh variety needs careful handling if the noodles have been refrigerated for several days. Cold rice noodles tend to dry up, harden and break easily into small pieces if not handled carefully. One way is to let them warm up to room temperature before frying. If the room is very cold, a faster way is to place the noodles in a colander and pour hot water over them. If the noodles are for soup, they can go straight from the fridge into a pot of boiling water.

The best-tasting broad rice noodles are those made with 100 per cent rice flour which makes them hard to handle as they are very soft. Commercial broad rice noodles usually have a small percentage of some other starch, such as tapioca or cornflour to make the noodles easier to handle. If you have no access to fresh broad rice noodles, but can get rice flour easily, you might want to try your hand at making your own (page 11). In Singapore, these sheets are cut into squares for the hearty Hokkien noodle dish of *kuay chap* (page 106). Steamed rice sheets are also used in that Cantonese dim sum favourite, *chee cheong fun,* which comes plain or stuffed with meat or vegetables, served with dressing (page 92).

Kuay tiao, whether dried or fresh is harder to find outside South East Asia than dried rice vermicelli, but not impossible. Even fresh *kuay tiao* appears in some big Asian stores occasionally, in the refrigerated sections, sometimes as sheets of uncut steamed dough. If fresh *kuay tiao* comes as a sheet, steam it to soften, then cut into strips or squares. Like dried rice vermicelli, dried broad rice noodles should be soaked in cold water until pliable, then boiled before frying or serving in soup. The length of time to soak and boil depends on the thickness and cut of the noodles. Care should be taken not to break up the noodles during the soaking, boiling and cooking stages.

Broad rice noodles taste best freshly cooked, as they clump up when cold. They also lose their texture quickly if left in a bowl of soup or if cooked with a sauce. They do not make good leftovers although reheating fried broad rice noodles in a microwave oven works quite well.

MOUSE-TAIL NOODLES

Known by the Cantonese name of *loh shi fun* which translates into "mouse-tail noodles" or *mee tai bak* in Hokkien, these noodles are always sold fresh. These short noodles are tapered at both ends, and are the least common of the rice noodles. Mouse-tail noodles are popular with children because they are easy to eat and very tasty in soup. Mouse-tail noodles are also delicious fried and as dressed noodles. Best of all, fresh mouse-tail noodles keep well and do not fall apart as easily as fresh rice vermicelli or fresh broad rice noodles. It also makes good party or picnic food because they do not clump up when cold.

OTHER SHAPES

Look out for dried noodles in other shapes such as these little shells (page 46). I found a bag of these in a little grocery store in Hong Kong.

RICE VERMICELLI

Singapore Noodles

This a popular dish known around the world, but it did not originate in Singapore.
I always try them whenever I see it on the menu when I travel.
Turmeric seems to figure prominently in the dish. Here is my version of it.

COOKING TIME: 20 MINUTES

4 Tbsp cooking oil

30 g (1 oz) onions, peeled and cut into cubes

1^1/$_2$ tsp salt

100 g (3^1/$_2$ oz) prawns (shrimps)

50 g (1^3/$_4$ oz) tomatoes, cubed

100 g (3^1/$_2$ oz) chicken/ pork, sliced into strips

50 g (1^3/$_4$ oz) carrots, peeled and cut into rounds

200 g (7 oz) cabbage, shredded

100 g (3^1/$_2$ oz) *choy sum*, cut into finger-lengths

300 g (11 oz) dried fine rice vermicelli, softened in cold water until pliable

2 eggs, cracked into a small bowl

SPICE PASTE
1 Tbsp meat curry powder (page 37)

1 tsp ground turmeric

1 Tbsp water

1. Prepare spice paste. Mix ingredients together to get a thick paste.

2. To fry noodles, heat 3 Tbsp oil in a wok and sauté onion until soft. Add spice paste and salt and sauté until fragrant.

3. Add prawns and tomato and fry until prawns are pink. Add chicken/ pork and cook until meat changes colour.

4. Add carrot and cabbage and fry for 30 seconds before adding *choy sum*.

5. Stir in rice vermicelli and fry until noodles are two-thirds done.

6. Make a well in the centre of the wok and add remaining oil. When oil is hot, add eggs. Spread eggs out, then cover with rice vermicelli and let eggs cook before stirring up rice vermicelli. Lower heat if noodles begin to stick or dry out. Sprinkle in some water if necessary.

7. Serve noodles hot.

Fried Rice Vermicelli with Fish Sauce and Lime Juice

This is Thai-style fried rice vermicelli but without the sugar or toasted chilli flakes. If possible, use bird's eye chillies so that the noodles have some bite. This dish keeps well.

COOKING TIME: 15 MINUTES

4 Tbsp cooking oil

1 Tbsp chopped garlic

100 g (3¹/₂ oz) prawns (shrimps), peeled

200 g (7 oz) fish cake (page 40), cut into strips

3 fresh red chillies, sliced

250 g (9 oz) bean sprouts, rinsed

100 g (3¹/₂ oz) carrots, peeled and cut into fine strips

300 g (11 oz) dried fine-medium rice vermicelli, softened in cold water until pliable

4 Tbsp fish sauce

1 bundle chives, cut into 2.5-cm (1-in) lengths

GARNISHING
Limes, halved

1. Heat oil in a wok and sauté garlic until fragrant.

2. Add prawns and fish cake followed by chilli strips, bean sprouts, carrot strips and rice vermicelli.

3. Mix well, then add fish sauce and chives and fry until noodles are tender but al dente.

4. Serve noodles garnished with lime halves.

Vegetarian Vermicelli with Five-Spice Powder

Garlic and onions are not used in traditional Chinese vegetarian cooking because
these bulbs are considered to be stimulating and therefore inappropriate for vegetarians.
However, my version of these noodles has garlic because noodles without it just does not
taste right to me. This recipe also works well with dried egg noodles.

COOKING TIME: 30 MINUTES

3 Tbsp cooking oil

1 Tbsp chopped garlic

50 g (1³/₄ oz) carrot, peeled
and cut into fine strips

200 g (7 oz) cabbage,
shredded

300 g (11 oz) dried fine-
medium rice vermicelli,
softened in cold water until
pliable

SAUCE
¹/₂ Tbsp chopped garlic

125 ml (4 fl oz / 1 cup)
water

1¹/₂ tsp salt

2 Tbsp light soy sauce

2 tsp dark soy sauce

¹/₂ tsp Chinese five-spice
powder

2 dried Chinese
mushrooms, rinsed and
softened in water, then cut
into thin strips

2 pieces bean curd sticks,
softened in cold water, then
cut into finger-lengths

GARNISHING
2 sweet bean curd slices,
rinsed, pat dry

Cooking oil for frying

CONDIMENTS
Pickled green chillies
(page 32)

1. Prepare garnish. Cut sweet bean curd slices into narrow strips.

2. Heat oil for frying and fry bean curd strips over low to medium heat
   until crisp. Take care not to burn bean curd. Set bean curd aside.
   Reserve oil for cooking sauce.

3. Prepare sauce. In a saucepan, reheat 1 Tbsp oil from cooking sweet
   bean curd and sauté chopped garlic until fragrant.

4. Add water, salt, soy sauces and five-spice powder. Bring to the boil,
   then add mushrooms and bean curd sticks. Simmer gently for
   30 minutes until liquid is reduced to about 4 Tbsp.

5. To cook noodles, heat 3 Tbsp oil and fry chopped garlic until fragrant
   and pale golden in colour. Add carrot and cabbage and mix well.

6. Stir in softened rice vermicelli, followed by sauce and its ingredients.
   Mix well and fry until noodles are tender but al dente and dry.

7. Serve garnished with sweet bean curd slices and pickled green chillies
   on the side.

Spicy Rice Vermicelli Fried with Herbs

Fresh herbs give this fried rice vermicelli its great flavour. Use whatever fresh herbs you have on hand. You can substitute the fresh variety with dried herbs but use just one kind. The easiest combination would be coriander leaves, spring onion and celery leaves, whether Chinese or western celery. Basil, mint and sawtooth coriander will give it a Thai/Vietnamese flavour.

COOKING TIME: 15 MINUTES

4 Tbsp cooking oil

1 Tbsp chopped garlic

100 g (3½ oz) fish cake (page 40), sliced into strips

100 g (3½ oz) prawns (shrimps), peeled

2 Tbsp light soy sauce

300 g (11 oz) bean sprouts

300 g (11 oz) dried fine-medium rice vermicelli, softened in cold water until pliable

1 tsp salt

1 Tbsp water

200 g (7 oz) fresh herb mix (coriander leaves (cilantro), spring onion (scallion), Chinese celery, turmeric leaves, basil and/or mint), chopped

SPICE PASTE

50 g (1¾ oz) fresh red chillies, seeded

50 g (1¾ oz) shallots, peeled

2 cloves garlic, peeled

1 Tbsp water

1. Prepare spice paste. Place ingredients into a blender and process until fine.

2. To fry noodles, heat 1 Tbsp oil in a wok and sauté garlic until fragrant and pale gold in colour. Add fish cake, prawns, 1 Tbsp light soy sauce and stir-fry until prawns turn pink. The mixture should be moist. Scoop mixture out into a bowl and set aside.

3. Heat remaining oil in the same wok and fry spice paste until oil rises to the top. Add bean sprouts and mix well, then stir in rice vermicelli, remaining light soy sauce, salt and water.

4. When noodles are about 1 minute away from being tender, stir in fish cake and prawns. Mix well and fry until noodles are tender but still al dente.

5. Stir in herb mix, mixing it well into the noodles. Remove from heat when herbs turn limp.

6. Serve noodles hot or cold.

Rice Vermicelli Fried with Soy Sauce

This family favourite was the very first dish that I learnt to cook as a teenager. In fact, I learnt to fry noodles before learning how to boil rice or make a curry.

COOKING TIME: 15 MINUTES

4 Tbsp cooking oil

1 Tbsp chopped garlic

100 g (3^1/$_2$ oz) pork, sliced into thin, narrow strips

100 g (3^1/$_2$ oz) prawns (shrimps), peeled

250 g (9 oz) *choy sum*, cut into finger-lengths, stems and leaves separated

250 g (9 oz) bean sprouts

300 g (11 oz) dried fine-medium vermicelli, softened in cold water until pliable

3 Tbsp light soy sauce

1 tsp dark soy sauce

^{1}/$_2$ tsp salt

CONDIMENTS

Fresh red chillies with light soy sauce (page 31) or garlic chilli sauce (page 34)

1. Heat oil in a wok and sauté garlic until fragrant and beginning to brown.

2. Add pork and when meat is almost cooked, add prawns.

3. When prawns turn pink, add *choy sum* stems and beans sprouts, then rice vermicelli followed by light and dark soy sauces. Mix well to colour noodles evenly.

4. Add *choy sum* leaves last and cover with rice vermicelli to cook greens. Fry until noodles are tender but still al dente.

5. Serve with a condiment of fresh red chillies and light soy sauce or garlic chilli sauce.

Rice Vermicelli Fried with Oyster Sauce

4 Tbsp cooking oil

1 Tbsp chopped garlic

2 fresh red chillies, seeded and cut into strips

3 Tbsp oyster sauce

400 g (14^1/$_3$ oz) shelled prawns (shrimps)

500 g (1 lb 1^1/$_2$ oz) sliced cabbage

300 g (11 oz) dried fine-medium vermicelli, softened in cold water until pliable

1 Tbsp light soy sauce

^{1}/$_2$ tsp salt

GARNISHING

Limes, halved

1. Heat oil in wok and sauté garlic and chilli strips for 30 seconds then add oyster sauce, prawns and cabbage. When prawns turn pink, stir in vermicelli, soy sauce and salt. Fry till noodles are tender but still al dente.

2. Serve with lime halves.

Fried Shan Noodles

KHOWSEN KHO

This fried rice noodle dish originates from the Shan plateau region of central Myanmar. An essential ingredient is fermented soybean powder *(ponyegyi)*. The fermented soybeans are dried into wafers and ground into a powder. Substitute *ponyegyi* with Chinese fermented soybean paste *(taucheo)*, dark Japanese miso or well-fermented Indonesian tempeh, if unavailable.

COOKING TIME: 1 HOUR

300 g (11 oz) belly pork, thinly sliced

$^1/_2$ tsp ground turmeric

1 tsp salt + a large pinch

300 g (11 oz) ripe tomatoes

300 g (11 oz) dried coarse rice vermicelli, softened in cold water until pliable or 600 g (1 lb 5$^1/_3$ oz) fresh coarse rice vermicelli

4 Tbsp lard (page 45)

100 g (3$^1/_2$ oz) onions, peeled and thinly sliced

2 Tbsp fermented soybean powder

1 Tbsp dark soy sauce

$^1/_2$ tsp ground black pepper

1 spring onion (scallion), cut into finger-lengths

PORK SOUP

1 litre (32 fl oz / 4 cups) water

500 g (1 lb 1$^1/_2$ oz) pork ribs

2 tsp salt

1 bunch spring onions (scallions), finely chopped

GARNISHING

3 eggs, beaten

$^1/_2$ tsp salt

1 Tbsp cooking oil

Limes, halved

1 bunch chives, chopped

$^1/_4$ cup fried garlic (page 30)

1. Prepare omelette for garnish. Beat eggs with salt, Heat oil in an omelette pan and make 2 omelettes. Roll omelettes up and cut into strips. Set aside.

2. Prepare pork soup. Bring water to boil and add pork ribs and salt. Simmer until water is reduced by nearly half and meat is tender. To serve, ladle soup and ribs into individual serving bowls and sprinkle some chopped spring onions. While soup is simmering, prepare to cook noodles. Rub belly pork with turmeric and a large pinch of salt. Set aside.

3. Using a sharp knife, peel tomato skin, then chop tomatoes finely.

4. Bring a pot of water to the boil and blanch noodles until nearly tender and still very al dente. The timing depends on whether fresh or dried coarse noodles are used. Drain noodles in a colander. Do not start boiling noodles until you are ready to fry them.

5. Heat lard in a wok and sauté onion until transparent and soft. Add marinated pork and fry until meat is cooked and fairly dry. Add tomatoes and remaining salt and cook until tomatoes are no longer watery. Stir in fermented soybean powder, soy sauce and pepper, then add blanched noodles.

6. Fry until noodles are tender but still al dente. Add spring onions last. Dish fried noodles out onto a large serving platter and top with omelette, lime halves, chives and fried garlic. Serve noodles with pork rib soup.

Fried Rice Vermicelli, Thai-Style

PAD THAI

This is a common Thai hawker and restaurant dish.

COOKING TIME: 20 MINUTES

5 Tbsp cooking oil

2 eggs, beaten

1 Tbsp chopped shallots

1 Tbsp chopped garlic

300 g (11 oz) dried fine rice vermicelli, softened in cold water until pliable

2 tsp raw dried red chilli paste (page 33)

50 g (1³/₄ oz) pork, thinly sliced

100 g (3¹/₂ oz) firm bean curd, sliced

200 g (7 oz) bean sprouts, rinsed

1 small bunch chives, cut into finger-lengths

SEASONING

4 Tbsp water

1 Tbsp tamarind paste

3 Tbsp fish sauce

2 Tbsp sugar

A few drops dark soy sauce

CONDIMENTS

1 Tbsp toasted red chilli flakes (page 35)

1 small bowl sugar

GARNISHING

150 g (5¹/₃ oz) peanuts, toasted and ground

100 g (3¹/₂ oz) bean sprouts, rinsed and tailed

Limes, halved

1. Prepare seasoning. Mix water with tamarind paste. Strain liquid and discard solids. Divide tamarind juice into 2 portions.

2. In one portion, stir in 2 Tbsp fish sauce, 1 Tbsp sugar and a few drops of dark soy sauce. In the other portion, stir in remaining fish sauce and sugar. Be sure you can tell them apart.

3. Start preparing to cook noodles. Heat a little oil in a frying pan and make 3 thin omelettes with beaten eggs. Roll omelettes up and shred.

4. Heat 3 Tbsp oil in a wok and fry shallots for 1 minute before adding garlic to brown.

5. Stir in noodles and tamarind juice with dark soy sauce. Mix well to colour noodles evenly and fry until noodles are tender but still al dente. Scoop noodles out and set aside.

6. Heat remaining oil in the wok and fry chilli paste until oil rises to the top. Add pork, bean curd and second bowl of tamarind juice with fish sauce. Fry until pork is cooked.

7. Stir in bean sprouts, chives, omelette strips and fried noodles and mix well.

8. Serve noodles on a large serving platter. Garnish with peanuts, raw bean sprouts and lime halves, and serve chilli flakes and sugar on the side.

Dry Rice Vermicelli, Malay-Style

DRY MEE SIAM

**The Malay name of this dish means "Siam noodles", the name Thailand
was known by before 1945, but there are doubts that this dish originated in Thailand!**
Mee siam is also served in a spicy gravy (page 82 and 84).

COOKING TIME: 15 MINUTES

4 Tbsp cooking oil

250 g (9 oz) firm bean curd, cut crosswise in half

85 ml (2½ fl oz / ⅓ cup) water

2 Tbsp tamarind paste

50 g (1¾ oz) onions, peeled and thinly sliced

300 g (11 oz) small prawns (shrimps), peeled

2 tsp sugar

1 tsp salt

250 g (9 oz) bean sprouts, rinsed

300 g (11 oz) dried fine rice vermicelli, softened in cold water until pliable

100 g (3½ oz) chives, coarsely chopped

SPICE PASTE

100 g (3½ oz) shallots

1 tsp dried prawn paste (*belacan*)

1 Tbsp water

2 Tbsp fermented soybean paste (*taucheo*)

2 Tbsp raw dried red chilli paste (page 33)

1. Prepare spice paste. Place shallots, dried prawn paste, water and fermented soybean paste in a blender and process until fine. Mix in chilli paste. Set aside.

2. Heat oil in a wok and fry bean curd to get a firm, brown skin. Leave to cool, then cut into small cubes and set aside.

3. Mix water with tamarind paste. Strain juice and discard solids. Set tamarind juice aside.

4. Reheat oil in the same wok and fry spice paste until oil rises to the top. Add onion and fry for 1 minute. The onion should still be firm.

5. Add prawns and fry until pink.

6. Stir in sugar, salt and tamarind juice and mix well.

7. Add bean sprouts and noodles, mixing well and frying until noodles are tender but still al dente.

8. Stir in chopped chives and bean curd cubes. Mix well, then dish out onto a large serving platter.

Crispy Thai Rice Noodles

MEE KROB

This Thai dish is very rich and is best served as an appetiser or snack. You may also pair it with rice, in which case, increase the quantity of meat and bean curd and reduce the rice vermicelli.

COOKING TIME: 30 MINUTES

300 g (11 oz) dried fine rice vermicelli

500 ml (16 fl oz / 2 cups) cooking oil

2 Tbsp chopped garlic

50 g (1³/₄ oz) shallots, peeled and thinly sliced

1 Tbsp fermented soybean paste *(taucheo)*, finely mashed

200 g (7 oz) pork/chicken/prawns (shrimps)

100 g (3¹/₂ oz) leeks, finely sliced

100 g (3¹/₂ oz) firm bean curd

2 eggs, beaten

1 tsp toasted red chilli flakes (page 35)

SEASONING

4 Tbsp fish sauce

1¹/₂ Tbsp Chinese white rice vinegar

200 g (7 oz) sugar

4 Tbsp water

GARNISHING

200 g (7 oz) bean sprouts, rinsed

1 bunch coriander leaves (cilantro), chopped

4 fresh red chillies, seeded and finely sliced

2 cloves pickled garlic (optional), sliced

1. Put dried rice vermicelli into a large plastic bag and break into shorter strands.

2. Heat oil in a wok and deep-fry vermicelli in small batches until pale gold in colour. It will take just seconds if the oil is hot enough. Scoop crisp vermicelli out very quickly and place on a large tray lined with paper towels.

3. Combine all ingredients for seasoning in a small bowl and set aside,

4. Remove all but 3 Tbsp oil from wok and sauté chopped garlic, shallots and fermented soybean paste until fragrant. Add pork/chicken/prawns, leeks and bean curd, stirring well.

5. Make a well in the centre of ingredients and add beaten eggs. Mix well with ingredients, then add seasoning and bring to the boil.

6. Stir in chilli flakes, crisp vermicelli and mix well, coating vermicelli with thick sweet sauce.

7. Dish out onto a large serving platter and garnish with raw bean sprouts, coriander leaves, sliced red chilli and pickled garlic.

8. Serve immediately, either on its own or with rice.

Vegetarian Rice Vermicelli, Indian-Style

This dish of fried noodles keeps well. It is great as picnic food even in hot weather
as there is no worry about meat spoiling. Vary the recipe by
substituting rice vermicelli with the various wheat noodles as desired.

COOKING TIME: 15 MINUTES

4 Tbsp cooking oil

50 g (1¾ oz) onions, peeled and thinly sliced

1 Tbsp chopped garlic

6 slices ginger, peeled and finely chopped

1 Tbsp raw dried red chilli paste (page 33)

100 g (3½ oz) tomatoes, cut into cubes

1½ tsp salt

100 g (3½ oz) firm bean curd, cut into cubes

100 g (3½ oz) cabbage, shredded

100 g (3½ oz) *choy sum*, cut into finger-lengths

50 g (1¾ oz) frozen peas

100 g (3½ oz) bean sprouts

300 g (11 oz) dried fine rice vermicelli, softened in cold water until pliable

1 spring onion (scallion), chopped

1. Heat oil in a wok and sauté onion, garlic and ginger until fragrant, then add chilli paste and fry until oil rises to the top.

2. Add tomato and salt and cook until tomato is soft.

3. Stir in bean curd, cabbage, *choy sum* and peas. Sauté until *choy sum* starts to change colour.

4. Add bean sprouts and noodles and mix well. Fry until noodles are tender but still al dente.

5. Stir in chopped spring onion and serve.

South Indian / Sri Lankan Fried Rice Noodles

FRIED IDYAPAM WITH CURRY LEAVES

Like any rice noodle, *idyapam* can also be fried with egg and onion.

COOKING TIME: 10 MINUTES

600 g (1 lb 5^1/$_3$ oz) *idyapam*

1 tsp chilli powder

1 tsp ground turmeric

4 Tbsp cooking oil

1 large onion, peeled and thinly sliced

1^1/$_2$ tsp salt

1 fresh green chilli, thinly sliced

3 stalks curry leaves, leaves picked and crushed

3 eggs

GARNISHING
1 fresh green chilli, thinly sliced

1. Prepare *idyapam* (page 10). Set aside.

2. Mix chilli powder and ground turmeric with a little water to form a paste.

3. Heat 3 Tbsp oil in a wok and sauté onion until soft. Add salt, green chilli, chilli and turmeric paste and curry leaves. Mix well.

4. Add *idyapam*, chopping it into small pieces as you stir. (Only the Chinese insist on keeping noodles long.)

5. Push noodles to one side of wok. Add remaining oil. When oil is hot, add eggs to cook, then cover with noodles. Let eggs set for at least 2 minutes, turning down heat if necessary to prevent noodles from burning, or sprinkle some water over noodles. Stir to mix eggs and noodles.

6. Serve *idyapam* hot with sliced green chillies on the side.

South Indian / Sri Lankan Rice Noodles with Coconut Soup

STEAMED IDYAPAM WITH SOTHI

600 g (1 lb 5^1/$_3$ oz) *idyapam* (page 10)

COCONUT SOUP (SOTHI)
200 ml (6^3/$_4$ fl oz) packaged coconut cream

1 litre (32 fl oz / 4 cups)

water/prawn stock

100 g (3^1/$_2$ oz) dried anchovies, rinsed

100 g (3^1/$_2$ oz) shallots, peeled and thinly sliced

6 fresh red and green chillies,

coarsely sliced

1 tsp salt

5 stalks curry leaves, leaves picked and crushed

^{1}/$_4$ tsp ground turmeric

125 ml (4 fl oz/^{1}/$_2$ cup) lime juice

1. Combine all ingredients for the soup except lime juice. Bring coconut soup to the boil.

2. Serve *idyapam* with a bowl of coconut soup and add lime juice to the soup to taste.

Arakan Rice Noodle Salad and Fish Soup

RAKHINE MONTI THOKE

This is a pungent dish what with the fish, fish sauce and dried prawn paste.
Fish is an important part of the diet in Arakan on the west coast of Myanmar. Pike-conger eel
(Fam. Muraenesocidae congresox talabonoides (Bleeker)) is the typical Arakan fish for this dish.

COOKING TIME: 30 MINUTES

300 g (11 oz) dried fine rice vermicelli

STOCK

1/2 tsp dried prawn paste (*belacan*)

3 cloves garlic, peeled

200 g (7 oz) fish

1 thumb-size knob galangal, peeled and bruised

750 ml (24 fl oz / 3 cups) water

1 Tbsp raw dried red chilli paste (page 33)

2 Tbsp fish sauce

1 Tbsp lime juice

DRESSING FOR NOODLES

1/2 cup Burmese fried garlic (page 30)

1/2 Tbsp dried prawns (shrimps)

2 Tbsp toasted ground chickpeas

2 tsp fermented soybean powder (see headnote page 55)

3 Tbsp water

2 Tbsp tamarind pulp

3 Tbsp fish sauce

6 bird's eye chillies, seeded and finely pounded

50 g (1 3/4 oz) potatoes (preferably Russet), boiled until soft, then peeled and finely mashed

GARNISHING

1 bunch coriander leaves (cilantro), chopped

6 shallots, peeled and thinly sliced

Limes, halved

1. Prepare stock. Grind dried prawn paste and garlic with 1 Tbsp water and set aside.

2. Put fish, galangal, water, chilli paste and fish sauce into a pot and bring to the boil, then lower heat and simmer for 10 minutes until fish is cooked. Remove fish, cool and flake flesh with a fork. Mash flesh finely. Set aside. Return fish bones to stock and simmer for another 5 minutes. Strain stock back into pot and discard solids. Add ground dried prawn paste with garlic and flaked fish to stock and return to the boil. Remove from heat and stir in lime juice.

3. Prepare dressing for noodles. Pound fried garlic chips to a powder in a mortar and pestle. Rinse dried prawns and remove any shells. Chop dried prawns finely, then dry-fry in a wok over low heat until crisp. Pound prawns to a powder in a mortar and pestle. Mix ground chickpea and soybean powder together. Set aside. Mix water into tamarind pulp and strain juice. Discard solids. Mix with fish sauce and chillies. Set aside.

4. To prepare noodles, bring a large pot of water to boil and blanch noodles until tender but still al dente. Drain well and place in a large bowl. Stir mashed potato and tamarind juice mixture into noodles, using chopsticks, or toss with salad forks. Add ground chickpea and soybean powder mixture and mix well.

5. To serve, divide noodles into serving bowls. Garnish with coriander leaves, shallots and lime halves. Serve dressed noodles with a small bowl of fish stock. The stock can be poured over the noodles or enjoyed separately.

Fried Noodles, Filipino-Style

PANCIT GUISADO

"Pancit" means noodles and *"guisado"* means fried. The noodles used can be fine rice vermicelli, egg noodles, wheat noodles *(mee sua)* or glass noodles. The word *"guisado"* and the addition of bay leaves are clues to the Spanish colonial heritage of the Philippines.

COOKING TIME: 15 MINUTES

2 dried Chinese mushrooms

375 ml (12 fl oz / 1¹/₂ cups) water

100 g (3¹/₂ oz) pork

100 g (3¹/₂ oz) chicken

2 Tbsp cooking oil

100 g (3¹/₂ oz) onions, peeled and finely chopped

2 Tbsp chopped garlic

2 Chinese sausages, thinly sliced

2 bay leaves, crushed

¹/₂ cup snow peas

100 g (3¹/₂ oz) cabbage, shredded

50 g (1³/₄ oz) carrots, peeled and thinly sliced

300 g (11 oz) dried fine-medium rice vermicelli, softened in cold water until pliable

1¹/₂ tsp salt

1 tsp ground white pepper

1 tsp sesame oil

1 Tbsp anatto oil (page 29)

GARNISHING

1 spring onion (scallion), chopped

1 bunch coriander leaves (cilantro), chopped

2 eggs, hard-boiled, peeled and sliced

Limes, halved

CONDIMENTS

Fresh red chillies with light soy sauce (page 31)

1. Rinse mushrooms and soak in 125 ml (4 fl oz / ¹/₂ cup) water to soften. Slice softened mushrooms and set aside soaking liquid for gravy.

2. Bring remaining water to the boil, then add pork and chicken until cooked. Cut cooled pork into thin, narrow strips and chicken into cubes. Set aside stock for use in gravy.

3. Heat oil in a wok and add onion and garlic. Fry until onion begins to turn transparent and garlic brown.

4. Stir in Chinese sausages and fry for 1 minute, then add bay leaves, stock and mushroom soaking liquid and bring to the boil.

5. Add mushrooms, snow peas, cabbage and carrot and cook for 1 minute.

6. Stir in noodles, salt and pepper and fry until noodles are tender but still al dente.

7. Stir in cooked chicken, pork, sesame oil and anatto oil and mix well.

8. Dish noodles out onto a large serving platter and top with garnishes. Serve with light soy sauce and fresh cut red chillies.

Filipino-Style Noodles in Prawn Sauce

PANCIT LUGLUG

Dried wheat noodles *(mee sua)* or Cantonese-style dried egg noodles can also be
used in place of the rice noodles in this recipe. Filipino cooks sweeten the noodles with
prawn juice, made either by pounding or blending raw prawn shells and heads
with water. The lard gives these rice noodles a fantastic mouth feel.

COOKING TIME: 20 MINUTES

600 g (1 lb 5¹/₃ oz) fresh
coarse rice vermicelli

SAUCE
2 Tbsp cornflour

250 ml (8 fl oz / 1 cup)
prawn stock (page 44)

1 large bunch Chinese
celery

4 Tbsp lard (page 45)

1 large onion, peeled and
finely chopped

1 Tbsp chopped garlic

100 g (3¹/₂ oz) pork, sliced
into thin strips

200 g (7 oz) peeled prawns
(shrimps), leaving tails
intact

2 Tbsp anatto oil (page 29)

Ground white pepper to
taste

GARNISHING
100 g (3¹/₂ oz) smoked,
flaked fish or smoked
oysters

100 g (3¹/₂ oz) pork
crackling, finely pounded
or cut into thin strips

1 spring onion (scallion),
chopped

1 bunch coriander leaves
(cilantro), chopped

Limes, halved

1. Prepare sauce. Stir cornflour into prawn stock and set aside.

2. Chop leaves of Chinese celery and cut stems into finger-lengths. Keep stems separate from chopped leaves.

3. Heat lard in a wok and sauté chopped onion and garlic until onion is transparent and garlic is starting to brown.

4. Stir in Chinese celery stems, pork and prawns and sauté until prawns turn pink.

5. Add prawn stock, anatto oil and pepper to taste. Stir well and bring to the boil. Stir in chopped celery leaves last.

6. To serve noodles, bring a pot of water to the boil. Blanch noodles until tender but al dente. Drain well and place noodles into serving bowls or plates.

7. Pour sauce over noodles and top with garnishes. Serve immediately.

Cambodian Laksa

A Singaporean friend was eating Cambodian *laksa* in the Phnom Penh home of a
Cambodian friend when she suddenly remembered that I was doing a book on Asian noodles.
She came home with a list of ingredients coupled with some vague instructions on what to do with
them. There were no instructions for the basil leaves, so I ground them with the rest of the spice
paste. The result was a lovely pale-green gravy that tasted vaguely like a Thai green curry.
(I was supposed to just chop and use them as a garnish!)

COOKING TIME: 45 MINUTES

250 g (9 oz) bean sprouts

600 g (1 lb 5¹/₃ oz) fresh medium-coarse rice vermicelli

SPICE PASTE

2 stalks lemongrass, finely cut

1 thumb-size knob fresh turmeric, peeled

¹/₂ Tbsp raw dried red chilli paste (page 33)

75 g (2¹/₂ oz) shallots

A handful of basil leaves

2 Tbsp water

GRAVY

1 litre (32 fl oz / 4 cups) water

500 g (1 lb 1¹/₂ oz) grated coconut

50 g (1³/₄ oz) salted fish

3 Tbsp cooking oil

2 Tbsp chopped garlic

¹/₂ Tbsp dried prawn paste (*belacan*), crumbled

100 g (3¹/₂ oz) chicken/pork, thinly sliced

100 g (3¹/₂ oz) prawns (shrimps), peeled, leaving tails intact

3 Tbsp fish sauce

³/₄ Tbsp sugar

GARNISHING

1 small bunch *laksa* leaves

200 g (7 oz) pineapple flesh, coarsely shredded

1 cup peanuts, roasted and ground

50 g (1³/₄ oz) cucumber, shredded

Limes, halved

4 fresh red chillies, seeded and sliced

1. Prepare spice paste. Combine ingredients in a blender and process until smooth. Set aside.

2. Prepare gravy. Mix water with grated coconut and squeeze through a muslin bag or cloth-lined sieve to obtain coconut milk. Set coconut milk aside in a bowl.

3. Rinse salted fish and remove any bones. Slice fish thinly and pound in a mortar and pestle until fine. Chop with a knife if necessary.

4. Heat oil in a saucepan and sauté garlic and dried prawn paste until fragrant. Stir in spice paste and sauté until fragrant and oil separates from paste.

5. Stir in ground salted fish and chicken/pork, and fry until meat is cooked. Add prawns and fry until prawns begin to turn pink. Add coconut milk, fish sauce and sugar and bring to the boil.

6. Prepare garnish. Pick *laksa* leaves and discard stalks. Rinse leaves well, then chop finely.

7. To serve noodles, bring a pot of water to the boil. Blanch bean sprouts for 10 seconds, then drain and divide into serving bowls. Return pot of water to the boil, then blanch noodles until tender but still al dente. Drain and divide into serving bowls. Ladle gravy with meat and prawns over noodles. Top with garnishes and serve immediately.

Rice Noodles in Coconut Gravy, Sarawak-Style
SARAWAK LAKSA

In Sarawak, East Malaysia, the wet markets sell ready-to-cook spice paste for Sarawak *laksa*. This thick black paste is boiled up in stock which is then strained and the pulp discarded. This recipe is my take on this particular spice paste which gives the best-tasting Sarawak *laksa* I have eaten. As in Singapore *laksa*, Hokkien *mee* (fresh cooked yellow wheat noodles) can be substituted for rice vermicelli. The stock for the gravy can be either chicken or prawn or a combination of both.

COOKING TIME: 30 MINUTES

250 g (9 oz) bean sprouts

320 g (11^1/$_3$ oz) dried fine-medium rice vermicelli, softened in cold water until pliable

SPICE PASTE
4 candlenuts

1 tsp dried prawn paste (*belacan*)

5 slices galangal, peeled

1 stalk lemongrass, finely cut

2 Tbsp water

1 Tbsp ground coriander

1^1/$_2$ Tbsp ground black pepper

4 Tbsp raw dried red chilli paste (page 33)

GRAVY
500 ml (16 fl oz / 2 cups) water

500 g (1 lb 1^1/$_2$ oz) grated coconut

5 Tbsp cooking oil

150 g (5^1/$_3$ oz) shallots, peeled and thinly sliced

1 Tbsp chopped garlic

2 tsp salt

GARNISHING
200 g (7 oz) chicken

200 g (7 oz) prawns (shrimps)

100 g (3^1/$_2$ oz) cucumber, shredded

Limes, halved

1. Prepare garnish. Bring 750 ml (24 fl oz / 3 cups) water to the boil in a pot, then lower heat to a simmer. Add chicken until cooked. Remove chicken and leave to cool before cutting meat into cubes. Set meat aside and reserve bones.

2. Reheat stock and boil prawns until pink. Remove, cool and peel prawns. Reserve prawn shells. Return prawn shells and chicken bones to stock and simmer for another 10 minutes. Strain stock and discard shells and bones. Reserve 500 ml (16 fl oz / 2 cups) stock for use in gravy.

3. Prepare spice paste. Blend candlenuts, dried prawn paste, galangal and lemongrass with 2 Tbsp water to a fine paste. Mix in ground coriander, pepper and chilli paste. Set aside.

4. Prepare gravy. Mix water with grated coconut and squeeze through a muslin bag or cloth-lined sieve to obtain coconut milk. Set aside. Heat oil in a pot and fry shallots to a nice dark brown. Halfway through, add chopped garlic. Stir in spice paste and fry until fragrant and oil separates from paste. Add reserved stock and salt. Bring to the boil. Add coconut milk and bring to a near-boil.

5. To serve noodles, bring a large pot of water to the boil. Blanch bean sprouts for 10 seconds, then drain and divide into serving bowls. Return water to the boil and cook noodles until tender but still al dente. Drain and divide into serving bowls. Ladle hot gravy over noodles, then garnish with chicken, prawns, shredded cucumber and limes. Serve immediately.

Rice Noodles in Fish Soup, Penang-Style

PENANG LAKSA

The fish traditionally used for this dish is wolf-herring, also called *dorab* or *ikan parang* (*Fam. Chirocentridae Chirocentrus dorab (Foskal)*). However, any soft-fleshed fish that flakes easily will do as well, including canned sardines in tomato sauce. If using the latter, discard the tomato sauce.

COOKING TIME: 45 MINUTES

1 torch ginger bud

1 large bunch *laksa* leaves

600 g (1 lb 5$^1/_3$ oz) fresh medium-coarse rice vermicelli

SPICE PASTE

150 g (5$^1/_3$ oz) shallots

1 tsp dried prawn paste (*belacan*)

100 g (3$^1/_2$ oz) fresh red chillies, seeded

2 Tbsp water

GRAVY

100 g (3$^1/_2$ oz) tamarind paste

1.25 litres (40 fl oz / 5 cups) water

600 g (1 lb 5$^1/_3$ oz) fish

4–6 large pieces sour fruit slices (*asam gelugor*)

GARNISHING

$^1/_2$ tsp salt

1 large onion, peeled and thinly sliced

200 g (7 oz) cucumber, cored and shredded

1 small bunch mint leaves

1 torch ginger bud

2 Tbsp black prawn paste (*haeko*)

3 Tbsp hot water

1 small head lettuce, shredded

1 small pineapple, peeled and flesh coarsely shredded

Limes, halved

1. Prepare spice paste. Combine all ingredients in a blender and process to a fine paste. Set aside.

2. Prepare gravy. Mix tamarind paste with water. Strain liquid into a large pot. Discard solids.

3. Add fish and sour fruit slices to pot and bring to the boil. Simmer gently until fish is cooked. Remove fish and leave to cool. Flake fish and set aside. Return fish bones and skin to pot and simmer for another 10 minutes. Strain stock and discard solids. Add spice paste to pot and bring to the boil.

4. Cut off and discard long stem of torch ginger bud. Halve bud and add to boiling gravy. Rinse *laksa* leaves complete with stalks and add to gravy. Simmer for 10 minutes. Remove and discard *laksa* leaves and ginger bud just before serving. Add flaked fish to pot and stir well. Return gravy to boil.

5. Meanwhile prepare garnish. Mix salt into sliced onion and leave to stand for 5 minutes. Squeeze juice from onion, then arrange on a serving platter. Soak shredded cucumber in cold water for 5 minutes. Drain well and arrange on serving platter. Pick mint leaves from stalks and rinse leaves clean. Pat dry with a paper towel, then arrange on serving platter. Chop torch ginger bud finely. Arrange on serving platter. Dilute black prawn paste with hot water to get an even pouring liquid. Pour diluted black prawn paste in a small bowl for drizzling over noodles. Arrange remaining garnishes on serving platter.

6. To serve noodles, bring a large pot of water to the boil. Blanch noodles until tender but still al dente. Divide into serving bowls.

7. Ladle hot fish gravy over noodles and garnish as desired.

Rice Noodles in Coconut Gravy, Singapore-Style

SINGAPORE LAKSA

Sometimes called *laksa lemak* (coconut *laksa*) because of the coconut milk in it, this hawker dish is found all over Singapore. An essential ingredient that makes this dish what it is, is *laksa* leaf *(Pericaria odorata, syn. Polygonum odoratum)* which is also known as Vietnamese or Cambodian mint, or *daun kesom* in Malay.

COOKING TIME: 30 MINUTES

200 g (7 oz) bean sprouts

600 g (1 lb 5^1/$_3$ oz) fresh coarse rice vermicelli or fresh cooked yellow wheat noodles

SPICE PASTE

50 g (1^3/$_4$ oz) shallots

1 thumb-size knob fresh turmeric, peeled

6 slices galangal

2 stalks lemongrass, sliced

5 candlenuts

1 tsp dried prawn paste (*belacan*)

2 Tbsp dried prawns (shrimps), rinsed and soaked in water until softened

2 Tbsp water

2 Tbsp ground coriander

2 Tbsp raw dried red chilli paste (page 33)

GRAVY

750 ml (24 fl oz / 3 cups) water

500 g (1 lb 1^1/$_2$ oz) grated coconut

6 Tbsp vegetable oil

500 ml (16 fl oz / 2 cups) chicken stock (page 44) or water

2 tsp salt

GARNISHING

1 bunch *laksa* leaves, stalks discarded and shredded

8 hard-boiled quail eggs, peeled

1 chicken drumstick, boiled and shredded

100 g (3^1/$_2$ oz) prawns (shrimps), boiled and peeled

200 g (7 oz) cucumber, shredded and soaked in cold water

2 Tbsp dried red chilli paste with dried prawns (page 33)

300 g (11 oz) blood cockles (*haam*), steamed and shelled (optional)

1. Prepare spice paste. Place all ingredients, except ground coriander and chilli paste, into a blender and process until fine. Mix in ground coriander and chilli paste.

2. Prepare gravy. Mix water with grated coconut and squeeze through a muslin bag or cloth-lined sieve to obtain coconut milk. Set aside.

3. Heat oil in a large pot and sauté spice paste until fragrant.

4. Add chicken stock/water and salt and bring to the boil. Add coconut milk and simmer until gravy is cooked through. Take care not to let coconut milk boil or it will separate.

5. To serve noodles, bring a pot of water to the boil. Blanch bean sprouts for 10 seconds, then drain well and divide into serving bowls.

6. Return pot of water to the boil, then blanch noodles until tender but still al dente. Drain and divide into serving bowls.

7. Ladle desired amount of gravy over noodles, then top with any combination of garnishes, with the exception of *laksa* leaves, which cannot be omitted.

8. Provide cooked dried red chilli paste on the side for those who prefer more heat. Serve immediately.

Rice Vermicelli in Spicy Coconut Gravy, Laotian-Style

KHAO POON NAM PHIK

This could be called Laotian *laksa*, variants of which are found all over South East Asia. Catfish is the typical Laotian choice for this dish, but a fish that flakes easily and has no tiny bones will do as well.

COOKING TIME: 1½ HOURS

500 g (1 lb 1½ oz) grated coconut

100 g (3½ oz) fresh red chillies, rinsed

600 g (1 lb 5⅓ oz) fresh medium-coarse rice vermicelli

500 ml (16 fl oz / 2 cups) water

1 Tbsp fried shallots (page 29), finely pounded

1 Tbsp fried garlic (page 30), finely pounded

1 bunch coriander leaves (cilantro), chopped

1 spring onion (scallion), chopped

½ cup basil leaves, chopped

½ cup sawtooth coriander, finely chopped

Lime juice to taste

1 tsp ground white pepper

FISH-PORK STOCK

500 ml (16 fl oz / 2 cups) pork stock (page 43)

1 large thumb-size knob galangal, peeled and bruised

300 g (11 oz) fish

3 Tbsp fish sauce

GARNISHING

200 g (7 oz) water convolvulus, rinsed and drained

6 Tbsp lard (page 45)

100 g (3½ oz) aubergine, cut into thick slices

100 g (3½ oz) yard-long beans, cut into finger-lengths

3 dried red chillies, seeded and wiped clean

Toasted red chilli flakes (page 35)

Fish sauce

1. Prepare stock. Place all ingredients into a saucepan and bring to the boil. Simmer until fish is cooked. Remove fish and cool before flaking flesh. Set flesh aside. Return fish bones to stock and simmer for another 5 minutes. Strain stock and discard solids.

2. Wrap grated coconut in muslin and squeeze to obtain thick cream. Set grated coconut aside and pour cream into a frying pan. Bring cream to boil, lower heat and stirring constantly, simmer until oil separates from cream. Continue stirring until coconut residue turns brown and fragrant. Transfer coconut residue to a small bowl and set aside as garnish. Leave oil in frying pan.

3. Grill chillies under a hot grill until soft. Seed chillies, then pound in a mortar and pestle to a paste. Add to frying pan with coconut oil. Heat oil and sauté pounded chilli paste until fragrant.

4. Add 500 ml (16 fl oz / 2 cups) water to squeezed grated coconut and extract second milk into a saucepan. Bring to the boil and stir in pork-fish stock. Add flaked fish, pounded fried shallots and garlic and cooked chilli paste. Add chopped herbs, pepper and lime juice to taste.

5. Prepare garnish. Cut water convolvulus into short lengths. Split stems lengthwise in half if thick. Heat 1 Tbsp lard in a wok and sauté water convolvulus for 10 seconds, until colour changes.

6. Heat 2 Tbsp lard in a frying pan and brown both sides of aubergine. Heat 1 Tbsp lard and sauté yard-long beans until colour changes, but beans are still crisp. Arrange on serving platter with other vegetables. Heat remaining 2 Tbsp lard and fry dried chillies until black. Discard chillies and leave chilli lard in frying pan.

7. To serve noodles, boil a large pot of water, then blanch rice vermicelli until tender but still al dente. Drain well, then stir noodles into hot chilli lard. Arrange dressed noodles in a serving platter with the garnishes and the pot of gravy nearby.

Rice Noodles in Fish Soup, Burmese-Style
MOHINGA

Mohinga can be called "Burmese *laksa*" because it has all the characteristics of
South East Asian *laksas*. It uses fish and typical South East Asian spices and herbs
such as lemongrass, chillies and dried prawn paste and has rice noodles. The Burmese typically
use catfish, but substitute with any fish that flakes easily such as mackerel.

COOKING TIME: 1 HOUR

600 g (1 lb 5^{1}/$_{3}$ oz) fresh fine-
medium rice vermicelli

SPICE PASTE
80 g (3 oz) shallots, peeled

3 cloves garlic, peeled

2.5-cm (1-in) knob galangal,
peeled

1 stalk lemongrass, thinly sliced

2 Tbsp water

1^{1}/$_{2}$ Tbsp raw dried red chilli
paste (page 33)

FISH STOCK
400 g (14^{1}/$_{3}$ oz) fish

2 Tbsp fish sauce

^{1}/$_{2}$ tsp salt

1.5 litres (48 fl oz / 6 cups) water

5 dried red chillies

1 tsp dried prawn paste (*belacan*)

1 stalk lemongrass, bruised

^{1}/$_{4}$ tsp ground turmeric

GRAVY
1 Tbsp rice

1 Tbsp chickpea flour

4 Tbsp water

4 Tbsp peanut oil

8 small shallots, peeled

1 unripe banana/plantain,
peeled; cut into 2-cm (1-in) thick
rounds

2 Tbsp toasted peanuts, finely
ground

GARNISHING
^{1}/$_{4}$ tsp ground turmeric

1 cup toasted chickpea flour

2 hard-boiled eggs, peeled; sliced

1 Tbsp Burmese fried garlic
chips (page 30)

100 g (3^{1}/$_{2}$ oz) fish cake (page 40),
thinly sliced

1 bunch coriander leaves
(cilantro), chopped

4 pieces Burmese *dhal* crackers
(page 43)

Toasted red chilli flakes
(page 35)

Limes, halved

Banana stem 12-cm (5-in) long,
sliced 1-cm (^{1}/$_{2}$-in) thick and
soaked

Banana flowers

1. Prepare spice paste. Place shallots, garlic, galangal, lemongrass and water in a blender and process until fine. Mix in chilli paste. Set aside.

2. Prepare fish stock. Place ingredients in a pot and bring to the boil, then lower heat and simmer until fish is cooked but still whole.

3. Remove fish from stock and leave to cool before flaking flesh. Set aside.

4. Return fish bones to the pot and simmer for another 10 minutes. Strain stock and discard solids.

5. Prepare gravy. In a dry wok over low heat, dry-fry rice to a beige colour, then pound to a powder. Dry-fry chickpea flour until light in texture, taking care not to burn flour. (This is also a good time to do step 10).

6. Mix rice powder and chickpea flour together with water to a smooth paste. Set aside and stir well just before adding to rest of gravy.

7. Heat oil in a large pot and fry spice paste until fragrant. Add fish stock, whole shallots and banana/plantain slices and simmer until banana/plantain and shallots are soft.

8. Stir in flaked fish and rice-flour mixture and bring to the boil. Transfer gravy to a large serving bowl and sprinkle in ground peanuts just before serving.

9. Prepare garnish. Bring a pot of water to the boil with ground turmeric and blanch banana stem for 1 minute. Drain and arrange on a platter for garnishes, together with other garnishes.

10. Dry-fry chickpea flour for 2 minutes until fragrant. Scoop flour into a small bowl and place on the platter for garnishes.

11. To serve noodles, bring a large pot of water to the boil, then blanch rice vermicelli until tender but al dente. Drain well and divide into individual serving bowls. Serve garnishes and gravy on the side for guests to help themselves.

Mohinga with Coconut Milk

This is a version of mohinga enriched with coconut milk and likely to be found
in the lowland areas of Myanmar. Some of the ingredients for mohinga such as
ground chickpea flour, toasted rice flour and fried garlic are sold ready-made in stores that carry
Burmese produce. Substitute with ground peanuts if ground chickpea flour is not available.

COOKING TIME: 1 HOUR

600 g (1 lb 5$^1/_3$ oz) fresh fine-medium rice noodles

STOCK
400 g (14$^1/_3$ oz) catfish/fish
30 g (1 oz) salted fish
3 Tbsp fish sauce
5 dried red chillies, rinsed
2 stalks lemongrass, bruised
1 litre (32 fl oz / 4 cups) water

SPICE PASTE
100 g (3$^1/_2$ oz) onions, peeled and coarsely sliced

3 cloves garlic, peeled
2.5-cm (1-in) knob ginger, peeled
$^1/_4$ tsp ground turmeric
1 tsp dried prawn paste (*belacan*)
2 Tbsp water
2 Tbsp raw dried red chilli paste (page 33)

GRAVY
375 ml (12 fl oz / 1$^1/_2$ cups) water
250 g (9 oz) grated coconut
4 Tbsp cooking oil

8 shallots, peeled
1 unripe banana/plantain, peeled; cut into 1-cm ($^1/_2$-in) slices
$^1/_2$ tsp salt
1 Tbsp rice
2 Tbsp chickpea flour

GARNISHING
1 cup Burmese fried garlic (page 30)
$^1/_2$ cup toasted ground chickpeas

1. Prepare stock. Combine all ingredients in a pot and boil. Simmer for 20 minutes or until fish is cooked but still whole. Carefully remove fish from stock and leave to cool before flaking flesh. Set flesh aside and return fish bones to stock. Return stock to the boil for a further 10 minutes, then strain and discard solids.

2. Prepare spice paste. Combine ingredients, except chilli paste, in a blender and process to a fine paste. Mix with chilli paste and set aside.

3. Prepare gravy. Mix 250 ml (8 fl oz / 1 cup) water into grated coconut, then squeeze through a muslin bag or cloth-lined sieve to obtain coconut milk. Discard grated coconut.

4. Heat oil in a large pot and sauté spice paste until fragrant. Spoon two-thirds of spice paste into a bowl and set aside. Place flaked fish into pot and sauté with remaining spice paste for 3 minutes. Scoop out and set aside. Return two-thirds spice paste to the pot and add strained stock, whole shallots, unripe banana/plantain and salt. Bring to the boil, then add flaked fish and coconut milk.

5. In a dry pan, dry-fry rice to a pale beige colour, then pound to a powder. Remove and set aside in a bowl. Using the same pan, dry-fry chickpea flour until light in texture and slightly browned. Place into bowl together with ground rice. Add remaining water to ground rice and flour mixture, stirring well to get rid of any lumps. Add to boiling gravy and stir well. Return to the boil.

6. To serve noodles, boil a large pot of water. Blanch noodles, then drain well and divide into serving bowls. Arrange garnishes on a large serving platter and gravy in a large bowl.

Rice Vermicelli with Coconut Cream, Thai-Style

KHANOM JEEN SAO NAM

The richness of barely-cooked coconut cream and raw shredded garnishes give this
noodle dish a tasty salad-like flavour and texture. The garnishes have to be very
finely shredded and the coconut cream carefully watched over as it cooks.
This dish is best served with tender, freshly-made rice vermicelli and fresh coconut milk.

COOKING TIME: 5 MINUTES

200 g (7 oz) bean sprouts

600 g (1 lb 5^1/$_3$ oz) fresh medium-coarse rice vermicelli

20 fish balls (page 40), boiled in water until cooked

GRAVY

300 ml (10 fl oz / 1^1/$_4$ cups) water

500 g (1 lb 1^1/$_2$ oz) grated coconut

3 Tbsp fish sauce

2 Tbsp sugar

SPICE PASTE

50 g (1^3/$_4$ oz) fresh red chillies, seeded

1 Tbsp dried prawns (shrimps), softened in cold water

GARNISHING

200 g (7 oz) fresh pineapple flesh, shredded

4 cloves garlic, peeled and cut into thin slivers

30 g (1 oz) young ginger, peeled and cut into thin slivers

Limes, halved

CONDIMENTS

Chopped bird's eye chillies with fish sauce

1. Prepare gravy. Mix water into grated coconut, then squeeze through a muslin bag or cloth-lined sieve to obtain thick coconut milk. Pour into a saucepan.

2. Prepare spice paste. Blend chillies and dried prawns in a blender until fine.

3. Add spice paste, fish sauce and sugar to coconut milk in saucepan. Heat to a near-boil, but do not allow coconut milk to boil up or the cream will separate.

4. To serve noodles, bring a large pot of water to the boil. Blanch bean sprouts for 10 seconds, then drain and divide into serving bowls.

5. Return water to the boil and blanch noodles until tender but still al dente. Divide into serving bowls.

6. Top noodles with shredded pineapple, garlic, ginger and fish balls. Pour hot coconut milk over and serve with lime halves and a small saucer of chopped bird's eye chillies with fish sauce.

Thai Coconut Rice Noodles
THE ORIGINAL MEE SIAM

Is this the original *mee siam*? This Thai recipe for rice noodles certainly uses many of the ingredients found in the various *mee siam* recipes of Singapore and Malaysia.

COOKING TIME: 30 MINUTES

250 g (9 oz) bean sprouts

600 g (1 lb 5^1/$_3$ oz) fresh medium-coarse rice vermicelli

GRAVY

1 litre (32 fl oz / 4 cups) water

2 Tbsp tamarind paste

500 g (1 lb 1^1/$_2$ oz) grated coconut

50 g (1^3/$_4$ oz) shallots, peeled and thinly sliced

2 Tbsp fermented soybeans *(taucheo)*, finely mashed

1 Tbsp sugar

1 tsp salt

2 Tbsp raw dried red chilli paste (page 33)

200 g (7 oz) chicken/pork, cut into thin strips

100 g (3^1/$_2$ oz) firm bean curd, cut into thin strips

100 g (3^1/$_2$ oz) chives, chopped

GARNISHING

2 eggs, beaten

Cooking oil for frying

Large limes, cut into wedges

3 fresh red chillies, seeded and sliced

1 bunch coriander leaves (cilantro), chopped

1 spring onion (scallion), cut into 2.5-cm (1-in) lengths

CONDIMENTS

Toasted red chilli flakes (page 35)

Sugar

1. Mix 125 ml (4 fl oz / ^{1}/$_2$ cup) water with tamarind paste. Strain juice and discard solids.

2. In a large bowl, mix grated coconut with remaining water, then squeeze through a muslin bag or cloth-lined sieve to obtain coconut milk.

3. Bring coconut milk to the boil in a saucepan and simmer gently for about 10 minutes or until a layer of oil begins to appear on top.

4. Add shallots, fermented soybeans, sugar, salt, tamarind juice and dried red chilli paste and simmer for 5 minutes. Add chicken/pork, bean curd and chives, and simmer until meat is cooked.

5. Meanwhile, prepare garnishes. Heat oil in a frying pan and make 2 omelettes with beaten eggs. Leave to cool, then roll omelettes up and cut into thin strips.

6. To serve noodles, bring a large pot of water to the boil. Blanch bean sprouts for 10 seconds and divide into serving bowls.

7. Return water to the boil, then blanch noodles until tender but al dente. Divide and add to the bean sprouts in the serving bowls, then ladle gravy over with some meat and bean curd.

8. Top with garnishes and serve hot with chilli flakes, sugar and limes on the side.

Rice Noodles in Fish Gravy, Thai-Style

KHANOM JEEN NAM YA

Is this Thai *laksa*? This dish is sometimes served in Thai homes for special occasions such as birthdays when long noodles are desired for their symbolism of long life. The usual fish soup, known as *nam ya* in Thai, can be dressed up with sliced chicken and prawns. Although the roots and chillies are usually ground to a paste for *nam ya*, they may also be very finely sliced and cooked until soft.

COOKING TIME: 1 HOUR

1 litre (32 fl oz / 4 cups) water

250 g (9 oz) mackerel, gutted and scaled

500 g (1 lb 1½ oz) grated coconut

4 Tbsp fish sauce

Cooking oil

30 g (1 oz) dried salted fish, rinsed and thinly sliced

600 g (1 lb 5⅓ oz) fresh medium-coarse rice vermicelli

SPICE PASTE

50 g (1¾ oz) garlic, peeled and quartered

100 g (3½ oz) shallots, peeled and coarsely sliced

2 stalks lemongrass, finely sliced

750 g (1 lb 11 oz) Chinese keys, scraped and sliced finely

5 slices galangal

½ Tbsp dried prawn paste (*belacan*)

10 dried red chillies, seeded and rinsed

250 ml (8 fl oz / 1 cup) water

GARNISHING

100 ml (3⅓ f l oz) water

500 g (1 lb 1½ oz) prawns (shrimps), peeled and deveined, leaving tails intact; reserve heads and shells

100 g (3½ oz) bean sprouts, rinsed and blanched

100 g (3½ oz) French beans, tailed, cleaned and blanched

1 cup basil leaves, rinsed and coarsely chopped

½ cup sawtooth coriander, rinsed and finely chopped

½ cup mint, rinsed and finely chopped

4 hard-boiled eggs, peeled and sliced

CONDIMENTS

Dried red chilli paste with dried prawns (page 33)

1. Prepare spice paste. Combine ingredients in a pot and simmer gently for about 10 minutes or until shallots are soft. Leave to cool, then pour into a blender and blend till smooth.

2. Bring 250 ml (8 fl oz / 1 cup) water to the boil in a pot and add fish to cook. When fish is cooked, remove and leave to cool. Flake flesh and add to blended spice paste in the blender. Blend till fine.

3. Return fish bones to pot and simmer for another 10 minutes. Strain stock and discard bones.

4. Mix 250 ml (8 fl oz / 1 cup) water into grated coconut in a large bowl, then squeeze through a muslin bag or cloth-lined sieve to obtain coconut milk. Set coconut milk aside.

5. Add remaining 500 ml (16 fl oz / 2 cups) water to squeezed grated coconut and extract second milk. Pour second milk into a large saucepan.

6. Add spice paste to second milk in saucepan and bring to the boil. Add strained fish stock and fish sauce and simmer for 3 minutes.

7. Add first coconut milk and stir well. Bring to a near-boil.

8. Heat some oil in a frying pan and fry salted fish over low heat until crisp. Drain fish and leave to cool, then pound until fine for sprinkling over gravy.

9. Prepare prawns for garnish. Bring water to the boil in a pot. Dip prawns in briefly and remove as soon as they turn pink and curl up. Do not overcook.

10. Place prawn shells and heads into pot and boil for 5 minutes. Strain stock and add to fish soup.

11. To serve noodles, bring a pot of water to the boil. Blanch noodles until tender but still al dente. Drain well and divide into serving bowls.

12. Garnish with blanched vegetables and chopped herbs, then ladle hot fish soup over. Top with prawns and hard-boiled egg. Serve hot.

Malay Mee Siam without Coconut Milk

This *mee siam* recipe came originally from my Malay neighbour who taught my mother how to do the dish. It is an interesting recipe because the gravy does not have any coconut milk.

COOKING TIME: 1 HOUR

600 g (1 lb 5¹/₃ oz) fresh coarse rice vermicelli

1 Tbsp chilli powder

4 Tbsp cooking oil

1 large onion, peeled and thinly sliced

¹/₂ tsp salt

300 g (11 oz) bean sprouts

SPICE PASTE

250 g (9 oz) shallots, peeled

1 tsp dried prawn paste (*belacan*)

1 Tbsp fermented soybeans (*taucheo*)

3 Tbsp raw dried red chilli paste (page 33)

GRAVY

1 litre (32 fl oz / 4 cups) water

100 g (3¹/₂ oz) tamarind paste

4 Tbsp cooking oil

1 tsp salt

2 Tbsp sugar

GARNISHING

400 g (14¹/₃ oz) prawns (shrimps), preferably very small and in their shells

¹/₄ tsp salt

1 tsp ground turmeric

Cooking oil for frying

1 large bunch chives, finely chopped

200 g (7 oz) firm bean curd, cut cross-wise into 4 slices

Limes, halved

CHILLI-ONION OMELETTE

1 fresh red chilli, seeded

1 small onion, peeled and cut into cubes

¹/₄ tsp salt

4 eggs, beaten

2 Tbsp cooking oil

CONDIMENTS

Dried red chilli paste with dried prawns (page 33)

1. Bring a large pot of water to the boil and blanch noodles until nearly tender and still al dente. Drain noodles in a colander. Using chopsticks, stir chilli powder into hot noodles. Set aside.

2. Heat oil in a wok and sauté onion for 1 minute. Onion should still be fairly firm. Stir in salt, bean sprouts and noodles and fry for 1 minute until noodles are evenly coloured and bean sprouts still very crisp. Dish out into a covered container.

3. Prepare spice paste. Place all ingredients, except chilli paste, into a blender and process to a fine paste. Mix in chilli paste and set aside.

4. Prepare gravy. Mix water with tamarind paste. Strain liquid and discard solids. Set aside. Heat oil in a large saucepan and fry spice paste until oil rises to the top. Add tamarind juice, salt and sugar and bring to the boil. Lower heat and simmer for 5 minutes.

5. Prepare garnish. If prawns are large, shell and split in half. Mix salt and turmeric into prawns. Set aside for a few minutes. Heat some oil in a wok and brown bean curd. Remove bean curd and pat dry with a paper towel and cut into small cubes. Leaving 2 Tbsp oil in wok, fry marinated prawns over high heat until dry and fragrant.

6. Prepare chilli-onion omelette. In a mortar and pestle, pound chilli and onion together till broken up but still fairly chunky. Mix salt, pounded chilli and onion with beaten eggs. Heat some oil in an omelette pan and fry egg mixture in several batches into firm omelettes. Cool, then slice into thin strips.

7. To serve noodles, place desired amount of noodles into a deep dish or bowl. Ladle hot gravy over and garnish as desired.

Rice Vermicelli, Saigon-Style

BUN SUONG

This is one of the simplest yet tastiest of noodle dishes.
The flavour comes from the fresh herbs in the fragrant soup.

COOKING TIME: 2 HOURS

600 g (1 lb 5$^1/_3$ oz) fresh coarse rice vermicelli

SOUP
2 litres (64 fl oz / 8 cups) pork stock (page 43)

600 g (1 lb 5$^1/_3$ oz) pork foreleg, chopped into pieces

1 Tbsp sugar

3 Tbsp fish sauce

$^1/_2$ tsp ground white pepper

1 Tbsp raw dried red chilli paste (page 33)

1 star anise

1 egg white, beaten

GARNISHING
Chopped mint leaves, basil leaves, sawtooth coriander, coriander leaves (cilantro) and *laksa* leaves

2 pieces prawn cakes (page 41), fried and thinly sliced

CONDIMENTS
Nuoc cham (page 38)

1. Prepare soup. Place pork stock and foreleg in a stockpot and bring to the boil. Skim off any scum that rises to the top. Lower heat, add sugar, fish sauce, pepper, chilli paste and star anise. Simmer for about 2 hours or until pork is tender.

2. With soup at a boil, stir in beaten egg white. Remove from heat.

3. To serve noodles, bring a pot of water to the boil, then blanch noodles until tender but al dente. Drain well and divide into serving bowls.

4. Ladle hot soup with a few pieces of pork over noodles. Garnish generously with chopped herbs and fried prawn cake.

5. Serve immediately with a saucer of *nuoc cham* on the side.

Rice Vermicelli in Coconut Gravy, Malay-Style
MEE SIAM WITH COCONUT GRAVY

This particular *mee siam* recipe has coconut milk in the gravy. It has that old-fashioned coconut milk flavour that I recall in the *mee siam* of an Indian *mee siam* hawker of more than 50 years ago.

COOKING TIME: 1 HOUR

125 ml (4 fl oz / $^1/_2$ cup) cooking oil

300 g (11 oz) dried fine rice vermicelli, softened in cold water until pliable

400 g (14$^1/_3$ oz) bean sprouts, rinsed

1 tsp salt

SPICE PASTE
250 g (9 oz) shallots

1 Tbsp dried prawn paste (*belacan*)

3 Tbsp fermented soybeans (*taucheo*), rinsed and mashed well

2 Tbsp water

$^1/_2$ cup raw dried red chilli paste (page 33)

GRAVY
750 ml (24 fl oz / 3 cups) water

400 g (14$^1/_3$ oz) grated coconut

100 g (3$^1/_2$ oz) tamarind paste

750 ml (24 fl oz / 3 cups) prawn stock (page 44)

$^1/_2$ tsp salt

1 Tbsp sugar

GARNISHING
Cooking oil for frying

100 g (3$^1/_2$ oz) firm bean curd, cut crosswise into thin layers

4 hard-boiled eggs, peeled and sliced

1 bunch chives, chopped

300 g (11 oz) prawns (shrimps), cleaned and boiled

Limes, halved

ONION SAMBAL
2 Tbsp cooking oil

50 g (1$^3/_4$ oz) onions, peeled, cut into quarters and thinly sliced

$^1/_2$ cup raw dried red chilli paste (page 33)

4 Tbsp water

$^1/_2$ Tbsp sugar

$^1/_4$ tsp salt

1. Prepare spice paste. Blend shallots, dried prawn paste and fermented soybeans with water till fine. Mix in chilli paste. Set aside. Heat oil in a wok and sauté spice paste until fragrant and oil separates from paste. Remove two-thirds of spice paste from wok and set aside.

2. Bring a pot of water to the boil and blanch noodles until nearly tender and still very al dente. Drain in a colander. Reheat remaining one-third spice paste in wok. Add bean sprouts and noodles and sauté for 1 minute. The bean sprouts should still be crisp. Mix well to colour noodles evenly.

3. Prepare gravy. Mix 500 ml (16 fl oz / 2 cups) water with grated coconut and squeeze though a muslin bag or cloth-lined sieve to obtain coconut milk. Mix tamarind paste with remaining water. Strain liquid and discard solids. Put tamarind juice, prawn stock, remaining two-thirds spice paste, salt and sugar into a saucepan and bring to the boil. Add coconut milk and return to near-boiling, taking care that coconut milk does not separate.

4. Prepare bean curd for garnish. Heat some oil in a wok and brown both sides of bean curd layers. Cut into small cubes.

5. Prepare onion *sambal*. Heat oil and fry onion until soft, then add chilli paste, water, sugar and salt. Lower heat and simmer gently for 10 minutes until mixture drops easily from a spoon when lifted .

6. To serve noodles, place desired amount of noodles into a deep dish or bowl. Ladle hot gravy over noodles, then top with garnishes according to taste. Serve with a saucer of onion *sambal* on the side. Squeeze lime juice over before eating.

Rice Noodles with Duck, Laotian-Style

KHAO POON NAM PED

Khao poon nam ped may be to Laotians what *pho* is to the Vietnamese.
Despite its apparent simplicity compared to *pho*, it is equally delicious.
Make it with chicken if duck is not available. With the large quantity of shredded
raw vegetables in it, the dish is rather like a noodle salad dressed with duck soup!

COOKING TIME: 3 HOURS

800 g ($1^3/_4$ lb) duck

1 bunch coriander leaves (cilantro)

1 stalk Chinese celery

1 spring onion (scallion)

1 thumb-size knob galangal

4 Tbsp fish sauce

2 litres (64 fl oz / 8 cups) water

600 g (1 lb $5^1/_3$ oz) fresh coarse rice vermicelli

GARNISHING

200 g (7 oz) winter bamboo shoots

1 tsp salt

1 litre (32 fl oz / 4 cups) water

1 bunch coriander leaves (cilantro), chopped

1 spring onion (scallion), chopped

$^1/_2$ cup basil leaves, finely chopped

$^1/_2$ cup sawtooth coriander, finely chopped

200 g (7 oz) unripe papaya, peeled and finely shredded

100 g ($3^1/_2$ oz) cabbage, finely shredded

CONDIMENTS

50 g ($1^3/_4$ oz) fresh red chillies, seeded and thinly sliced

Fish sauce

1 Tbsp sugar

1. Rinse duck clean, pluck out any feather shafts and cut off bishop's nose (the tail part).

2. Rinse coriander leaves, Chinese celery and spring onion, then blanch with hot water to soften them. Knot greens into bundles.

3. Put duck, knotted greens, galangal, fish sauce and water into a large stockpot and bring to the boil. Skim off any scum that rises to the top, then lower heat and simmer gently for 3 hours until duck is tender and stock is reduced to about 1 litre (32 fl oz / 4 cups).

4. Remove duck and leave to cool before shredding meat. Discard bones. Scoop out solids from stock and return duck meat to pot. Keep stock hot.

5. Prepare garnish. Place bamboo shoots, salt and water into a pot and simmer for 30 minutes. Discard water and cool bamboo shoots, then shred very finely with a sharp knife.

6. Mix shredded bamboo shoots and remaining garnishes together in a mixing bowl.

7. To serve noodles, bring a pot of water to the boil. Blanch noodles until tender but still al dente. Drain well and divide into serving bowls.

8. Top noodles with garnishes, then ladle hot stock with a serving of duck meat over.

9. Serve hot with small saucers of fresh red chillies, fish sauce and sugar on the side.

Cambodian Rice Noodles in Fish Soup

NUM P'CHOK

The Cambodians use a freshwater fish like snakehead or catfish in this soup.
The soup is thickened with roasted rice flour which may be bought ready-made.
Prahok (fermented fish) is to Cambodians what *padek* is to Laotians and dried prawn paste
to Malays and Indonesians. Substitute with canned pickled anchovies if unavailable.

COOKING TIME: 30 MINUTES

500 g (1 lb 1 1/2 oz) snakehead/
catfish/tilapia

1 litre (32 fl oz / 4 cups) water

2 Tbsp roasted rice flour

3 Tbsp cooking oil

2 Tbsp fish sauce

1 Tbsp sugar

300 g (11 oz) fine or coarse rice
vermicelli, softened in cold water
until pliable

SPICE PASTE

4 slices galangal

2 stalks lemongrass, thinly sliced

20 g Chinese keys, scraped clean

1 thumb-size knob fresh
turmeric, scraped clean

2 spring onions (scallions)

3 cloves garlic, peeled

1/2 Tbsp *prahok* (Cambodian
fermented fish)

4 Tbsp water

GARNISHING

1 cup *laksa* leaves, chopped

2 cups banana flower (optional)

200 g (7 oz) cabbage, shredded

200 g (7 oz) bean sprouts, tailed
and rinsed

1 cucumber, cored and shredded

CONDIMENTS

Tuk trey chu p'em (page 36)

1. Prepare spice paste. Combine all ingredients in a blender and process to a fine paste. Set aside.

2. Put fish and 875 ml (28 fl oz) water in a pot and bring to the boil. Simmer until fish is cooked. Remove fish. When cool, flake flesh and set aside.

3. Return fish bones and skin to pot and simmer for another 10 minutes. Strain stock and discard solids.

4. Mix remaining 125 ml (4 fl oz / 1/2 cup) water into roasted rice flour and set aside. Stir well again before adding to soup.

5. Heat oil in a large pot and fry spice paste for 2 minutes. Add flaked fish and fry for another 5 minutes until fragrant.

6. Add fish stock, fish sauce and sugar. Bring to the boil, then stir in rice flour paste and return to the boil.

7. Prepare garnish and combine. Divide into serving bowls.

8. To serve noodles, bring a pot of water to the boil and blanch noodles until tender but still al dente. The length of time will depend on the type of noodles chosen.

9. Drain noodles well and divide into serving bowls and top with garnishes. Ladle hot soup over and serve immediately with a condiment of *tuk trey chu p'em* (page 36).

Coarse Rice Vermicelli with Beef

There was once a hawker stall in a coffee shop in Singapore's Hock Lam Street that
was famous for beef noodles. The broad rice noodles came in beef soup or
were dressed and served with a bowl of beef soup. In this recipe,
I have turned the soup into a thick sauce to go with fresh coarse rice noodles.

COOKING TIME: 15 MINUTES

200 g (7 oz) bean sprouts, rinsed

600 g (1 lb 5^1/$_3$ oz) fresh coarse rice vermicelli

Chopped coriander leaves (cilantro), Chinese celery and spring onions (scallions)

GRAVY

500 ml (16 fl oz / 2 cups) beef stock (page 44)

1 clove garlic, peeled and sliced

2.5 cm (1 in) cinnamon stick

1 star anise

^{1}/$_2$ tsp Chinese five-spice powder

^{1}/$_2$ tsp salt

^{1}/$_2$ tsp dark soy sauce

2 Tbsp light soy sauce

^{1}/$_4$ tsp ground white pepper

300 g (11 oz) beef, thinly sliced

2 Tbsp + 1 tsp cornflour

2 Tbsp water

CONDIMENTS

Fresh red chilli-vinegar sauce (page 33)

1. Prepare gravy. Place all ingredients, except beef, cornflour and water, into the pot and bring to the boil. Simmer for 10 minutes, then scoop out and discard solids.

2. Mix 1 tsp cornflour into beef slices together with a pinch of salt and a few drops of oil.

3. Mix remaining 2 Tbsp cornflour with water and stir into hot gravy. Add sliced beef at the same time and bring to the boil.

4. To serve noodles, bring a large pot of water to the boil. Blanch bean sprouts for 10 seconds, then drain and divide into serving bowls.

5. Return water to the boil, then blanch noodles until tender but still al dente. Drain well and divide into serving bowls on top of bean sprouts.

6. Ladle some gravy and beef over noodles and garnish with chopped coriander, Chinese celery and spring onion. Serve hot with fresh chilli sauce with vinegar on the side.

Rice Vermicelli in Satay Sauce

SATAY BEE HOON

This hawker dish is not easily found in food centres in Singapore. It is a classic Singapore fusion dish, combining Chinese and Malay elements. The dish usually includes softened dried squid which is difficult to find outside Asia. I have omitted it in this recipe.

COOKING TIME: 45 MINUTES

300 g (11 oz) water convolvulus

100 g (3½ oz) pork, thinly sliced

100 g (3½ oz) prawns (shrimps), peeled, leaving tails intact

2 cups blood cockles (*haam*) (optional)

300 g (11 oz) dried fine rice vermicelli, softened in cold water until pliable

SPICE PASTE

1 stalk lemongrass, finely sliced

4 slices galangal

100 g (3½ oz) shallots, peeled

2 cloves garlic, peeled

½ tsp dried prawn paste (*belacan*)

2 Tbsp water

1 Tbsp raw dried red chilli paste (page 33)

SATAY SAUCE

750 ml (24 fl oz / 3 cups) water

¼ cup tamarind paste

3 Tbsp cooking oil

3 Tbsp sugar

1½ tsp salt

2 cups peanuts, toasted and ground

1. Rinse water convolvulus, then cut off roots. Halve stems and cut into finger-lengths.

2. Bring a pot of water to the boil and cook pork and prawns. Drain and set aside.

3. Rinse cockles in several changes of cold water to get rid of any mud and sand. Pour boiling water over cockles or dip cockles into boiling water for 5 seconds. Leave to cool before shucking. Set aside.

4. Prepare spice paste. Place ingredients , except chilli paste, into a blender and process to a fine paste. Mix in chilli paste and set aside.

5. Prepare satay sauce. Mix water and tamarind paste. Strain liquid and discard solids.

6. Heat oil in a saucepan and fry spice paste until fragrant and oil separates from paste.

7. Add tamarind juice, sugar and salt and bring to the boil.

8. Stir in ground peanuts last. (Ground peanuts will swell and thicken the sauce. If re-heating leftover satay sauce, dilute with tamarind juice or hot water.)

9. To serve noodles, bring a pot of water to the boil. Blanch water convolvulus for 10 seconds, then drain well and divide into deep serving plates.

10. Return water to the boil and blanch noodles until tender but still al dente. Drain well and divide into serving plates.

11. Garnish noodles with boiled pork, prawns and cockles, then ladle hot satay sauce over. Serve immediately.

Foochow Fried Rice Flour Cakes

Dried rice flour cake can be found in Chinese grocery stores.
They are also called "new year cake" *(nian gao)* perhaps
because their texture resembles sweet rice cakes of the same name,
or because they were traditionally served during the Chinese New Year.
In the Philippines, sweet rice cakes are known as *"tikoy"*.

COOKING TIME: 30 MINUTES

320 g (11$^1/_3$ oz) dried rice flour cake (page 18), soaked in water for 12 hours

SAUCE
500 g (1 lb 1$^1/_2$ oz) clams

1 litre (32 fl oz / 4 cups) water

$^1/_3$ cup cornflour

250 ml (8 fl oz / 1 cup) cooking oil

3 Tbsp chopped garlic

200 g (7 oz) prawns (shrimps), peeled, leaving tails intact

1 tsp salt

2 Tbsp light soy sauce

GARNISHING
1 spring onion (scallion), chopped

1 bunch coriander leaves (cilantro), chopped

1. Prepare sauce. Rinse clams and place in a pot with water. Bring to the boil, then lower heat and simmer for 1 minute. Discard any unopened clams and empty shells. Remove clams from stock and set aside.

2. Rest stock before measuring out 750 ml (24 fl oz / 3 cups) into another pot, taking care not to stir up sandy deposits at bottom of pot.

3. Ladle 125 ml (4 fl oz / $^1/_2$ cup) clam stock into a bowl and stir in cornflour. Stir well again just before adding to noodles.

4. Bring a pot of water to the boil. Add rice cakes and boil for 2 minutes until rice cakes are soft but not melting together. Drain well. (Boiled rice cakes must be cooked straight away. If allowed to cool, they will stick together.)

5. Heat oil in a wok and fry hot, boiled rice cakes quickly. Drain rice cakes and spread them out on a plate.

6. Leave 2 Tbsp oil in wok and reheat. Fry garlic until fragrant. Add prawns and when they turn pink, stir in clam stock, salt, light soy sauce, rice cakes and clams. When ingredients are heated through, stir in clam stock-cornflour mixture and bring to the boil.

7. Garnish with chopped greens and serve immediately.

KUAY TIAO (BROAD RICE NOODLES)

Steamed Rice Sheet
CHEE CHEONG FUN

A Cantonese specialty, *chee cheong fun* is basically rice noodles in sheet form.
These sheet noodles can be eaten plain with a generous dressing of chopped spring onions,
toasted sesame seeds and good dark soy sauce, or filled with prawns, crabmeat or
Chinese red roast pork. Create your own combinations.

PREPARATION TIME: 5–10 MINUTES

Fresh rice noodles
(*chee cheong fun*) (page 11)

TOPPING A
Chopped spring onions
(scallions)

Chopped coriander leaves
(cilantro)

Fried shallots (page 29)

Shallot oil (page 29)

TOPPING B
Sesame oil

Toasted sesame seeds

Chopped spring onions
(scallions)

Dark soy sauce

TOPPING C
2 Tbsp black prawn paste
(*haeko*)

125 ml (4 fl oz / $\frac{1}{2}$ cup) hot
water

TOPPING D
2 Tbsp cooked dried red
chilli paste (page 32)

2 Tbsp shallot oil (page 29)

3 Tbsp hot water

1. Prepare *chee cheong fun* and garnish with your choice of topping A, B, C or D.

2. If using topping C, stir prawn paste into hot water to get sauce of pouring consistency.

3. If using topping D, combine chilli paste, shallot oil and hot water in a microwave safe dish with a cover. Place in the microwave oven and cook on High for 2 minutes, stirring after 1 minute.

Penang-Style Fried Broad Rice Noodles

PENANG CHAR KUAY TIAO

The island of Penang in West Malaysia has very good *char kuay tiao* and some insist it is better than Singapore *char kuay tiao* because the broad rice noodles are more tender. Penang *char kuay tiao* is different from the Singapore version in not having sweet dark sauce but chives. The same recipe is used to fry mouse-tail noodles, a Penang hawker favourite which is not found in Singapore.

COOKING TIME: 10 MINUTES

5 Tbsp lard (page 45)

2 Tbsp chopped garlic

600 g (1 lb 5¹/₃ oz) fresh broad rice noodles

1 Tbsp cooked dried red chilli paste (page 32)

2 Tbsp light soy sauce

300 g (11 oz) bean sprouts, rinsed

1 tsp dark soy sauce

1 tsp salt

3 eggs

2–3 Tbsp water

100 g (3¹/₂ oz) fish cake (page 40), sliced

100 g (3¹/₂ oz) prawns (shrimps), boiled and peeled, leaving tails intact

300 g (11 oz) blood cockles (*haam*), steamed and shelled (optional)

1 large bunch chives, cut into finger-lengths

1. Heat 4 Tbsp lard in a wok and fry garlic until fragrant.

2. Stir in noodles, chilli paste and light soy sauce and fry for 30 seconds. Add bean sprouts and mix well.

3. Make a well in the centre of noodles, add remaining spoonful of lard and eggs. Break up yolks and spread eggs out. Cover eggs with noodles and let eggs set into chunks before them turning over.

4. Sprinkle water over noodles if noodles begin to stick to the bottom of pan. Add fish cake, prawns, chives and blood cockles, if using, and mix well with noodles. Serve hot.

Singapore-Style Fried Broad Rice Noodles
(Singapore Fried Kuay Tiao)

For a Singapore-style dish, omit the chives and add 2 tsp sweet dark soy sauce at step 4.

Broad Rice Noodles Fried with Beef

FRIED BEEF KUAY TIAO

Beef and broad rice noodles are a classic combination be they in soup or fried.
This Cantonese-style preparation is found in Chinese restaurants all over the world.

COOKING TIME: 5 MINUTES

300 g (11 oz) beef

4 Tbsp cooking oil

2 Tbsp chopped garlic

600 g (1 lb 5¹/₃ oz) fresh broad rice noodles

A few drops dark soy sauce

2 Tbsp light soy sauce

300 g (11 oz) *choy sum*, cut into finger-lengths

MARINADE

A large pinch bicarbonate of soda (optional)

2 tsp cornflour

3 tsp light soy sauce

A few drops dark soy sauce

¹/₂ Tbsp cooking oil

1 Tbsp water

THICKENER

2 Tbsp cornflour

500 ml (16 fl oz / 2 cups) water

¹/₂ tsp salt

2 Tbsp light soy sauce

A few drops dark soy sauce

1 tsp sesame oil

1 tsp ground white pepper

GARNISHING

Chopped spring onions (scallions)

Chopped coriander leaves (cilantro)

CONDIMENTS

Pickled green chillies (page 32)

1. Slice beef thinly across the grain and into narrow strips.

2. Combine all ingredients for marinade, then mix into beef slices. Leave for 10 minutes.

3. Prepare thickener. Mix all ingredients together.

4. To fry noodles, heat 3 Tbsp oil in a wok and sauté chopped garlic until fragrant. Add noodles and dark and light soy sauces. Cook for 1 minute, stirring noodles around constantly. Dish out and divide into serving plates. Heat remaining 1 Tbsp oil in the same wok and sauté *choy sum* until beginning to turn limp. Add marinated beef and stir-fry for 10 seconds.

5. Stir thickener, then add to wok. Stir to mix and bring to the boil. Ladle sauce with meat and vegetables over noodles and garnish with chopped coriander and spring onions.

6. Serve immediately with pickled green chillies on the side.

Cantonese-Style Fried Noodles in Seafood Sauce

Substitute beef with mixed raw seafood (fish, prawns, squid) and dispense with marinade. All other ingredients remain the same. Broad rice noodles may be substituted with rice vermicelli or dried egg noodles (ee meen). To get the "wok-hei" or wok fragrance, tilt the wok into the high flames to set the oil alight and char the noodles.

Fried Broad Rice Noodles with Chives and Salted Fish

Use the kind of salted fish that breaks up into little shreds and not the kind that dissolves. This recipe was inspired by a dish of broad rice noodles fried with chives and salted fish that I had in a Teochew restaurant some years ago. I added mustard cabbage stems because salted fish goes well with this slightly bitter vegetable.

COOKING TIME: 15 MINUTES

100 g (3^1/$_2$ oz) salted fish

4 Tbsp cooking oil

200 g (7 oz) mustard cabbage stems, thinly sliced

50 g (1^3/$_4$ oz) carrots, peeled and cut into fine strips

2 Tbsp chopped garlic

200 g (7 oz) boneless firm-fleshed white fish or fish cake (page 40), sliced

600 g (11 oz) fresh broad rice noodles

1 tsp salt

100 g (3^1/$_2$ oz) chives, cut into finger-lengths

^{1}/$_2$ tsp ground white pepper

1. Rinse salted fish well and pat dry. Remove bones if any, then slice thinly.

2. Heat oil in a wok and deep-fry salted fish until nicely brown and fragrant. Drain and leave to cool, then pound salted fish or shred by hand. Set fish aside and do not clean wok.

3. Bring a pot of water to the boil, then blanch mustard cabbage stems and carrot for 10 seconds. Drain and set aside.

4. Using the same wok for frying salted fish, sauté chopped garlic until starting to brown. Add blanched mustard cabbage and carrot and stir-fry for 1 minute. Remove and set aside.

5. Using the same wok, fry sliced fish or fish cake for 1 minute in remaining oil, then add noodles and salt. Fry for 1 minute.

6. Stir in mustard cabbage, carrot, chives and shredded salted fish. Mix well. When chives begin to turn limp, remove from heat.

7. Dish out into a large serving platter and serve immediately.

Vietnamese Beef Noodle Soup

PHO BO

Beef *pho* is the noodle dish that most associate with Vietnam, although pork
(*mi quang*, page 104) and chicken noodle soups are also common there.
These soups are served with a thin-cut rice noodle known as *banh pho* or rice sticks.
Fresh thin-cut rice noodles *(kuay tiao)* can also be used.

COOKING TIME: 2 HOURS

250 g (9 oz) bean sprouts

600 g (1 lb 5^1/$_3$ oz) fresh thin-cut rice noodles

200 g (7 oz) beef, thinly sliced

SOUP

1 kg (2 lb 3 oz) beef bones and ribs with some meat

100 g (3^1/$_2$ oz) onions, peeled and quartered

6 cm (2.5 in) cinnamon stick

2 star anise

1 thumb-size knob old ginger, peeled and bruised

1 thumb-size knob galangal, peeled and bruised

2.5 litres (80 fl oz / 10 cups) water

^{1}/$_2$ tsp salt

3 Tbsp fish sauce

2 tsp sugar

GARNISHING
Chopped basil, mint, *laksa* leaves, Chinese celery and sawtooth coriander

CONDIMENTS
Nuoc cham (page 38)

1. Prepare garnish. Select generous helpings of herbs. Rinse herbs, then pick leaves of basil, mint and *laksa* leaves. Discard stalks. Leaves can be kept whole or chopped. Chop Chinese celery and sawtooth coriander. Set aside.

2. Prepare soup. Place all ingredients into a large stockpot and bring to the boil. Skim off any scum that rises to the top. Lower heat and simmer for 2 hours or until stock is reduced by half.

3. To serve noodles, bring a pot of water to the boil. Blanch bean sprouts for 10 seconds, then drain and divide into serving bowls.

4. Return water to the boil, then blanch noodles until tender but al dente. Drain and divide into serving bowls.

5. While waiting for water for blanching to boil, return soup to the boil. Soup should be boiling hot when ladled over noodles.

6. Place sliced beef over noodles in serving bowls, then ladle boiling soup over to cook beef lightly.

7. Garnish with herbs and serve with *nuoc cham* on the side.

Vietnamese Rice Noodles in Chicken Soup
(Pho Ga)

Make a chicken soup using the same ingredients as for Vietnamese Beef Noodle Soup. Top with cooked shredded chicken instead of beef.

Broad Rice Noodles in Beef Soup, Thai-Style

Rice noodles in beef soup is a popular Thai hawker dish and customers can choose from
a range of rice noodles to go with the soup. Instead of sliced beef, some hawkers use beef balls.
Prepare this dish according to your preference. Use any kind of rice noodles and
beef balls if available. You can also use meat balls (page 41) for a change.

COOKING TIME: 10 MINUTES

1 litre (32 fl oz / 4 cups)
beef stock (page 44)

1/2 tsp salt + 1 large pinch

2 Tbsp garlic oil (page 30)

200 g (7 oz) beef, thinly
sliced across the grain

300 g (11 oz) bean sprouts

600 g (1 lb 5 1/3 oz) fresh
broad rice noodles

DRESSING (SERVES 1)

1 Tbsp fish sauce

1 tsp sugar

1 tsp vinegar

1 bird's eye chilli, chopped

GARNISHING

1 bunch coriander leaves
(cilantro), chopped

1 small bunch Chinese
celery, chopped

1 spring onion (scallion),
chopped

CONDIMENTS

Thai chilli-vinegar dip
(page 34)

1. Bring stock to the boil with 1/2 tsp salt.

2. Heat garlic oil in a pan and sauté beef for 10 seconds. Sprinkle a large
   pinch of salt over beef, then remove from heat.

3. Prepare dressing. Mix all ingredients in a serving bowl. Repeat for the
   number of servings.

4. Bring a pot of water to the boil and blanch bean sprouts for
   10 seconds. Drain well and divide into serving bowls with dressing.

5. Return water to the boil and blanch noodles until tender but still
   al dente. Drain well and divide into serving bowls. Stir dressing
   into noodles.

6. Ladle hot soup over noodles and top with a helping of beef and garlic
   oil. Garnish with coriander leaves, Chinese celery and spring onion.

7. Serve immediately with Thai vinegar-chilli dip on the side.

Broad Rice Noodles in Curry Sauce

SINGAPORE-STYLE CURRY HOR FUN

This is a broad rice noodle dish with a chicken curry sauce and is to be distinguished from curry *mee*, Kuala Lumpur-style (page 152), which is Hokkien *mee* in a chicken curry soup.

COOKING TIME: 45 MINUTES

300 g (11 oz) *choy sum*

600 g (1 lb 5⅓ oz) fresh broad rice noodles or 300 g (11 oz) dried fine rice vermicelli

SPICE PASTE
200 g (7 oz) shallots, peeled

75 g (2½ oz) garlic

125 ml (4 fl oz / ½ cup) water

¾ cup meat curry powder (page 37)

CHICKEN CURRY SAUCE
750 ml (24 fl oz / 3 cups) water

500 g (1 lb 1½ oz) grated coconut

2 Tbsp tamarind paste

4 Tbsp cooking oil

6 cm (2.5 in) cinnamon stick

2 cloves

2 cardamom pods

500 g (1 lb 1½ oz) chicken, chopped into small pieces

1½ tsp salt

1. Prepare spice paste. Place shallots and garlic in a blender and process with a little of the water until fine. Mix in remaining water and curry powder to get a thick paste.

2. Prepare curry sauce. Mix two-thirds of water with grated coconut, then squeeze through a muslin bag or cloth-lined sieve to obtain coconut milk. Set aside.

3. Mix water with tamarind paste. Strain liquid and discard solids. Set aside.

4. Heat oil in a pot. Fry cinnamon, cloves and cardamom pods for 1 minute. Add spice paste and fry until fragrant and oil separates from paste.

5. Add chicken and salt and mix well. Fry for a few minutes, then stir in tamarind juice and bring to the boil.

6. Add coconut milk and bring to the boil. Lower heat and simmer until chicken is cooked. Turn off heat and leave curry sauce to stand for several hours for flavours to develop before serving.

7. To serve noodles, bring a pot of water to the boil. Blanch *choy sum* for 10 seconds, then drain well and set aside.

8. Return pot of water to the boil, then blanch noodles until tender but still al dente. Drain well and divide into deep serving bowls.

9. Ladle pieces of chicken and curry sauce over noodles. Top with blanched *choy sum* and serve immediately.

Phnom Penh Noodle Soup

This is a very popular noodle soup in Cambodia. It is sometimes called Nam Vang noodle soup, Nam Vang being the Vietnamese name for Phnom Penh, the capital of Cambodia. The noodle soup is found all over Cambodia and customers can choose to have either broad rice noodles or egg noodles in the soup.

COOKING TIME: 2 HOURS

300 g (11 oz) dried rice vermicelli or dried egg noodles, softened in cold water until pliable

100 g (3^1/$_2$ oz) Chinese red roast pork (page 42), thinly sliced

100 g (3^1/$_2$ oz) boiled, shredded chicken

200 g (7 oz) prawns (shrimps), boiled and peeled, leaving tails intact

12 fish balls (page 40)

SOUP

500 g (1 lb 1^1/$_2$ oz) chicken bones

500 g (1 lb 1^1/$_2$ oz) pork bones

1 dried squid, rinsed

1 Tbsp dried prawns (shrimps)

1 thumb-size knob old ginger, bruised

1 star anise

2 cloves garlic

100 g (3^1/$_2$ oz) salted mustard cabbage

2 litres (64 fl oz / 8 cups) water

3 Tbsp fish sauce

^{1}/$_2$ Tbsp sugar

^{1}/$_2$ tsp salt

2 Tbsp cooking oil

50 g (1^3/$_4$ oz) onions, peeled and finely chopped

1 Tbsp chopped garlic

GARNISHING

200 g (7 oz) bean sprouts, tails removed, rinsed

^{1}/$_2$ cup coriander leaves (cilantro)

^{1}/$_2$ cup basil leaves

^{1}/$_2$ cup *laska* leaves

^{1}/$_2$ cup sawtooth coriander, chopped

1 spring onion (scallion), chopped

Limes, halved

CONDIMENTS

Tuk trey chu p'em (page 36)

1 cup roasted peanuts

Garlic chilli sauce (page 34)

1. Prepare soup. Put all ingredients, except fish sauce, sugar, salt, oil, onion and garlic, into a large pot and bring to the boil. Skim off any scum that rises to the top, then lower heat and simmer until liquid is reduced by half. Discard solids. Stir in fish sauce, sugar and salt. Heat oil in a wok and fry onion and garlic until fragrant and brown. Add to soup.

2. Prepare garnish. Toss bean sprouts and herbs together, then divide into serving bowls.

3. To serve noodles, bring a pot of water to the boil. Blanch noodles until tender but al dente. Drain well and divide into serving bowls on top of garnish.

4. Ladle hot soup over and top with Chinese red roast pork, chicken, prawns, fish balls and lime halves. Serve immediately with condiments on the side.

Broad Rice Noodles in Spicy Sichuan Vegetable Soup

Sichuan vegetable soup is often served with rice, but as this recipe shows,
it is also delicious with rice noodles. Preserved Sichuan vegetable comes pickled in chilli
and salt and should be soaked in several changes of cold water to get rid of excess salt
before using, but it should not be soaked until it turns bland either. Do a test to get the
right level of saltiness before cooking. This recipe works well with other rice noodles too.

COOKING TIME: 10 MINUTES

1 tsp light soy sauce

A few drops dark soy sauce

A pinch of salt

2 tsp sesame oil

150 g ($5^{1}/_{3}$ oz) pork/
chicken, cut into
matchsticks

600 g (1 lb $5^{1}/_{3}$ oz) fresh
broad rice noodles

2 tsp cornflour

SOUP
100 g ($3^{1}/_{2}$ oz) preserved
Sichuan vegetable

1.25 litres (40 fl oz / 5 cups)
pork/chicken stock
(page 43/44)

200 g (7 oz) soft bean curd,
cut into cubes

100 g ($3^{1}/_{2}$ oz)
chrysanthemum leaves

A pinch of salt

GARNISHING
1 bunch coriander leaves
(cilantro), chopped

1 spring onion (scallion),
chopped

1 Tbsp fried garlic
(page 30)

CONDIMENTS
Fresh red chillies with light
soy sauce (page 31)

1. Mix light and dark soy sauces, salt and sesame oil into pork/chicken and leave for 10 minutes.

2. Prepare soup. Rinse Sichuan vegetable and slice thinly. Soak in several changes of cold water but be careful not to over-soak.

3. Bring stock to the boil, then add Sichuan vegetable and simmer for 10 minutes. Stir in marinated pork/chicken and bean curd. Bring to the boil and simmer for 2 minutes.

4. Add chrysanthemum leaves and salt. Remove from heat when leaves change colour.

5. To prepare noodles, bring a pot of water to the boil, then blanch noodles until tender but still al dente. Drain well and divide into serving bowls.

6. Ladle hot soup over noodles and garnish with fried garlic, chopped spring onion and coriander leaves. Serve immediately.

Vietnamese Rice Noodles with Stewed Pork

MI QUANG

This soup goes well with any type of rice noodles, from broad rice noodles, to coarse and fine rice vermicelli, in both fresh and dried form. The herbs can either be chopped or kept whole.

COOKING TIME: 1 HOUR

4 lettuce leaves, shredded

200 g (7 oz) bean sprouts

600 g (1 lb 5$^1/_3$ oz) fresh broad rice noodles

1 cup peanuts, toasted and ground

1 cup Vietnamese rice crackers (optional), crushed, or 1 cup pork crackling, chopped

HERBS

1 small bunch basil leaves

1 small bunch mint leaves

1 small bunch *laksa* leaves

1 small bunch sawtooth coriander

SOUP

1 Tbsp dried prawns (shrimps)

300 g (11 oz) belly pork

1.25 litres (40 fl oz / 5 cups) water

2 Tbsp cooking oil

2 spring onions (scallions), chopped

$^1/_2$ tsp prawn paste (*belacan*)

2 Tbsp fish sauce

1 tsp salt

1 tsp freshly ground black pepper

150 g (5$^1/_3$ oz) tomatoes, coarsely chopped

CONDIMENTS

Nuoc cham (page 38)

1. Rinse herbs. Pick basil, mint and *laksa* leaves and discard stalks. Set aside. Chop sawtooth coriander.

2. Prepare soup. Clean dried prawns, remove shell and any inedible bits. Rinse in cold water, then chop until fine. Set aside.

3. Place belly pork into a large pot with 1.25 litres (40 fl oz / 5 cups) water and bring to the boil. Lower heat and simmer for 15 minutes until pork is cooked. Remove pork, leave to cool, then slice into thin strips, keeping layers of fat with lean. Set pork aside and reserve water for use in stock.

4. In a separate pot, heat oil and fry chopped spring onions for 1 minute, then add the chopped dried prawns and fry for 2 minutes until fragrant.

5. Add sliced pork and fry for 3 minutes. Add water used to boil pork and all remaining soup ingredients except tomatoes. Simmer over low heat until pork is tender and soup reduced by about one-third.

6. Add tomatoes and simmer for another 5 minutes until tomatoes are soft.

7. To serve noodles, arrange herbs and shredded lettuce in serving bowls.

8. Bring a large pot of water to the boil and blanch bean sprouts for 10 seconds. Drain and divide into serving bowls.

9. Return water to the boil and blanch noodles until tender but still al dente. Drain well and divide into serving bowls.

10. Top with ground peanuts and crushed rice crackers or pork crackling. Ladle hot soup over with a helping of pork slices. Serve with *nuoc cham* on the side.

Rice Noodle Squares in Pork Soup

KUAY CHAP

This is a Singapore hawker dish of rice noodle squares in a hearty soup served with braised meats that originally included tripe. As tripe is seldom eaten today, I have adapted this dish. In Singapore, noodle stalls in wet markets sell rice sheets for *kuay chap*.

COOKING TIME: 1 HOUR

750 ml (24 fl oz / 3 cups) pork stock (page 43)

1 tsp salt

1 star anise

1 Tbsp fried shallots (page 29)

600 g (1 lb 5^1/$_3$ oz) rice noodle squares

BRAISED MEAT

200 g (7 oz) belly pork, cut into cubes

50 g (1^3/$_4$ oz) pork skin

50 g (1^3/$_4$ oz) soybean puffs, cut into bite-size squares

200 g (7 oz) firm bean curd, cut into cubes

1 Tbsp dark soy sauce

2 Tbsp light soy sauce

1 litre (32 fl oz / 4 cups) water

A large pinch of ground white pepper

2 cloves garlic, peeled

1 tsp Chinese five-spice powder

4 hard-boiled eggs, shelled

CONDIMENTS

Fresh red chilli-vinegar sauce (page 33)

1. Prepare braised meat. Put all ingredients, except hard-boiled eggs, into a pot and simmer over low heat for 1 hour or until belly pork and pork skin are tender but still whole. There should be about half the original amount of liquid left.

2. When meat is done, add hard-boiled eggs and simmer for another 5 minutes to colour eggs.

3. About 30 minutes before meat is done, bring pork stock, salt, star anise and fried shallots to the boil in a pot, then lower heat and simmer for 10 minutes until fragrant.

4. If using dried rice noodle squares, cook in boiling water until tender but still al dente. Divide into serving bowls. If using fresh wet market noodle squares, blanch in boiling water for 10 seconds.

5. Ladle hot stock over rice noodle squares and serve with a dish of braised meat and a saucer of fresh red chilli-vinegar sauce on the side.

6. Slice pork belly and pork skin into small pieces and halve or quarter eggs. Place into a serving bowl and ladle gravy over. The braised meat can be served in individual portions or on a large serving platter as a communal dish.

MOUSE-TAIL NOODLES

Fried Mouse-Tails, Thai-Style

Fresh mouse-tail noodles fry well as this recipe shows. You may also substitute with
dried rice noodles or fresh coarse rice vermicelli. Do not use fresh
broad rice noodles as they do not stand up well to repeated stirring.

COOKING TIME: 15 MINUTES

5 Tbsp cooking oil

4 cloves garlic, peeled and chopped

4 shallots, peeled and thinly sliced

600 g (1 lb 5¹/₃ oz) fresh mouse-tail noodles

1 Tbsp cooked dried red chilli paste (page 30)

100 g (3¹/₂ oz) pork/ chicken/prawns (shrimps), cut meat into matchsticks; peel and devein prawns

200 g (7 oz) firm bean curd, cut into strips

1 spring onion (scallion), cut into finger-lengths

300 g (11 oz) bean sprouts

2 eggs

SEASONING

¹/₃ cup water

2 Tbsp tamarind paste

3 Tbsp sugar

4 Tbsp fish sauce

GARNISHING

50 g (1³/₄ oz) roasted peanuts, ground

1 spring onion (scallion), chopped

A handful of basil leaves

1 bunch coriander leaves (cilantro), chopped

Limes, halved

1. Prepare seasoning. Mix water with tamarind paste. Strain liquid and discard solids. Mix tamarind juice with sugar and fish sauce. Set aside.

2. Heat 2 Tbsp oil in a wok and fry garlic and shallots until nicely brown. Add noodles and 2 Tbsp seasoning mixture. Fry for 1 minute or a little longer if noodles are firm. If necessary, sprinkle a little water over noodles to help soften them. Remove from wok and set aside.

3. Add 1 Tbsp oil to the same wok and fry chilli paste for 1 minute. Add meat/prawns and fry for another minute.

4. Stir in bean curd and spring onion and three-quarters of bean sprouts.

5. Stir in remaining seasoning mixture and fry for 1 minute. Dish out. Set aside.

6. Heat remaining 1 Tbsp oil in the wok and add eggs, breaking yolks up and spreading eggs out to cook and set.

7. Return noodles and other fried ingredients to wok and mix well with fried eggs.

8. Turn off heat and stir in remaining raw bean sprouts. Dish out into a large serving plate, garnish and serve immediately.

Spicy Fried Mouse-Tail Noodles

This dish was created when I needed to bring something to a picnic. Needless to say, these noodles went down rather well. Fried mouse-tail noodles keep well and make good leftovers.

COOKING TIME: 10 MINUTES

4 Tbsp cooking oil

2 Tbsp chopped garlic

100 g (3$\frac{1}{2}$ oz) prawns (shrimps), peeled and deveined

100 g (3$\frac{1}{2}$ oz) fish cake (page 40), thinly sliced

300 g (11 oz) Tientsin cabbage (page 34), thinly sliced

600 g (1 lb 5$\frac{1}{3}$ oz) mouse-tail noodles

50 g (1$\frac{3}{4}$ oz) carrots, peeled and cut into matchsticks

1 tsp dark soy sauce

2 Tbsp light soy sauce

$\frac{1}{2}$ tsp salt

1 Tbsp cooked dried red chilli paste (page 33)

1. Heat oil in a wok and sauté garlic until fragrant. Add prawns and fish cake, then Tientsin cabbage and mix well.

2. When vegetables are limp, stir in noodles, carrot, dark and light soy sauces, salt and chilli paste and mix well.

3. Fry for 3 minutes, turning noodles over in wok constantly. If noodles start to stick, sprinkle in a few spoonfuls of water.

4. Serve hot or at room temperature.

Penang-Style Fried Mouse-Tail Noodles

The ingredients and method of cooking are the same as those for Penang-Style Fried Broad Rice Noodles (page 94). Just use 600 g (1 lb 5$\frac{1}{3}$ oz) fresh mouse-tail noodles in place of the broad rice noodles.

Fried Mouse-Tail Noodles with Chilli Bean Sauce

This is a Cantonese-style preparation, meaning that the meat is marinated in cornflour and egg white to give the cooked meat a smooth texture. Peanut oil is another ingredient that marks this out as a Cantonese dish. The hot chilli bean sauce is the northern or Sichuan touch and the fresh red chillies the South East Asian influence. Other rice noodles (fresh coarse rice vermicelli, dried thin-medium rice vermicelli or fresh broad rice noodles) may be substituted for mouse-tail noodles. If using fresh broad rice noodles, the noodles should be added after the meat and before the garlic and bean sauce. For a stronger flavour, use the stems of Chinese celery in place of Western celery.

COOKING TIME: 10 MINUTES

600 g (1 lb 5^1/$_3$ oz) fresh mouse-tail noodles

4 Tbsp peanut oil

100 g (3^1/$_2$ oz) celery, thinly sliced

1 Tbsp hot chilli bean sauce

4 slices ginger, finely chopped

2 fresh red chillies, seeded and thinly sliced

^{1}/$_2$ Tbsp chopped garlic

A few drops dark soy sauce

1 spring onion (scallion), chopped

1 bunch coriander leaves (cilantro), chopped

MEAT AND MARINADE
300 g (11 oz) beef/lean pork

A pinch of bicarbonate of soda

^{1}/$_4$ tsp salt

2 tsp light soy sauce

1 tsp sesame oil

1 tsp Chinese cooking wine

^{1}/$_2$ tsp ground white pepper

1 tsp cornflour

1 egg white

SAUCE
250 ml (8 fl oz / 1 cup) water

^{1}/$_2$ tsp sugar

2 tsp Chinese cooking wine

2 tsp sesame oil

1 Tbsp cornflour

^{1}/$_2$ tsp salt

^{1}/$_2$ tsp dark soy sauce

1. Prepare meat and marinade. Slice beef/pork across the grain into thin matchsticks. Mix bicarbonate of soda into meat, then add salt, light soy sauce and sesame oil, and lastly cornflour and egg white. Leave to marinate for 10 minutes.

2. Prepare sauce. Combine ingredients in a bowl and stir well before adding to wok.

3. Prepare noodles. Bring a pot of water to the boil, then blanch mouse-tail noodles until tender but al dente. Drain well.

4. Heat peanut oil in a wok and cook marinated meat. Beef will take about 10 seconds and pork a little longer. Add celery and fry for another 30 seconds. Leaving oil in the wok, remove meat and celery and set aside.

5. Stir chilli bean sauce, ginger, chillies and garlic into hot oil and sauté for 1 minute before adding rice noodles and dark soy sauce to colour noodles. Fry for 1 minute, then add sauce mixture and stir well.

6. Stir in fried meat, spring onion and coriander leaves. Dish out onto a serving platter and serve hot.

Thai-Style Mouse-Tail Noodles in Soup

This dish is prepared with sugar and fish sauce, and uses fish sauce, vinegar and
bird's eye chilli as a condiment, giving it a Thai flavour. This recipe can also be prepared with
other kinds of rice noodles. The quantities given for the soup serves between four and six,
but the seasoning for the noodles is for a single serving.

COOKING TIME: 10 MINUTES

1 litre (32 fl oz / 4 cups) chicken
stock (page 44)

1^1/$_2$ tsp salt

3 tsp sugar

1 tsp white rice vinegar

200 g (7 oz) bean sprouts

600 g (1 lb 5^1/$_3$ oz) mouse-tail
noodles

DRESSING (SERVES 1)

1 tsp toasted red chilli flakes
(page 35)

1 Tbsp fish sauce

1 Tbsp garlic oil

GARNISHING

Lettuce leaves

200 g (7 oz) Chinese red roast
pork (page 42), sliced

1 bunch coriander leaves
(cilantro), chopped

1 spring onion (scallion),
chopped

^{1}/$_2$ Tbsp fried garlic (page 30)

3 Tbsp roasted peanuts, ground

CONDIMENTS

Thai chilli-vinegar dip (page 34)

1. Bring stock to the boil in a pot, then stir in salt, sugar and
   vinegar. Lower heat and leave stock to simmer.

2. Prepare dressing. Combine chilli flakes, fish sauce and garlic oil
   in a serving bowl. Repeat for the number of servings.

3. Bring a large pot of water to the boil, then blanch bean sprouts
   for 10 seconds. Drain well and divide into prepared serving
   bowls.

4. Return water to the boil and blanch noodles until tender but al
   dente. Drain well and divide into serving bowls on top of bean
   sprouts. Stir to mix well with dressing.

5. Ladle hot soup over noodles and top with a lettuce leaf, slices
   of roast pork, coriander leaves, spring onion, fried garlic and
   ground peanuts.

6. Serve immediately with Thai chilli-vinegar dip on the side.

Wheat Noodles

There are many kinds of noodles made from wheat, ranging from simple pinched wheat-water-egg doughs found in the Himalayan regions, to fresh, cooked wheat noodles found in South East Asia and dried wheat noodles made by the East Asians. The basic dough is made with water, wheat flour and salt, with egg in some varieties. The dough is rolled thin and cut out or extruded, then dried or partially cooked and sold as fresh noodles. Fresh noodles keep for up to a week in the refrigerator. Most wheat noodles can also be dried and stored without refrigeration. Although all wheat noodles are made with wheat flour, the taste and texture varies and they do not make perfect substitutes for one another. The difficulty in substituting wheat noodles is also due to tradition, where certain noodles are associated with certain preparations. Changing the noodle thus means that the dish will taste different from the original. Hence the particular kind of noodle required is always specified.

HOKKIEN MEE (FRESH COOKED WHEAT NOODLES)

The most popular kind of wheat noodles in places with large numbers of Chinese from Fujian province is Hokkien *mee*. Sometimes referred to as yellow *mee* in South East Asia because of the tradition of adding yellow colouring, these wheat noodles do not have egg as an ingredient and may not always be coloured yellow, although they will still have a slight yellow tint from the alkali salts or bicarbonate of soda added to the flour paste. Like rice vermicelli, Hokkien *mee* is made from a semi-cooked paste of wheat flour that is extruded into boiling water, parboiled, then oiled to keep the strands apart. These cooked noodles are sometimes labelled as "Taiwan noodles" in the United States where they may be found in the refrigerator section of large Asian stores. They are a light yellow colour and may be extruded as round strands or thicker strips. Because Hokkien *mee* is parboiled, it is preferable to under cook these fresh noodles.

PLAIN WHEAT NOODLES

These simple noodles made of wheat flour, water and salt are found in many parts of Asia including the Himalayan mountain region and the islands of South East Asia. One of the best-known plain wheat noodles is *mee sua*, a Hokkien-style noodle that comes as "sua" meaning "thread" as well as "coarse". The Hokkien phrase "*mee sua*" or Chinese phrase "*mian sian*" translates into "thread noodles". Spelt "*misua*" in the Philippines where it is a popular noodle, *mee sua* may also be labelled as "flour vermicelli" or "wheat vermicelli". Coarse wheat vermicelli appears fresh or semi-fresh in large amounts during the Chinese Lunar New Year season in Singapore. During this period, they are often labelled "longevity noodles" because many Hokkiens cook these very long noodles as a symbol of long life at the start of the New Year. *Mee sua* is also eaten on other special occasions such as birthdays and, once upon a time, was consumed as part of the wedding ritual.

Like *mee sua*, Japanese *somen* is a thin wheat noodle which may also be flavoured with egg (*tamago somen*), green tea (*cha somen*) and pickled plum (*ume somen*), the noodles being yellow, green and pink respectively to distinguish them from plain *somen* (white). *Mee sua* and *somen* are usually sold dried or served in soup or, in the case of *somen*, also eaten cold with a dipping sauce. Japanese *somen*, Korean *somyon* and Chinese *mee sua* are interchangeable.

Another plain wheat noodle is Japanese udon (page 16) which may come fresh, dried, already boiled, flat or round, plain or flavoured. Udon is usually hearty fare eaten in soup or fried,

although *hiyamugi* is a thinner, round udon that is also eaten cold.

Plain wheat noodles need not always be in straight strands, round or flat. They can be shaped. One of the prettiest is bow-tie noodles known as *chhu tagi* (page 171) from Ladakh on the edge of the Tibetan plateau. This shape allows the noodles to be popped into a hearty meat and vegetable stew without falling apart.

Northern Chinese *la mian* (pulled noodles) is a wheat noodle made by pulling soft wheat dough into long and thin strands. Pulling dough into noodles is harder to do than it looks. *La mian* comes both fresh and dried although the fresh variety is not easy to find outside of areas without a large community of Northern Chinese. Dried *la mian* is no match for fresh *la mian* in both flavour and texture, and you might want to make your own fresh plain wheat noodles by rolling and cutting the dough (page 12).

Not to be forgotten among the wheat noodles is instant noodles, an invention of Ando Momofuku, a Nissin employee who in 1958 came up with a cake of dried noodles that could be turned into a quick meal in a matter of minutes. His inspiration came from the Japanese preference for Chinese-style noodles called ramen.

Today, there is almost no place in the world where instant noodles are not to be found. Japanese astronaut Noguchi Soichi even brought it to outer space in 2005. Instant noodles are fried or baked into cakes during manufacturing, allowing the noodles to be eaten straight out of the packet as a quick, filling snack, as is done in Nepal where distances to be covered on foot are long and places remote. Instant noodle manufacturers are now marketing these pre-cooked noodles in large cakes without the instant seasoning mixes for frying or serving in soup.

A noodle that is included here is Japanese soba or buckwheat noodles although buckwheat flour is not milled from a cereal but seeds. Soba are thin noodles that come dried or frozen and may be served cold in summer, in hot soup in winter or fried. Soba is also popular in Korea. Buckwheat flour has to be mixed with grated mountain yam or yam starch to get a dough elastic enough to be rolled out and cut. Another method is to make a paste of buckwheat and wheat flour and extrude the stiff paste into boiling water, rather like making Hokkien *mee*. Making soba is not easy which makes it something of an art, or you may want to resort to using an ancient Japanese peasant technique of pinching the dough. Wholemeal buckwheat flour (available in health food sections in some countries) gives a very dark noodle with plenty of fibre. This dark grey soba is known as *yabu* soba. Soba becomes lighter when made with more highly refined buckwheat flour, the whitest being *gozen* soba made from the most refined buckwheat flour. Soba is also flavoured with, among other things, green tea, black sesame seeds and yuzu lime rind.

EGG NOODLES

Wheat noodles are also made with egg (page 13) and Chinese egg noodles vary in taste, texture and appearance. They can be fresh, dried or pre-fried and dried. A Cantonese pre-fried egg noodle is called "*ee meen*" or "*ee fu meen*" in Cantonese and these brittle dried noodles are usually in round cakes of a deep shade of brown. Fresh *ee meen* is sometimes on the menu of Chinese restaurants where these noodles may be handmade in the kitchen. Fresh *ee meen* which has a delicious egg flavour is not deep-fried. Dried egg noodles vary in thickness from flat narrow-cut strands to fine round strands and may also be flavoured with seafood such as prawns. To add to the confusion, there are dried wheat noodles that look like dried egg noodles but do not have egg in them. They are sometimes labelled "vegetarian noodles". Read the ingredients label for a guide to what is actually in them.

Dried egg noodles are often dried in individual serving portions and are a good substitute for a fresh wheat noodle known to Singaporeans as *mee kia* (little noodles) which may not have egg in them. *Mee kia* comes in thin strands with a broad-cut flat variation known as *mee pok*. The term "*mee pok*" could be a corruption of the Hokkien word, "*poh*", meaning "flat" or "fine". The thinner and more translucent the *mee pok*, the better the flavour and bite. Well-made—and well-prepared—*mee pok* is one of the best-tasting noodles ever. On the other hand, thick and overcooked *mee pok* can also be one of the most awful.

While some commercial *mee kia* and *mee pok* can be a trifle pasty and lack a good bite, this cannot be said of the variety called Hong Kong noodles (not to be confused with the cooked dish called Hong Kong Noodles). In Singapore, these fresh noodles are usually found in the refrigerator section of supermarkets. They have an excellent bite and are almost wiry. Noodle shops in Hong Kong serve up similar noodles.

In the United States, a fresh Chinese noodle found in many Asian stores taste very much like Hong Kong noodles. These fresh noodles come from noodle factories in California where many Cantonese migrants settled in the 19th century. These noodles freeze well.

WHEAT NOODLES

Foochow Fried Mee

Fat Hokkien *mee* is braised in a rich seafood stock seasoned generously with garlic. The result is a hearty dish for seafood lovers. You may use surf clams *(Fam. Veneridae Paphai undulata Born)* known as *remis* in Malay, or *hoy lai* or *hoy huaan* in Thai, ridged sand clams *(Fam. Veneridae Circe scripta (Linnaeus), Venus scripta)*, or waved sand clams *(Fam. Veneridae Anomalacardia squamosa (Linnaeus), Venus squamosa)* in this dish.

COOKING TIME: 20 MINUTES

100 g (3¹/₂ oz) pork, thinly sliced

3 Tbsp cooking oil

200 g (7 oz) prawns (shrimps), peeled, leaving tails intact

2 Tbsp chopped garlic

600 g (1 lb 5¹/₃ oz) fresh fat Hokkien *mee*

1 tsp salt

A few drops dark soy sauce

2 Tbsp light soy sauce

1 spring onion (scallion), cut into finger-lengths

3 Tbsp cornflour, mixed with 4 Tbsp water

SEAFOOD STOCK

500 g (1 lb 1¹/₂ oz) clams

500 ml (16 fl oz / 2 cups) water

250 ml (8 fl oz / 1 cup) prawn stock (page 44)

MARINADE FOR PORK

1 tsp light soy sauce

A pinch of ground white pepper

¹/₂ tsp sesame oil

1 tsp cornflour

1 tsp water

CONDIMENTS

Fresh red chillies with light soy sauce (page 31)

1. Prepare seafood stock. Rinse clams and place in a pot with water. Bring to the boil, then lower heat and simmer for about 1 minute or until clams open up. Remove clams from stock and discard any empty shells or unopened clams. Set clams aside for frying.

2. Rest clam stock for 30 minutes to let sandy deposits from clams sink to the bottom. Pour stock into another pot and discard bottom layer with sand.

3. Pour prawn stock into pot with clean clam stock.

4. Prepare pork. Combine marinade for pork and place pork in to marinate for 10 minutes. Heat 1 Tbsp oil in a wok and fry pork until it changes colour. Dish out and set aside.

5. Heat another 1 Tbsp oil in the wok and fry prawns until they change colour. Dish out and set aside with pork.

6. Add remaining oil to wok and fry garlic until fragrant.

7. Stir in noodles, 750 ml (24 fl oz / 3 cups) seafood stock, salt and soy sauces and simmer for 10 minutes with wok covered. Stir occasionally.

8. Add pork, prawns, clams and spring onions. Stir cornflour mixture, then add to wok. Bring to the boil and allow sauce to thicken.

9. Dish out onto a large serving platter and serve immediately with sliced red chillies in light soy sauce on the side.

Fried Hokkien Mee

ROCHOR MEE

This Singapore noodle dish was once called Rochor *mee* because the original version was believed to be from a street hawker located in the Rochor area next to the Seven-Storey Hotel. Today, it is better known as fried Hokkien *mee*, getting its name from the noodles used. Although Hokkien *mee* leftovers can be rather mushy, it is very acceptable as leftovers.

COOKING TIME: 30 MINUTES

$^{1}/_{2}$ tsp salt

3 Tbsp light soy sauce

500 ml (16 fl oz / 2 cups) pork stock (page 43)

6 Tbsp lard (page 45)

2 Tbsp chopped garlic

2 eggs, cracked into a bowl

300 g (11 oz) Hokkien *mee*

300 g (11 oz) fresh coarse rice vermicelli

300 g (11 oz) bean sprouts

100 g ($3^{1}/_{2}$ oz) prawns (shrimps), boiled and peeled leaving tails intact

100 g ($3^{1}/_{2}$ oz) belly pork, boiled and cut into thin strips

100 g ($3^{1}/_{2}$ oz) squid, boiled, cooled and cut into thin rings

1 bundle chives, cut into finger-lengths

GARNISHING

Limes, halved

CONDIMENTS

Fresh red chillies with light soy sauce (page 31) or dried red chilli paste with dried prawns (page 33)

1. Mix salt and light soy sauce into stock and have it ready near the wok. The stock is added to the noodles during frying to prevent the noodles drying out. Reserve 4 Tbsp for adding to the noodles at the end of frying.

2. Heat 3 Tbsp lard in a wok until very hot, then stir in 1 Tbsp chopped garlic. When fragrant, add eggs, break up yolks and spread eggs around hot wok, turning and chopping cooked eggs into smaller pieces as they set. Spoon some stock over eggs.

3. Add Hokkien *mee* and rice vermicelli and mix well, stir-frying with generous additions of stock. Cover noodles to cook in steam for 5 minutes.

4. Stir in bean sprouts and mix well.

5. Make a well in the centre of noodles, add remaining lard and when hot, add rest of chopped garlic. Fry garlic for 1 minute, then mix into noodles.

6. Stir in cooked prawns, belly pork, squid and chives together with remaining stock.

7. Dish out and garnish with lime halves. Serve hot with either condiment.

Kuala Lumpur Fried Hokkien Mee

The noodles used in this dish is thick Hokkien *mee*, sometimes called "fat noodles" because
it is so chunky. It is the Kuala Lumpur version of Singapore's fried Hokkien *mee*.
Once, while visiting Kuala Lumpur, Malaysia, I came across a noodle stall in a coffeeshop where a
long patient queue had formed, waiting for a taste of the hawker's fried fat noodles.
I joined the queue. The noodles were so good that I stopped over on my way to the airport
to take some home to enjoy in Singapore. This is my version of it. The secret to these noodles
lies in the amount of lard and the quality of the dark soy sauce used.

COOKING TIME: 20 MINUTES

6 Tbsp lard (page 45)

1 Tbsp chopped garlic

600 g (1 lb 5^1/$_3$ oz) fat Hokkien *mee*

250 ml (8 fl oz / 1 cup) pork stock (page 43)

1^1/$_2$ Tbsp dark soy sauce

2 Tbsp light soy sauce

200 g (7 oz) prawns (shrimps), boiled and peeled

100 g (3^1/$_2$ oz) fish cake (page 40), sliced

300 g (11 oz) *choy sum*

Sambal belacan with lime juice (page 31)

1. Heat lard in a wok until hot, then add garlic and sauté until fragrant.

2. Add noodles, stir well, then add stock, dark and light soy sauces and stir well. Lower heat and cover wok to cook for about 3 minutes, stirring occasionally and taking care not to let noodles burn. Add a bit more stock if necessary.

3. When noodles are tender, stir in cooked prawns, fish cake and vegetables. Add more stock if noodles start to stick to the bottom of the pan. The noodles should be moist but not drowned in gravy. Noodles are done when vegetables change colour.

4. Serve hot with some *sambal belacan* in lime juice on the side.

Dry Fish Ball Noodles, Chaozhou-Style

This is one of the most common hawker noodle dishes in Singapore. Customers can choose any of these noodles to make up the dish: fine rice vermicelli, fresh egg noodles (*mee pok* and *mee kia*), fresh broad rice noodles or fresh mouse-tail noodles. In addition to fish balls and sometimes, sliced fish cake, the traditional garnishes include sliced pork liver and minced pork. A bowl of hot stock is always served with the dry noodles. This recipe serves one. Prepare more servings as desired.

COOKING TIME: 15 MINUTES

50 g (1³/₄ oz) bean sprouts

Fresh egg noodles (*mee kia* or *mee pok*) or 150 g (5¹/₃ oz) fresh broad rice noodles or 80 g (3 oz) dried fine rice vermicelli, soaked in cold water until pliable

DRESSING FOR NOODLES

¹/₂–1 Tbsp dried red chilli paste with dried prawns (page 33) or to taste

1 Tbsp Chinkiang black vinegar or to taste

1 Tbsp light soy sauce or Thai fish sauce

1¹/₂ Tbsp lard (page 45)

¹/₂ Tbsp fried shallots (page 29)

GARNISHING

3–5 fish balls (page 40), depending on size

4 slices fish cake (page 40)

1 lettuce leaf

50 g (1³/₄ oz) minced pork (optional)

1. Prepare dressing for noodles. Mix all ingredients in a serving bowl or deep plate. The amount of chilli paste and black vinegar can be adjusted to taste.

2. Bring a pot or water to the boil, then blanch bean sprouts for 10 seconds. Drain well and set aside.

3. Return water to the boil, then blanch noodles until tender but al dente. Drain well and place on prepared serving bowl or plate. Stir noodles into dressing.

4. Top noodles with fish balls, fish cake, lettuce leaf and blanched bean sprouts. If using minced pork, blanch meat in some boiling pork stock and serve soup as an accompaniment to the noodles. Serve hot.

Braised Noodles

LOR MEE

Although the phrase *"lor mee"* means braised noodles, the noodles in this dish
are not braised. Instead, the meat is braised in a fragrant sauce and a little of
it poured over the blanched noodles. The final dish is dry.

COOKING TIME: 1 HOUR

1 litre (32 fl oz / 4 cups) water

$1/4$ cup cornflour

500 g (1 lb $1^1/_2$ oz) pork ribs with meat

1 thumb-size knob old ginger, peeled and bruised

1 star anise

$1/2$ tsp Chinese five-spice powder

1 Tbsp dark soy sauce

$1/2$ Tbsp fried shallots (page 29)

$1^1/_2$ tsp salt

$1/2$ tsp ground white pepper

200 g (7 oz) bean sprouts

600 g (1 lb $5^1/_3$ oz) Hokkien *mee*

GARNISHING

1 stalk Chinese celery, chopped

1 bunch coriander leaves (cilantro), chopped

1 spring onion (scallion), chopped

CONDIMENTS

Garlic chilli sauce (page 34)

1. Mix 125 ml (4 fl oz / $1/2$ cup) water with cornflour. Stir mixture well again just before adding to stock.

2. Put remaining water into a stockpot with pork ribs and ginger and bring to the boil. Skim off any scum that rises to the top.

3. Add star anise, five-spice powder, dark soy sauce, fried shallots and salt. Lower heat and simmer until meat is soft and stock reduced to about one-third.

4. Stir in pepper and cornflour mixture to thicken stock. Set aside.

5. To serve noodles, bring a pot of water to the boil and blanch bean sprouts for 10 seconds. Drain well and divide into serving bowls.

6. Return water to the boil and blanch Hokkien *mee* until tender but still firm. Drain well and divide into serving bowls.

7. Ladle hot stock over noodles together with some pieces of pork ribs.

8. Garnish with chopped herbs and serve with a generous helping of garlic chilli sauce. The chilli sauce should be stirred into the noodles before eating.

Balinese Fried Noodles

This spice paste is unusual in that it is cooked into a sauce that is then added to the noodles during the frying. You can double and make extra for another day.

COOKING TIME: 30 MINUTES

600 g (1 lb 5¹/₃ oz) fresh wheat noodles or 300 g (11 oz) dried egg noodles

4 Tbsp cooking oil

3 eggs, beaten

1 onion, peeled and sliced

200 g (7 oz) prawns (shrimps), peeled and deveined

400 g (14¹/₃ oz) cabbage, shredded

1 medium carrot, peeled and cut into fine strips

SPICE PASTE
100 g (3¹/₂ oz) ripe tomatoes

125 ml (4 fl oz / ¹/₂ cup) cooking oil

50 g (1³/₄ oz) shallots, peeled and thinly sliced

2 cloves garlic, peeled and sliced

100 g (3¹/₂ oz) fresh red chillies, seeded and coarsely chopped

4 slices ginger

1 stalk lemongrass, finely sliced

4 Tbsp water

2 tsp sugar

1 tsp salt

1 Tbsp Indonesian sweet dark soy sauce *(kicap manis)*

GARNISHING
Fried shallots (page 29)

Limes, halved

1. Prepare spice paste. Using a sharp knife, peel tomatoes, then chop coarsely.

2. Heat oil in a saucepan and fry shallots until soft. Add garlic and sauté for 1 minute. Add remaining ingredients and simmer for 3 minutes. Leave mixture to cool, then blend into a thick paste. Reheat spice paste and simmer until oil separates from paste.

3. Bring a pot of water to the boil and blanch noodles until nearly tender but still very al dente. Drain well and set aside.

4. Heat a bit of oil in a wok and make omelettes from beaten eggs. Cut into thin strips.

5. Heat remaining oil in the wok and sauté onion for 1 minute. Add prawns and when they turn pink, add cabbage and carrot and fry for 1 minute.

6. Stir in cooked spice paste and noodles. Fry for 1–2 minutes until noodles are tender but still al dente. Add omelette strips.

7. Garnish with fried shallots and lime halves and serve immediately.

Fried Nyonya Mee

Although also eaten at other times, this particular dish is one of the standard dishes prepared in many Straits Chinese homes in Singapore for the Chinese New Year's Eve reunion dinner. The noodles symbolise long life and every member of the family was supposed to partake of it.

COOKING TIME: 10 MINUTES

4 Tbsp cooking oil

30 g (1 oz) shallots, peeled and thinly sliced

$^1/_2$ Tbsp chopped garlic

1 Tbsp fermented soybeans (*taucheo*), rinsed and mashed well

100 g (3$^1/_2$ oz) pork/ chicken, thinly sliced

200 g (7 oz) prawns (shrimps), peeled, leaving tails intact

200 g (7 oz) *choy sum*, cut into finger-lengths

200 g (7 oz) bean sprouts

1$^1/_2$ tsp salt

600 g (1 lb 5$^1/_3$ oz) Hokkien *mee*

250 ml (8 fl oz / 1 cup) pork/prawn/chicken stock (page 43/44)

Sambal belacan with lime juice (page 31)

1. Heat oil in a wok and fry shallots until golden brown. Remove fried shallots and set aside. Leave oil in wok.

2. Stir in chopped garlic and fermented soybeans and when garlic is fragrant, add meat, prawns, *choy sum*, bean sprouts and salt.

3. When prawns turn pink, add noodles and stock. Mix well and bring to the boil. Cook for about 2 minutes, then stir in fried shallots.

4. Serve noodles hot with a condiment of *sambal belacan* and lime juice on the side.

Hong Kong-Style Dry Noodles
HONG KONG KON LOH MEEN

In Hong Kong, there are noodle shops that serve only this particular dish. It can be topped with a variety of roast meats for which the Cantonese are well-known, such as roast duck or roast chicken. An additional plate of blanched vegetables dressed with oyster sauce or garlic oil can be ordered to supplement the few stalks of vegetables that come with the noodles. In Singapore, fresh thin Hong Kong egg noodles (*mee kia*) sold in the supermarkets are often labelled 'Hong Kong noodles'. This recipe serves one. Prepare more as necessary.

COOKING TIME: 10 MINUTES

$1^1/_2$ Tbsp peanut oil

$^1/_2$ Tbsp light soy sauce

2 Tbsp oyster sauce

100 g ($3^1/_2$ oz) *choy sum*

120 g ($4^1/_2$ oz) fresh Hong Kong egg noodles (page 14)

100 g ($3^1/_2$ oz) Chinese red roast pork (page 42)/roast duck/roast chicken/roast pork, sliced

CONDIMENTS
Hong Kong dried chilli oil (page 35)

Pickled green chillies (page 32)

1. Mix peanut oil, light soy sauce and oyster sauce on a serving plate. Set aside.

2. Bring a pot of water to the boil, then blanch *choy sum* for 10 seconds. Drain well and set aside.

3. Return water to the boil and blanch noodles until tender but al dente. Remove with a wire strainer, then rinse under cold water or drop noodles into a cold water bath. Return noodles to the boiling water for 10 seconds, or use the two-pot method (page 20).

4. Drain noodles well, then stir into dressing on prepared serving plate.

5. Top dressed noodles with blanched *choy sum* and sliced roast meat. Serve with Hong Kong chilli oil and pickled green chillies.

Penang-Style Dry Noodles
PENANG-STYLE KON LOH MEEN

The Penang hawker version of Cantonese dry noodles or *"kon loh meen"* usually has no chilli sauce in the dressing. Those who want some heat in their noodles must ask for it or eat the pickled green chillies that accompany the dish. This recipe serves one. Prepare more as necessary.

COOKING TIME: 15 MINUTES

100 g (3¹/₂ oz) *choy sum*, cut into finger-lengths

120 g (4¹/₂ oz) thin Cantonese fresh egg noodles (*mee kia*)

50 g (1³/₄ oz) Chinese red roast pork (page 42), thinly sliced

Wontons in soup (page 157) (optional)

DRESSING
1¹/₂ Tbsp lard (page 45)

1 tsp sesame oil

¹/₂ Tbsp dark soy sauce

1 Tbsp light soy sauce

¹/₂ tsp ground white pepper

CONDIMENTS
Pickled green chillies (page 32)

1. Prepare dressing. Mix dressing ingredients on a serving plate and set aside.

2. Bring a large pot of water to the boil and blanch *choy sum* for 10 seconds. Drain well and set aside.

3. Return water to the boil and blanch noodles until tender but al dente. Remove with a wire strainer, then rinse under cold water or drop noodles into a cold water bath. Return noodles to the boiling water for 10 seconds, or use the two-pot method (page 20).

4. Drain noodles well, then stir into dressing on prepared serving plate.

5. Top with blanched *choy sum* and sliced red roast pork.

6. Serve dry noodles with pickled green chillies and a small bowl of wonton soup if desired.

Kon Loh Meen, Singapore-Style

All the ingredients remain the same as the recipe above except for the dressing. Dressing B is what I remember from a North Bridge Road coffeeshop stall run by two Cantonese women who were always clad in white samfoo and white trousers.

DRESSING A
1¹/₂ Tbsp lard (page 45)

1¹/₂ Tbsp light soy sauce

1 tsp oyster sauce

1 Tbsp garlic chilli sauce (page 34)

DRESSING B
1¹/₂ Tbsp lard (page 45)

¹/₂ tsp sesame oil

1¹/₂ Tbsp light soy sauce

¹/₂ Tbsp garlic chilli sauce (page 34)

1 tsp ground white pepper

Dry Wheat Noodles, Sarawak-Style
SARAWAK KOLO MEE

The name of this dish, "*kolo mee*", is probably a corruption of the Cantonese phrase "*kon loh meen*" meaning dry noodles. The dish is from Sarawak, East Malaysia. The recipe calls for fresh wheat noodles, so you can make your own (page 14), or use thin dried egg noodles if desired.

COOKING TIME: 20 MINUTES

3 Tbsp cooking oil

50 g (1³/₄ oz) shallots, peeled and finely chopped

1 Tbsp fermented soybeans *(taucheo)*, finely mashed

200 g (7 oz) minced pork

¹/₂ Tbsp sugar

¹/₂ Tbsp light soy sauce

A few drops dark soy sauce

250 g (9 oz) *choy sum*, cut into finger-lengths

600 g (1 lb 5¹/₃ oz) fresh plain wheat noodles (page 12)

200 g (7 oz) prawns (shrimps), boiled and peeled

Wontons in soup (page 157)

DRESSING (SERVES 1)
1 Tbsp light soy sauce

1 Tbsp shallot oil (page 29)

CONDIMENTS
Cooked dried red chilli paste (page 32)

1. Mix dressing ingredients on a serving plate. Repeat for the number of servings. Set aside.

2. Heat oil in a pot and fry shallots until golden brown and fragrant. Stir in fermented soybeans, mix well, then add minced pork and fry for 1 minute.

3. Stir in sugar, light and dark soy sauces and simmer until meat is cooked. Set aside.

4. Bring a pot of water to the boil and blanch *choy sum* for 10 seconds. Drain well and set aside.

5. Return water to the boil and blanch noodles until tender but still al dente. Drain well and divide into prepared serving plates. Stir noodles into dressing on prepared serving plates.

6. Top dressed noodles with vegetables, prawns and a helping of minced pork and sauce. Serve immediately with cooked dried red chilli paste and a small bowl of wontons in soup.

Egg Noodles in Sesame Sauce with Shredded Chicken

The quality of this dish will depend on the quality of the sesame paste used. There are two types of sesame paste, black or white, depending on the seeds used, although white is more commonly available. You may also replace sesame paste with smooth peanut butter for a different flavour. Fresh thin egg noodles, *la mian* or fresh *ee meen* can be substituted for dried *ee meen* if desired.

COOKING TIME: 10 MINUTES

400 ml (13 fl oz) chicken stock (page 44)

250 g (9 oz) chicken

2 Tbsp sesame oil

300 g (11 oz) dried *ee meen*

SESAME PASTE SAUCE

1/4 cup + 2 Tbsp sesame paste

1/2 Tbsp dark soy sauce

2 Tbsp light soy sauce

1 tsp salt

2 tsp Chinese chilli oil (page 35)

GARNISHING

1 small cucumber, shredded

1 spring onion (scallion), chopped

1. Bring chicken stock to the boil in a pot, then add chicken and simmer until cooked. Remove chicken and leave to cool before shredding meat.

2. Return chicken bones to stock and simmer for another 10 minutes. Strain stock and return to pot. Discard solids. There should be about 300 ml (10 fl oz / 1 1/4 cups) stock.

3. Prepare sauce. Add ingredients for sesame paste sauce to chicken stock in pot and bring to the boil. Remove from heat and let sauce stand to meld flavours while noodles are being prepared.

4. Spoon sesame oil onto a large plate for dressing noodles.

5. Bring a large pot of water to the boil and cook noodles until tender but al dente. Drain well, then toss in sesame oil before dividing into individual serving bowls.

6. Spoon some sesame paste sauce into each bowl of noodles, then top with shredded chicken. Garnish with cucumber and spring onion. Serve immediately.

Cantonese Duck Noodles

If roast duck is unavailable, use roast chicken or turkey. Pickled ginger slices are sold in glass bottles in Asian stores, or if preferred, make a quickie pickle. Use the recipe for pickled green chillies (page 32) but replace green chillies with 50 g (1³/₄ oz) thinly sliced young ginger.

COOKING TIME: 10 MINUTES

¹/₂ Cantonese roast duck

600 g (1 lb 5¹/₃ oz) fresh egg noodles or fresh Hong Kong noodles

200 g (7 oz) chrysanthemum leaves, blanched, or 4 lettuce leaves, shredded

1 Tbsp pickled ginger, finely shred

1 spring onion (scallion), cut into finger-lengths

1 bunch coriander leaves (cilantro), cut into finger-lengths

DRESSING FOR DUCK (SERVES 1)

1 tsp sesame oil

1 Tbsp garlic oil

Ground white pepper to taste

DRESSING FOR NOODLES (SERVES 1)

1 Tbsp light soy sauce

¹/₂ Tbsp oyster sauce

1 tsp sesame oil

1 Tbsp garlic oil

1. Shred duck meat and discard skin and bones. Divide into 3–4 portions as needed, then mix each portion well with dressing for duck meat.

2. Prepare dressing for noodles. Mix ingredients together on a serving plate. Repeat for the number of servings.

3. Bring a large pot of water to the boil and cook noodles until tender but still al dente. Remove with a wire strainer and dip into a cold water bath or rinse under a cold water tap. Return noodles to boiling water for 10 seconds. Drain well.

4. Divide noodles into prepared serving plates and stir into dressing.

5. Top dressed noodles with dressed duck meat and blanched or shredded greens. Garnish with pickled ginger, spring onions and coriander leaves.

Noodles with Braised Duck

1.5 kg (3 lb 41/2 oz) duck

1.5 litres (48 fl oz / 6 cups) water

1 tsp Chinese five-spice powder

1 large thumb-size knob old ginger

1 tsp salt

1 Tbsp dark soy sauce

2 Tbsp light soy sauce

1 tsp ground white pepper

Combine 1.5 kg duck with water and bring to the boil. Scoop out scum that rises to the top. Add rest of ingredients and simmer till duck is tender. To serve, follow steps 3 and 4 above but omit sesame oil in dressing and substitute with garlic chilli sauce (page 34) or cooked dried chilli paste (page 32).

Fried Udon with Kimchi and Mushrooms, Korean-Style

This is a tasty way to have your kimchi and noodles in one dish. It is also quick to prepare.

COOKING TIME: 30 MINUTES

300 g (11 oz) kimchi (page 39)

250 g (9 oz) pork/prawns (shrimps)

1 tsp sesame oil

1 tsp raw dried red chilli paste (page 33)

$^1/_2$ tsp + $^1/_4$ tsp salt

300 g (11 oz) dried udon

3 Tbsp cooking oil

1 small onion, peeled and thinly sliced

4 dried Chinese mushrooms, softened in water and sliced

1$^1/_2$ Tbsp light soy sauce

3 cloves garlic, peeled and cut into slivers

1 spring onion (scallion), cut into finger-lengths

1 bunch coriander leaves (cilantro), cut into finger-lengths

CONDIMENTS
Korean sesame salt (page 38)

1. If kimchi is too chunky, cut into thinner slices. Squeeze out juices but keep for use later, if needed.

2. If using pork, cut into julienne strips. If using prawns, shell but keep tails intact. Mix sesame oil, dried red chilli paste and $^1/_4$ tsp salt into pork/prawns. Marinate for 15 minutes.

3. Bring a pot of water to the boil and cook udon using the boil-discard-add method (page 20) until the udon is tender but still al dente.

4. While udon is cooking, heat oil in a wok and sauté onion for 1 minute, then add pork/prawns and mushrooms and stir-fry until meat is cooked.

5. Add kimchi, drained udon, soy sauce and remaining salt and mix well. Stir-fry for 2 minutes or until kimchi is thoroughly heated.

6. Stir in garlic slivers, spring onion and coriander leaves. Dish out into a large serving platter and serve with Korean sesame salt.

Indian Mee Goreng

You will not find Indian *mee goreng* in India. It is found only in Singapore and Malaysia where South Indian food hawkers use Hokkien *mee* to yield this Singapore classic. The Indian hawker from whom I bought *mee goreng* when I was young would flavour the noodles with a large dollop of curry gravy from one of his nearby pots.

COOKING TIME: 20 MINUTES

2 Tbsp meat curry powder (page 37)

1 Tbsp water

4 Tbsp cooking oil

50 g (1³/₄ oz) onions, peeled and cut into cubes

1¹/₂ tsp salt

200 g (7 oz) prawns (shrimps) (optional), peeled, leaving tails intact

100 g (3¹/₂ oz) peas

100 g (3¹/₂ oz) large tomatoes, cut into cubes

600 g (1 lb 5¹/₃ oz) Hokkien *mee*

100 g (3¹/₂ oz) potatoes, boiled, peeled and cut into cubes

2 Tbsp tomato sauce

¹/₂ tsp dark soy sauce

300 g (11 oz) bean sprouts

2 eggs

1 fresh green chilli, coarsely sliced

GARNISHING
Limes, halved

1. Mix curry powder and water in a small bowl to a paste.

2. Heat 3 Tbsp oil in a wok and fry cubed onion until soft. Stir in salt and curry paste and fry until curry is fragrant.

3. Add prawns if using and when they turn pink, add peas, tomato, noodles, cubed potatoes, tomato sauce and dark soy sauce. Mix well to colour noodles evenly.

4. Add bean sprouts last to prevent overcooking.

5. Make a well in the centre of the wok. Add remaining 1 Tbsp oil, then break eggs into hot oil and cover with noodles. Lower heat to let eggs set without burning noodles.

6. Stir in green chilli, then dish out and serve hot with lime halves.

Cantonese-Style Egg Noodles with Crabmeat and Prawns

Any kind of fresh mushrooms can be used for this dish. "Velveting" or marinating prawns or meat with egg white or cornflour and seasoning before frying is a typical Chinese cooking technique.

COOKING TIME: 20 MINUTES

100 g (3^1/$_2$ oz) prawns (shrimps), peeled and deveined

300 g (11 oz) Tientsin cabbage, shredded

600 g (1 lb 5^1/$_3$ oz) or 300 g (11 oz) fresh egg noodles/ thin dried egg noodles, soaked in water until pliable

3 Tbsp peanut oil

1 Tbsp chopped garlic

100 g (3^1/$_2$ oz) fresh mushrooms, wiped clean and sliced

1 spring onion (scallion), cut into finger-lengths

100 g (3^1/$_2$ oz) crabmeat

1 egg, beaten

MARINADE FOR PRAWNS

2 tsp peanut oil

^{1}/$_2$ tsp sesame oil

2 tsp light soy sauce

^{1}/$_2$ tsp sugar

^{1}/$_2$ tsp salt

^{1}/$_2$ Tbsp cornflour

SAUCE

500 ml (16 fl oz / 2 cups) chicken stock (page 44)

1 Tbsp light soy sauce

^{1}/$_2$ Tbsp oyster sauce

1 tsp salt

1 tsp sugar

1 tsp sesame oil

A large pinch ground white pepper

2 Tbsp cornflour, mixed with 2 Tbsp water

2 Tbsp water

CONDIMENTS

Pickled green chillies (page 32)

1. Combine marinade for prawns in a bowl, then mix in the prawns to marinate for 10 minutes.

2. Bring a pot of water to the boil, then blanch shredded Tientsin cabbage for 30 seconds. Remove with a wire strainer, then use a large spoon to press cabbage against wire strainer to get excess water out. Return water to the boil and cook noodles until tender but still al dente. Remove and rinse under a cold water tap. Drain well and set aside.

3. Heat 1 Tbsp oil in a wok and fry noodles for 1 minute. Dish out onto a serving plate. Heat ^{1}/$_2$ Tbsp oil in the same wok and fry blanched Tientsin cabbage for 10 seconds. Arrange over noodles. Keep noodles and cabbage warm. Heat another ^{1}/$_2$ Tbsp oil in the wok and fry marinated prawns until they begin to turn pink. Remove and set aside.

4. Prepare sauce. Mix all ingredients, except cornflour mixture in a bowl and set aside.

5. Heat remaining 1 Tbsp oil in the wok and sauté chopped garlic until fragrant.

6. Stir in mushrooms, spring onion, prawns, crabmeat and sauce mixture. Bring to the boil, then stir in cornflour mixture. Return to the boil and stir in beaten egg, mixing well.

7. Pour sauce over noodles and cabbage. Serve immediately with pickled green chillies on the side.

Nepali-Style Fried Egg Noodles

TAREKO CHAU CHAU

Dried egg noodles called *chau chau* can be found in markets and stores all over Kathmandu, the Himalayan kingdom that is the Mecca of mountaineers. Instant noodles are also easily found, and these are often fried with vegetables. Instead of keeping the strands of noodles long and unbroken, Nepalese cooks break up the brittle noodles before cooking so it is easier to eat them with a spoon. (I must say that I prefer my noodles in long strands!) There is also a tendency to boil the noodles until they are very soft. Prepare the noodles the way you like them.

COOKING TIME: 30 MINUTES

600 g (1 lb 5$\frac{1}{3}$ oz) fresh egg noodles (page 12)

4 eggs, beaten

4 Tbsp ghee (clarified butter)

1 large onion, about 100 g (3$\frac{1}{2}$ oz), peeled and thinly sliced

4 slices ginger, finely chopped

1 tsp ground cumin

1 tsp chilli powder

1 Tbsp water

1$\frac{1}{2}$ tsp + $\frac{1}{2}$ tsp salt

200 g (7 oz) cabbage, shredded

100 g (3$\frac{1}{2}$ oz) tomatoes, cut into cubes

1 medium carrot, peeled and cut into rounds

1 tsp garam masala (page 37)

GARNISHING

Sliced green chillies

Lemon slices

1 onion, peeled and cut into narrow wedges

1. Bring a pot of water to the boil and blanch noodles until tender but still al dente. Rinse noodles under a cold water tap. Drain well and set aside.

2. Beat eggs with $\frac{1}{2}$ tsp salt. Heat a little ghee in a wok and make several thin omelettes with beaten eggs. Cut omelettes into thin strips and set aside.

3. Heat remaining ghee in the wok and fry onion and chopped ginger until fragrant. Stir in ground cumin and chilli powder, 1 Tbsp water and 1$\frac{1}{2}$ tsp salt. Mix well.

4. Add cabbage, tomato and carrot and fry until cabbage is limp but still crisp. Stir in egg strips and noodles and fry for 1 minute.

5. Sprinkle garam masala over fried noodles, then dish out and garnish with sliced green chillies, lemon slices and raw onion wedges. Serve hot.

Sichuan Cha Jiang Mian

This is a Northern Chinese favourite and simple to do even when you cannot get bottled chilli bean paste. To make your own, just combine chilli powder with fermented soybean paste (*taucheo* or red miso). Northern Chinese *la mian* is available dried although fresh is better. Try making your own homemade wheat noodles (page 13). *Cha chiang mian* was probably the inspiration for the Korean-Chinese sauce known as *cha jiang* sauce, which can be served with either noodles or rice (page 194).

COOKING TIME: 20 MINUTES

2 Tbsp cooking oil

1 Tbsp chopped garlic

2 Tbsp chilli bean paste

200 g (7 oz) minced pork

1 Tbsp cornflour, mixed with 125 ml (4 fl oz / ¹/₂ cup) chicken stock (page 44)

300 g (11 oz) dried *la mian* or 600 g (1 lb 5¹/₃ oz) fresh *la mian*

3 slices ginger, finely chopped

SEASONING

1 Tbsp Chinese chilli oil (page 35)

¹/₂ Tbsp sesame oil

1 Tbsp light soy sauce

1 tsp dark soy sauce

2 tsp sugar

¹/₄ tsp salt

GARNISHING

1 small cucumber, shredded

1. Mix seasoning ingredients together in a small bowl. Set aside.

2. Heat oil in a wok and sauté garlic and chilli bean paste for 1 minute. Stir in minced pork and seasoning mixture and bring to the boil. Simmer for 2 minutes.

3. Stir cornflour mixture and add to wok. Bring sauce to the boil.

4. Bring two pots of water to the boil. Blanch *la mian* in one pot, adding a cup of cold water after 5 minutes. When cooked but still a dente, drain and rinse noodles under a cold water tap, then swirl noodles in the pot of clean boiling water. Drain noodles well and divide into serving plates.

5. Spoon meat sauce over noodles and garnish with shredded cucumber. Serve immediately.

Hong Kong Noodles

Just as "Singapore Noodles" did not originate from Singapore, nor is it found in Singapore,
so too "Hong Kong Noodles" cannot be found in Hong Kong. In Singapore, however,
"Hong Kong Noodles" is a popular dish served in many seafood restaurants. What gives
this dish its Cantonese flavour is that it uses dried egg noodles.

COOKING TIME: 20 MINUTES

300 g (11 oz) dried egg noodles

4 Tbsp cooking oil

1 onion, peeled and cut into thin rings

2 tsp chopped garlic

100 g ($3^1/_2$ oz) Chinese red roast pork (page 42), cut into matchsticks

100 g ($3^1/_2$ oz) small prawns (shrimps), peeled

A few drops dark soy sauce for colour

2 eggs

2 fresh red chillies, seeded and thinly sliced

4 leaves lettuce, shredded

1 spring onion (scallion), cut into finger-lengths

1 bunch coriander leaves (cilantro), chopped

SEASONING

1 tsp salt

2 Tbsp light soy sauce

$^1/_2$ tsp ground white pepper

2 tsp sugar

GARNISHING

Limes, halved

1. Combine ingredients for seasoning in a small bowl and set aside.

2. Bring a pot of water to the boil and cook egg noodles until al dente. Drain well.

3. Heat 3 Tbsp oil in a wok and sauté onion and garlic until fragrant.

4. Add pork and prawns and fry until prawns are cooked.

5. Stir in seasoning mixture and cooked noodles. Mix well, then sprinkle in some dark soy sauce to colour noodles.

6. Make a well in the centre of the wok and add remaining 1 Tbsp oil. When oil is hot, crack eggs into oil and spread eggs out. Cover with noodles and let eggs set in large pieces. Add a sprinkling of water if noodles begin to stick to the wok.

7. When eggs are cooked, stir in chillies, lettuce, spring onion and coriander leaves. Mix well, then remove from heat. The lettuce should still be raw and crunchy.

8. Dish out onto a large serving platter and squeeze lime halves over noodles. Serve hot.

Chinese New Year Longevity Noodles

Fresh or semi-dried coarse wheat vermicelli, labelled as "Longevity noodles", make their appearance during the Chinese New Year season in Singapore where there is a large Hokkien community. It is a tradition to eat these noodles at least once during the 15-day celebration. Substitute "longevity noodles" with udon (page 16) or fresh plain wheat noodles (page 12).

COOKING TIME: 30 MINUTES

4 dried Chinese mushrooms, softened in 4 Tbsp water

600 g (1 lb 5¹/₃ oz) fresh thick wheat noodles (*mee sua*)

5 Tbsp cooking oil

1 Tbsp chopped garlic

100 g (3¹/₂ oz) pork, thinly sliced

200 g (7 oz) prawns, (shrimps) peeled

1 tsp salt

200 g (7 oz) *choy sum*, cut into finger-lengths

1 medium carrot, peeled and cut into fine strips

2 Tbsp light soy sauce

CONDIMENTS

Sambal belacan with lime juice (page 31)

Pickled green chillies (page 32)

Pickled radish (page 38)

Kimchi (page 39)

1. Squeeze excess water from soaked, softened mushrooms and slice thinly or cut in quarters. Set soaking liquid aside for use when frying noodles.

2. Bring a pot of water to the boil and cook the noodles using the boil-discard-add method (page 20) until noodles are tender but still al dente. Drain noodles in a colander and stir a bit of oil into noodles to prevent clumping. Set aside.

3. Heat oil in a wok and sauté garlic until fragrant. Add pork and mushrooms and sauté until pork changes colour.

4. Add prawns and when they turn pink, add salt and *choy sum*. Stir well.

5. Add noodles, mushroom soaking liquid and light soy sauce. Mix well and fry until noodles are tender.

6. Serve noodles hot with your choice of condiments on the side.

Prawn Mee Soup, Penang-Style

Penang-style prawn *mee* is spicier and is usually served with more pork than
Singapore-style prawn *mee*. Like Singapore-style prawn *mee*, the Hokkien *mee*
in this recipe can be combined with fine rice vermicelli.

COOKING TIME: 2 HOURS

500 ml (16 fl oz / 2 cups)
prawn stock (page 44)

300 g (11 oz) prawns
(shrimps)

400 g (14^1/$_3$ oz) water
convolvulus

200 g (7 oz) bean sprouts

600 g (1 lb 5^1/$_3$ oz) Hokkien
mee or substitute half with
rice vermicelli

STOCK
1.5 litres (48 fl oz / 6 cups)
water

1 kg (2 lb 3 oz) pork ribs
with meat

1 pig's tail, chop into short
lengths

1^1/$_2$ tsp salt

1 Tbsp cooked dried red
chilli paste (page 32)

1 Tbsp fried shallots
(page 29)

1 tsp dried prawn paste
(*belacan*)

GARNISHING
^{1}/$_4$ cup fried shallots
(page 29)

CONDIMENTS
Cooked dried red chilli
paste (page 33)

1. Bring prawn stock to the boil, then drop in prawns. When prawns
   turn pink, remove and leave to cool before peeling. Leave tails intact.

2. Return prawn shells and heads to prawn stock and simmer for
   10 minutes. Scoop out and discard shells.

3. Prepare stock. Put water, pork ribs and pig's tail into a stockpot and
   bring to the boil. Skim off any scum that rises to the top.

4. Add remaining ingredients for stock and simmer over low heat until
   stock is reduced by about a third. This should take about 1^1/$_2$ hours.

5. Add prawn stock to pork stock and return to the boil. Keep stock hot.

6. Prepare water convolvulus by rinsing clean and cutting into short
   lengths. If stems are thick, split them in half. Bring a pot of water to
   the boil and blanch water convolvulus for 10 seconds. Drain well and
   divide into serving bowls.

7. Return water to the boil and blanch bean sprouts for 10 seconds.
   Drain well and divide into serving bowls with water convolvulus.

8. Return water to the boil a third time and blanch Hokkien *mee* until
   tender but al dente. If combining Hokkien *mee* with rice vermicelli,
   boil both types of noodles separately.

9. Ladle hot stock over noodles with pieces of meat, pig's tail and some
   prawns. Garnish with fried shallots and serve hot with cooked dried
   red chilli paste on the side.

Prawn Mee Soup, Singapore-Style

This noodle soup is found all over Singapore. While Hokkien *mee*
is the usual noodle used in this dish, some like to combine it with
fine rice vermicelli which can also replace the wheat noodles completely.

COOKING TIME: 1 HOUR

750 ml (24 fl oz / 3 cups) water

600 g (1 lb 5^1/$_3$ oz) large prawns
(shrimps)

500 g (1 lb 1^1/$_2$ oz) raw prawn
shells

500 ml (16 fl oz / 2 cups) pork
stock (page 43)

2 tsp salt

400 g (14^1/$_3$ oz) water convolvulus

250 g (9 oz) bean sprouts

600 g (1 lb 5^1/$_3$ oz) Hokkien
mee or substitute half with rice
vermicelli

GARNISHING

1 cup fried shallots (page 29)

CONDIMENTS

Fresh red chillies with light soy
sauce (page 31) or red chilli
powder

1. Bring 500 ml (16 fl oz / 2 cups) water to the boil in a pot and cook prawns in their shells until they turn pink. Do not overcook. Remove prawns and leave to cool before peeling. Leave tails intact. Reserve stock and shells.

2. Heat a pot large enough to contain stock. When pot is very hot, place raw prawn shells and reserved shells from cooked prawns in and sauté until shells change colour and pot is coated with a dark brown-black layer of prawn juices.

3. Pour stock from boiling prawns as well as remaining 250 ml (8 fl oz / 1 cup) water into pot. Bring to the boil and simmer for 15 minutes over low heat. The stock should be a dark grey colour. Scoop out and discard shells.

4. Add pork stock and salt to pot and return to the boil.

5. Meanwhile prepare water convolvulus by rinsing clean and cutting into short lengths. If stems are thick, split into half.

6. Bring a large pot of water to the boil and blanch bean sprouts for 10 seconds. Drain well and divide into serving bowls.

7. Return water to the boil and blanch water convolvulus for 10 seconds. Drain well and divide into serving bowls on top of bean sprouts.

8. Return water to the boil a third time and blanch Hokkien *mee* until tender but still al dente. If Hokkien *mee* is to be combined with rice vermicelli, boil both types of noodles separately as they require different cooking times.

9. Ladle hot soup over noodles and top with boiled prawns. Garnish with fried shallots and serve hot with your choice of red chillies with light soy sauce or red chilli powder.

Mee Soup, Javanese-Style

COOKING TIME: 15 MINUTES

1.25 litres (40 fl oz / 5 cups) prawn stock (page 44)

2 Tbsp fried shallots (page 29)

100 g (3¹/₂ oz) tomatoes, chopped

2 red chillies, seeded and sliced

1¹/₂ tsp salt

1 Tbsp ground black pepper

200 g (7 oz) prawns (shrimps), peeled, leaving tails intact

50 g (1³/₄ oz) bean sprouts

50 g (1³/₄ oz) *choy sum*, cut into finger-lengths

50 g (1³/₄ oz) cabbage, shredded

500 g (1 lb 5¹/₃ oz) fresh wheat noodles or 300 g (11 oz) dried egg noodles

50 g (1³/₄ oz) firm bean curd, cubed

50 g (1³/₄ oz) potatoes, boiled, peeled and cubed

GARNISHING

1 medium tomato, cut into quarters

2 hard-boiled eggs, peeled and quartered

1 spring onion (scallion), cut into finger-lengths

1. Place prawn stock, fried shallots, tomato, chillies, salt and black pepper into a saucepan and simmer for 15 minutes.

2. Add prawns and when they turn pink, stir in bean sprouts, *choy sum* and cabbage and cook for 1 minute.

3. Rinse noodles and add to soup together with bean curd and potato cubes. Bring soup to the boil and simmer until noodles are tender but al dente. If using dried egg noodles, boil noodles until tender before adding to soup.

4. Divide noodles and vegetables into serving bowls. Garnish with tomato and egg wedges and a sprinkling of spring onions. Serve immediately.

Noodles in Indonesian Chicken Soup

SOTO MEE

This fusion dish in Singapore combines Indonesia's famous *soto ayam* (chicken soup) with Hokkien *mee* or fine rice vermicelli. In Indonesia, the soup itself is often served with cubes of *ketupat* (rice cake) or glass noodles. While the noodles are interchangeable, Chinese celery and coriander leaves are a must.

COOKING TIME: 1 HOUR

200 g (7 oz) bean sprouts

600 g (1 lb 5¹/₃ oz) Hokkien *mee* or 300 g (11 oz) dried fine rice vermicelli

SPICE PASTE

30 g (1 oz) ginger, peeled and ground

2 cloves garlic, peeled and ground

2 Tbsp water

2 tsp ground coriander

1 tsp ground cumin

2 tsp ground turmeric

2 tsp ground white pepper

SOUP

2 Tbsp cooking oil

30 g (1 oz) onions, peeled and finely sliced

4 cm (1¹/₂ in) cinnamon stick

4 cloves

4 cardamoms pods

2 stalks lemongrass, bruised

400 g (14¹/₃ oz) chicken drumstick or breast

1.25 litres (40 fl oz / 5 cups) chicken stock (page 44)

1¹/₂ tsp salt

BERGEDEL (POTATO CAKE)

250 g (9 oz) potatoes, boiled, peeled and mashed

¹/₄ tsp salt

1 Tbsp chopped spring onions (scallions)

1 egg, beaten

Cooking oil for frying

GREEN CHILLI SAUCE

50 g (1³/₄ oz) green chillies, seeded

1 Tbsp water

¹/₄ tsp salt

GARNISHING

2 Tbsp fried shallots (page 29)

1 large bunch coriander leaves (cilantro), chopped

3 stalks Chinese celery, chopped

1. Prepare spice paste. Grind ginger and garlic with water in a blender until fine, then spoon into a bowl and mix well with powdered spices. Set aside.

2. Prepare soup. Heat oil in a saucepan and sauté onion, cinnamon, cloves and cardamoms until onion is golden brown. Add spice paste and sauté for 2 minutes.

3. Add lemongrass, chicken, stock and salt and bring to the boil. Lower heat and simmer for 30 minutes until chicken is cooked.

4. Remove chicken from soup and when cool enough to handle, shred chicken and set aside with other garnishes. Return bones to soup and simmer for another 10 minutes.

5. Prepare *bergedel*. Mix mashed potatoes, salt and spring onion, then form into 4 patties. Heat oil. Dip patties into beaten egg and fry until nicely brown. Fry remainder of beaten egg into a thin omelette and slice finely.

6. Prepare green chilli sauce. Place ingredients into a blender and process until fine. Store in a jar, refrigerate, and use as needed.

7. To serve noodles, bring a pot of water to the boil and blanch bean sprouts for 10 seconds. Drain well and divide into serving bowls.

8. Return water to the boil and blanch Hokkien *mee* or rice vermicelli until tender but al dente. Drain well and divide into serving bowls on top of bean sprouts.

9. Ladle hot soup over noodles and top with shredded chicken, sliced egg and *bergedel*. Garnish with fried shallots, coriander and celery. Serve with green chilli sauce on the side for those who like it hot.

Curry Mee, Kuala Lumpur-Style

Kuala Lumpur-style curry *mee* is closely related to Singapore-style curry *hor fun* (broad rice noodles) but the two dishes are not the same. The Kuala Lumpur-style dish uses Hokkien *mee* or fine rice vermicelli and is served in a thin curry soup topped with a thick curry sauce and chicken. The Singapore-style dish uses fresh broad rice noodles dressed with a thick curry sauce (page 100).

COOKING TIME: 1 HOUR

600 g (1 lb 5¹/₃ oz) Hokkien *mee* or 300 g (11 oz) dried fine rice vermicelli

300 g (11 oz) bean sprouts

SPICE PASTE
250 g (9 oz) shallots, peeled
100 g (3¹/₂ oz) garlic, peeled
180 ml (6 fl oz / ³/₄ cup) water
1 cup meat curry powder (page 37)

CHICKEN CURRY SAUCE
1 litre (32 fl oz / 4 cups) water
500 g (1 lb 1¹/₂ oz) grated coconut
3 Tbsp tamarind paste
4 Tbsp cooking oil
6 cm (2¹/₂ in) cinnamon stick
2 cloves
2 cardamom pods

500 g (1 lb 1¹/₂ oz) chicken, chopped into small pieces

1 tsp salt

CURRY SOUP
4 large pieces deep-fried soybean puffs

750 ml (24 fl oz / 3 cups) chicken stock (page 44)

1 tsp salt

1. Prepare spice paste. Place shallots and garlic in a blender and process with a little water until fine. Set aside. Mix remaining water and curry powder together to get a thick paste. Set aside.

2. Prepare curry sauce. Mix half the water into grated coconut, then squeeze through a muslin bag or cloth-lined strainer to extract coconut milk. Set aside.

3. Mix half the remaining water into squeezed coconut, then squeeze again through a muslin bag or cloth-lined strainer to extract second milk. Set aside for use in curry soup.

4. Mix remaining water into tamarind paste. Strain liquid and discard solids. Divide tamarind juice into 2 portions.

5. Heat oil in a pot and sauté cinnamon, cloves, cardamoms, ground shallots and garlic until fragrant. Add curry powder paste and fry until oil separates from paste. Set half the fried curry paste aside for use in curry soup.

6. Add chicken, salt and 1 portion of tamarind juice to pot and bring to the boil. Add first coconut milk and bring to the boil. Lower heat and simmer until chicken is cooked.

7. Prepare curry soup. Rinse deep-fried soybean puffs in cold water and squeeze dry. Cut puffs into bite-size pieces, as they will swell in soup. Place all ingredients, second coconut milk and remaining portion of fried curry paste and tamarind juice into a pot and bring to the boil.

8. Prepare to serve noodles. Bring a pot of water to the boil and blanch bean sprouts for 10 seconds. Drain well and divide into serving bowls.

9. Return water to the boil, then blanch Hokkien *mee* or rice vermicelli until tender but al dente. Drain well and divide into serving bowls on top of bean sprouts.

10. Ladle hot curry soup and deep-fried soybean puffs over noodles and top with curry sauce and pieces of chicken. Serve immediately.

Boiled Yellow Noodles, Malay-Style
MEE REBUS

**Although the Malay name for this dish means "boiled *mee*", this dish is anything but plain.
The noodles are served in a thick, rich gravy with varied garnishes.**

COOKING TIME: 45 MINUTES

250 g (9 oz) bean sprouts

600 g (1 lb 5¹/₃ oz) Hokkien *mee*

THICKENER

3 Tbsp cornflour

2 Tbsp plain flour

4 Tbsp water

350 g (12 oz) sweet potatoes

SPICE PASTE

100 g (3¹/₂ oz) shallots, peeled

50 g (1³/₄ oz) garlic, peeled

2 Tbsp dried red chilli paste
(page 33)

¹/₂ thumb-sized knob fresh
turmeric, peeled

6 slices galangal

1 tsp dried prawn paste (*belacan*)

2 Tbsp water

GRAVY

4 Tbsp cooking oil

2 Tbsp fermented soybeans
(taucheo), finely mashed

¹/₂ Tbsp sugar

1 tsp salt

1 litre (32 fl oz / 4 cups) prawn
stock (page 44)

¹/₂ tsp dark soy sauce

GARNISHING

100 g (3¹/₂ oz) firm bean curd

Cooking oil for frying

1 cup *grago* (tiny dried prawns in
their shells)

Fried shallots (page 29)

4 hard-boiled eggs, peeled and
halved

1 bunch Chinese celery, chopped

1 spring onion (scallion), chopped

1 bunch coriander leaves
(cilantro), chopped

Fresh green chillies

Limes, halved

1. Prepare thickener. Mix cornflour and plain flour, then add water and stir to get a smooth paste. Set
   aside. Scrub sweet potatoes clean, then boil until soft. Remove and leave to cool before peeling and
   mashing through a sieve. Discard fibres and set aside.

2. Prepare spice paste. Place ingredients, except chilli paste, in a blender and process to get a fine
   paste. Add chilli paste last.

3. Prepare gravy. Heat oil in a pot and sauté spice paste until fragrant. Stir in mashed fermented
   soybeans and fry for 1 minute. Add sugar and salt, then pour in prawn stock and bring to the boil.
   Mix some stock into mashed sweet potatoes to form a thick soup, then add sweet potato mixture to
   stock. Stir in cornflour mixture and bring to the boil.

4. Prepare garnishes. Cut bean curd across into three thin layers and fry in hot oil until brown on both
   sides. Remove and leave to cool before cutting into cubes. Rinse *grago* briefly, then pat dry with
   paper towels. Reheat oil and fry *grago* until crisp. Drain well, then store in an airtight jar.

5. To serve noodles, bring a pot of water to the boil and blanch bean sprouts for 10 seconds. Divide
   into deep plates. Return water to the boil, then blanch Hokkien *mee* until tender but still al dente.
   Drain well and divide into serving plates on top of bean sprouts. Ladle hot gravy over noodles and
   garnish with fried shallots, *grago*, egg, chopped greens, limes and green chillies.

Burmese Curry Noodles

OHN NO KHAUK SWE

These noodles are served in a curry soup, like curry *mee*, Kuala Lumpur-style (page 152).
Burmese wheat noodles or wheat vermicelli is coloured yellow and looks like
yellow Hokkien *mee* but has a more chewy texture. Make your own
egg noodles (page 12) or wheat noodles (page 12) for use in this recipe.

COOKING TIME: 1 HOUR

600 g (1 lb 5^1/$_3$ oz) fresh simple egg noodles or fresh plain wheat noodles or 300 g (11 oz) dried egg noodles

SPICE PASTE
50 g (1^3/$_4$ oz) garlic, peeled

150 g (5^1/$_3$ oz) shallots, peeled

2 Tbsp water

1 Tbsp raw dried red chilli paste (page 33)

SOUP
500 g (1 lb 1^1/$_2$ oz) grated coconut

1 litre (32 fl oz / 4 cups) water

600 g (1 lb 5^1/$_3$ oz) chicken, cut into 4 pieces

^{1}/$_2$ tsp salt

1 tsp ground turmeric

3 Tbsp cooking oil

3 Tbsp fish sauce

THICKENER
2 Tbsp chickpea flour/soybean flour

4 Tbsp cold water

GARNISHING
Burmese *dhal* crackers (page 43) or 50 g (1^3/$_4$ oz) dried egg noodles

2 large onions, peeled and thinly sliced

^{1}/$_4$ tsp salt

2 hard-boiled eggs, peeled and cut into quarters

Limes, halved

Toasted red chilli flakes (page 35)

1. Prepare spice paste. Place garlic, shallots and water in a blender and process until fine. Mix in chilli paste. Set aside.

2. Prepare soup. Mix grated coconut with 250 ml (8 fl oz / 1 cup) water, then squeeze through a muslin bag or cloth-lined sieve to get coconut milk. Pour into a saucepan and boil, then lower heat and simmer for 10 minutes continuously to bring oil to the top. Stir often to prevent cream from catching the bottom of the pan. Add remaining 750 ml (24 fl oz / 3 cups) water to grated coconut and squeeze again to obtain second milk. Pour into a clean saucepan large enough to hold milk and chicken. Add chicken, salt and turmeric, then bring to the boil and simmer until chicken is cooked. Remove chicken and leave to cool before shredding meat. Set meat aside and return bones to second milk. Simmer for another 10 minutes, then discard bones.

3. Prepare thickener. Mix together flour and water to get a thick paste. Stir small quantities of hot soup into paste and mix well to smooth out lumps. Pour this mixture into hot soup and stir well.

4. In a frying pan, heat 3 Tbsp oil and fry spice paste until oil separates from paste. Set aside two-thirds of fried spice paste for curry soup, then stir in shredded chicken and fry for 2 minutes.

5. Prepare garnish. If using dried egg noodles instead of *dhal* crackers, heat some oil in a wok and deep-fry dried egg noodles in small batches until crisp. Remove from oil, cool, then crumble fried egg noodles into a screw-top bottle to keep crisp. Remove all but 2 Tbsp oil from wok. Skip this step if using *dhal* crackers. Season half the onions with ^{1}/$_4$ tsp salt, then squeeze out liquid. Fry other half

of onion strips in 2 Tbsp hot oil until brown. Remove browned onion and set aside oil for dressing cooked noodles.

6. Arrange garnish in small plates or bowls around noodles placed on a large serving platter. Have ready individual serving plates or bowls.

7. To serve noodles, bring a large pot of water to the boil and cook noodles until done but still al dente. Drain noodles well, then stir cooked noodles into oil used for browning fried onion garnish. This is to prevent noodles from clumping together when cool, if the noodles are to be served Burmese-style on one large platter. Guests help themselves to the noodles. Ladle hot soup over noodles and top with a large spoonful of shredded chicken and various garnishes. Crumble *dhal* crackers/fried noodles over noodles before serving.

Cantonese Fried Egg Noodles in Soybean Puff Soup

EE MEEN IN TAU POK SOUP

Most noodle stalls in wet markets in Singapore and Malaysia also sell fish balls,
fish cakes and assorted vegetables and soybean products stuffed with fish paste.
The assortment of stuffed vegetables and soybean products is collectively known as
yong tau foo, which can be cooked in soup and served a choice of noodles or rice.
My favourite is deep-fried soybean puffs stuffed with fish paste.

COOKING TIME: 10 MINUTES

1 Tbsp cooking oil

1 Tbsp chopped garlic

1 litre (32 fl oz / 4 cups) chicken stock (page 44)

1¹/₂ tsp salt

16 triangles or small squares stuffed deep-fried soybean puffs

200 g (7 oz) *choy sum*, cut into finger-lengths

1 spring onion (scallion), chopped

1 bunch coriander leaves (cilantro), chopped

300 g (11 oz) dried *ee meen*, soaked in water until pliable

1. Heat oil in a pan and sauté garlic until it begins to brown. Add chicken stock and salt and bring to the boil.

2. Add soybean puffs and simmer until fish paste is cooked.

3. Add *choy sum*, spring onion and coriander leaves and return to the boil. Remove from heat.

4. Bring a large pot of water to the boil, then cook softened *ee meen* until tender but still al dente. Remove with a wire strainer, rinse in cold water, then drain well and divide into serving bowls.

5. Ladle hot soup, soybean puffs and greens over noodles. Serve with red chillies and light soy sauce on the side.

Wonton Noodle Soup

Although a small bowl of wonton soup is commonly served with Cantonese dry noodle preparations such as *kon loh meen* or Hong Kong dry noodles, noodles in wanton soup are also popular. Make wontons ahead of time but cook only just before serving.

COOKING TIME: 10 MINUTES

1 Tbsp cooking oil

1 Tbsp chopped garlic

1 litre (32 fl oz / 4 cups) chicken stock (page 44)

1¹/₂ tsp salt

200 g (7 oz) *choy sum*, cut into finger-lengths

1 spring onion (scallion), chopped

1 bunch coriander leaves (cilantro), chopped

300 g (11 oz) dried *ee meen*, soaked in water until pliable

WONTON WRAPPERS

150 g (5¹/₃ oz) plain flour

¹/₄ tsp salt

¹/₂ tsp bicarbonate of soda

1 Tbsp beaten egg

1 Tbsp cold water

Cornflour for dusting

WONTON FILLING

50 g (1³/₄ oz) minced pork

50 g (1³/₄ oz) minced prawns (shrimps)

50 g (1³/₄ oz) water chestnuts, peeled and finely chopped

1 tsp sesame oil

¹/₂ tsp salt

2 tsp cornflour

¹/₂ tsp ground white pepper

CONDIMENTS

Fresh red chillies with light soy sauce (page 31)

1. Follow steps 1–5 as for Cantonese fried egg noodles in soybean puff soup (page 156) but substitute stuffed soybean puffs with wontons.

2. Prepare wonton wrappers. Sift flour, salt and bicarbonate of soda into a mixing bowl. Make a well in the centre and add egg and cold water. Mix in flour and knead into a smooth, stiff dough. Rest dough in a sealed plastic bag for 1 hour. Dust a working surface with tapioca flour/cornflour, then roll dough out as thinly as possible into a neat rectangle. Cut dough into 10-cm (4-in) squares and dust liberally with cornflour. Stack wrappers on top of one another and keep sealed in a plastic bag to prevent drying out.

3. Combine ingredients for wonton filling. Put a teaspoonful of filling in the centre of a wrapper. Fold wrapper over filling to form a triangle, then bring together the two facing corners and seal at the centre with a dab of water. Repeat until ingredients are used up. Set aside in a covered container and cook only when noodles are ready.

4. To cook wontons, bring a pot of water to the boil and cook wontons for 3 minutes, depending on size of wontons. Wontons are ready when they float.

Northern Chinese Wheat Noodles in Sichuan Hot-Sour Soup

LA MIAN IN SICHUAN HOT-SOUR SOUP

Sichuan hot and sour soup is very hearty and goes well with wheat noodles such as *la mian*.

COOKING TIME: 30 MINUTES

100 g (3¹/₂ oz) chicken/pork, cut into matchsticks

2 dried Chinese mushrooms, soaked in water until softened

2 pieces wood ear fungus, softened in water

1 Tbsp cooking oil

4 slices ginger, finely chopped

1 tsp garlic

1.25 litres (40 fl oz / 5 cups) chicken stock (page 44)

100 g (3¹/₂ oz) bamboo shoots, shredded

100 g (3¹/₂ oz) soft bean curd, cut into small cubes

600 g (1 lb 5¹/₃ oz) fresh *la mian*

1 bunch coriander leaves (cilantro), chopped

1 spring onion (scallion), chopped

MARINADE FOR MEAT

1 tsp light soy sauce

1 tsp cornflour

¹/₂ tsp sesame oil

SEASONING FOR SOUP

2 Tbsp light soy sauce

1 tsp dark soy sauce

5 Tbsp Chinkiang black vinegar

1 tsp sugar

1 tsp salt

2 tsp sesame oil

1 Tbsp Chinese chilli oil (page 35)

THICKENER

3 Tbsp cornflour

3 Tbsp water

A large pinch of ground white pepper

1. Combine marinade ingredients in a bowl and add chicken/pork. Leave to marinate for 15 minutes.

2. Trim and discard woody stems of Chinese mushrooms and slice thinly. Trim and discard tough woody ends of wood ear fungus, then cut into thin strips.

3. Heat oil in a saucepan and stir-fry marinated chicken/pork until the colour changes. Remove and set aside with sauce from pan. Using the same pan, sauté ginger and garlic for 1 minute. Pour in chicken stock and bring to the boil.

4. Add bamboo shoots, bean curd, mushrooms and wood ear fungus and simmer for 10 minutes. Combine seasoning for soup in a bowl. Add cooked chicken/pork with sauce to pan, and when stock returns to the boil, stir in seasoning.

5. Prepare thickener. Mix cornflour, water and pepper together and stir well just before adding to hot soup.

6. To serve noodles, bring a pot of water to the boil and cook *la mian* until tender but still al dente using the boil-discard-add method (page 20). Drain well and divide into serving bowls.

7. Ladle hot stock with some chicken/pork, mushrooms and wood ear fungus over and garnish with coriander leaves and spring onion. Serve immediately.

Penang-Style Birthday Noodle Soup

PENANG BIRTHDAY MEE SUA

Amongst the Penang Straits Chinese, this was a traditional dish served to
a loved one celebrating a birthday. The noodle soup should be prepared just before
serving as *mee sua* turns soggy very quickly. This recipe serves one.

COOKING TIME: 10 MINUTES

1 pig's kidney

1/2 Tbsp cooking oil

2 tsp chopped garlic

2 slices ginger

500 ml (16 fl oz / 2 cups)
pork stock (page 43)

1 Tbsp minced pork

30 g (1 oz) pig's liver, sliced

1/2 tsp salt

1/4 tsp ground white pepper

50 g (1³/₄ oz) fine wheat
vermicelli (*mee sua*)

1 hard-boiled egg, dyed red
with food colouring

GARNISHING
1 Tbsp chopped spring
onions (scallions)

CONDIMENTS
Dark soy sauce

1. To clean kidney, split it in half crosswise and trim off smelly renal
    tubes. Cut away white parts. Using a sharp knife, score outside of
    kidney with a criss-cross pattern, then cut into bite-size rectangles.
    Soak pieces of kidney in several changes of cold water until kidney is
    free of urine.

2. Heat oil in a small pot and fry garlic and ginger until light brown.
    Add stock and bring to the boil.

3. Add minced pork and stir quickly to break meat up.

4. Add kidney and liver slices and salt and pepper and cook for
    1 minute.

5. Rinse noodles quickly under a cold tap, then add to boiling soup.
    Stir and cook for 1 minute.

6. Garnish with spring onion and serve immediately with dyed hard-
    boiled egg and a dip of dark soy sauce.

Sweet Birthday Noodles

A Straits Chinese friend told me how she used to look forward to enjoying a bowl of *mee sua* every year, as a birthday treat when she was a child. It would be served for breakfast. This recipe serves one.

COOKING TIME: 5 MINUTES

1 Tbsp sugar

1 *pandan* leaf, knotted

250 ml (8 fl oz / 1 cup) water

1 bundle (25 g / 1 oz) fine wheat vermicelli (*mee sua*)

1 egg

1. Put sugar, *pandan* leaf and water in a pot and bring to the boil. When sugar has melted, discard *pandan* leaf.

2. Rinse noodles quickly under a cold water tap, then add to boiling syrup. Return syrup to the boil, then lower heat and simmer for 1 minute.

3. Crack egg into pot and turn off heat. Cover pot to semi-cook egg for 2 minutes.

4. Dish out into a bowl without breaking egg yolk and serve immediately.

Straits Chinese Wedding Noodles

I was told that it was once a Straits Chinese custom for the new bride to serve her husband a bowl of sweet noodles as a symbol of their wedded life. The sharpness of the ginger, the sweetness of the soup and the red dates (good luck) were symbolic of the different elements of married life. Naturally, the recipe serves one and feminists will object to the male chauvinist symbolism!

COOKING TIME: 5 MINUTES

1 thumb-size knob ginger, peeled and bruised

1 Chinese red date, pitted and cut into thin shreds

1 Tbsp sugar

250 ml (8 fl oz / 1 cup) water

1 bundle (25 g / 1 oz) fine wheat vermicelli (*mee sua*)

1. Place ginger, red date, sugar and water in a pot and bring to the boil. Lower heat and simmer for 5 minutes. Remove and discard ginger.

2. Rinse noodles quickly under a cold water tap, then add to boiling syrup. Cook for 1 minute. Serve immediately.

Tibetan Noodle Soup

THUKPA

Thukpa is a generic Tibetan word for any soup or stew combined with noodles.
This particular *thukpa* uses fresh homemade egg noodles and can also be called Chinese *thukpa*.
Himalayan mountain cheese, called *churpe*, comes in rock-hard cubes that must be softened in
water for several hours before it can be eaten or grated. It is not available outside the
Himalayan regions. Substitute with grated cheddar.

COOKING TIME: 30 MINUTES

A large pinch of bicarbonate of soda (optional)

200 g (7 oz) mutton/beef/chicken, thinly sliced

3 Tbsp cooking oil

1 onion, about 100 g (3^1/$_2$ oz), peeled and finely chopped

1 tsp chilli powder

^{1}/$_2$ tsp ground turmeric

1^1/$_2$ tsp salt

^{1}/$_4$ tsp ground black pepper

1.25 litres (40 fl oz / 5 cups) water

100 g (3^1/$_2$ oz) fresh green peas

150 g (5^1/$_3$ oz) tomatoes, cut into quarters

600 g (1 lb 5^1/$_3$ oz) fresh egg noodles (page 12)

2 Tbsp grated cheddar cheese

CONDIMENTS
Fresh red or green chillies

1. Knead bicarbonate of soda into sliced meat if using mutton or a tough cut of beef and leave to marinate for 15 minutes. Omit this step if using chicken.

2. Heat oil in a saucepan and sauté onion until fragrant. Add chilli powder, ground turmeric and meat. Stir well.

3. Add salt, pepper and water and simmer over low heat until meat is tender. There should be about 1 litre (32 fl oz / 4 cups) soup left when meat is tender. Add more water to make up this amount if necessary.

4. Stir in peas and tomatoes and continue to simmer until peas are tender.

5. When peas are nearly tender, bring a separate pot of water to the boil and blanch noodles until tender but al dente. Add cooked noodles to soup.

6. Divide into serving bowls and sprinkle grated cheese on top. Serve immediately with fresh red or green chillies on the side.

Korean Noodles in Soy Milk

K'ONGGUKSU

This is an interesting way to use soybean milk. Use a flavoured thin wheat noodle such as *ume somen* or *chasoba* to make a very pretty dish. This dish is quick-cooking, but the preparation is rather long. In Singapore, you can shorten the process by buying unsweetened soybean milk. Or look for unsweetened soybean milk in supermarkets. However, note that these dairy milk substitutes tend to be flavoured with vanilla.

COOKING TIME: 5 MINUTES

200 g (7 oz) dried soybeans

1.25 ml (40 fl oz / 5 cups) water

1 small cucumber

1$\frac{1}{2}$ tsp salt

Cooking oil for frying

1 egg, beaten

300 g (11 oz) Korean *somyon*

1 tomato, cut into 8 wedges

Nori strips, a handful

CONDIMENTS
Korean sesame salt
(page 38)

1. Rinse soybeans and soak overnight in a basin of cold water. The following day, boil beans in 1.25 litres (40 fl oz / 5 cups) water for 10 minutes, then cool and process beans together with cooking liquid using a blender until fine.

2. Strain soy milk through a fine muslin cloth placed over a sieve into a large saucepan or stock pot. Discard pulp.

3. Bring soy milk to the boil, taking care that milk does not boil over. Stir 1 tsp salt into soy milk.

4. Cut cucumber into thin strips and rub remaining salt into them. Let stand for 10 minutes, then squeeze water out.

5. Heat some oil in a frying pan and make a large thin omelette using beaten egg. Cut into very thin strips.

6. Bring a large pot of water to the boil and boil *somyon* until tender but still al dente. Remove noodles and rinse in cold water, then drain well. Divide into serving bowls.

7. Ladle hot soy milk over noodles and garnish with wedges of tomato, salted cucumber strips, egg and nori strips. Serve immediately with Korean sesame salt.

Cold Buckwheat Noodles, Pyongyang-Style
PYONGYANG NYAENG MYON

There are different ways of preparing cold buckwheat noodles but the dish with this particular combination of beef, pear and pickled radish is said to have originated from Pyongyang in North Korea. Make the broth the day before so that it can be chilled and the fat removed easily. The broth also has to be clear which means filtering the stock through a piece of muslin or coffee filter held over an appropriate size sieve. The pickled radish gives this Korean summer dish its piquancy and the Korean pear its sweetness. The cooking time is long because of the stock and beef brisket.

COOKING TIME: 3 HOURS

300 g (11 oz) dried buckwheat noodles

1 spring onion (scallion), chopped

150 g (5^1/$_3$ oz) soft bean curd, cut into cubes

8 thin slices Korean pear

Pickled radish (page 38)

BROTH
500 g (1 lb 1^1/$_2$ oz) beef bones

500 g (1 lb 1^1/$_2$ oz) beef brisket

2 litres (64 fl oz / 8 cups) water

4 slices old ginger

3 cloves garlic, peeled

^{1}/$_2$ tsp black peppercorns

1^1/$_2$ Tbsp white rice vinegar

1–1^1/$_2$ Tbsp light soy sauce

^{1}/$_2$ tsp salt

CONDIMENTS
Korean sesame salt (page 38)

1. Prepare broth a day ahead. Put all broth ingredients into a stockpot and bring to the boil. Lower heat and simmer gently for about 3 hours or until stock is reduced to half and beef brisket is tender.

2. Remove beef brisket and discard bones. Leave broth to cool before refrigerating overnight.

3. The following day, scoop out congealed fat, then strain broth through a piece of muslin or paper coffee filter. Slice beef brisket thinly. Keep broth chilled.

4. Prepare noodles. Have ready an ice-cold water bath.

5. Bring a large pot of water to the boil and boil noodles until done but still al dente. Remove noodles and place into cold water bath.

6. Drain noodles well and divide into serving bowls, twirling noodles into a heap.

7. Ladle chilled broth into bowl, but do not submerge noodles. Place slices of pear, beef brisket and a few strands of pickled radish on top of noodles. Top with cubes of bean curd and sprinkle with chopped spring onions.

8. Serve cold with Korean sesame salt.

Sukiyaki Udon

Sukiyaki is the quintessential Japanese one-pot meal that can be done as a fancy table-top cook-it-yourself dish with some boiled udon on hand for adding to the *sukiyaki*. Or if udon in *sukiyaki* is really the goal, cook it in the kitchen and serve in individual bowls. Although traditional *sukiyaki* has *shiritaki*, a noodle made from the starch of devil's taro (see Glossary), *shiritaki* is not easy to find outside of places with large Japanese communities. It has been omitted in this recipe, but use it if you can find it. You can also substitute with *konnyaku* which is made from the same starch and comes as a speckled greyish slab of jelly Look for *sukiyaki* beef which comes thinly sliced with a layer of succulent fat if you have access to a well-stocked Japanese supermarket. It may even include that piece of suet that is used to oil the *sukiyaki* pan at the start of cooking.

COOKING TIME: 20 MINUTES

300 g (11 oz) dried udon

300 g (11 oz) *sukiyaki* beef

2 Tbsp sake

100 g (3^1/$_2$ oz) firm bean curd

1 piece suet (beef fat), about 4 x 4-cm (1.5 x 1.5-in)

3 stalks leeks, cut into 3-cm (1-in) lengths

8 fresh shiitake mushrooms, caps wiped, thickly sliced or cut into quarters

250 g (9 oz) chrysanthemum leaves, cut into 3-cm (1-in) lengths

SAUCE

4 Tbsp Japanese light soy sauce

1 Tbsp Japanese dark soy sauce

4 Tbsp mirin (sweet cooking sake)

1^1/$_2$ Tbsp sugar

180 ml (6 fl oz / ^{3}/$_4$ cup) water or water from soaking dried mushrooms (from preparing another recipe)/dashi (page 45)

CONDIMENTS

Shichimi togarashi (page 36)

Pickled vegetables such as radish or kimchi (page 39)

1. Bring a large pot of water to the boil and cook udon until tender but al dente. Drain well and divide into serving bowls.

2. If thinly sliced *sukiyaki* beef is not available, prepare your own. Freeze a piece of beef until firm but not rock-hard. Using a sharp knife, slice beef across the grain as thinly as you can. Marinate beef in sake for 15 minutes.

3. Heat a little oil in a frying pan and brown bean curd. Cut into thick slices and set aside.

4. Prepare sauce. Mix ingredients for sauce together in a small pot, then simmer for 1 minute to dissolve sugar. Wipe a *sukiyaki* pan or a deep frying-pan with suet for 2 minutes to extract oil. Discard suet. Pour enough sauce into prepared pan to form a 0.5-cm (^{1}/$_4$-in) layer in pan and bring it to the boil.

5. Spread pieces of beef flat in pan and cook for 20 seconds. Add more sauce as it dries out. Set aside cooked beef. Put remaining sauce into pan and bring to the boil. Add bean curd, leeks and mushrooms and simmer for 1 minute until leeks are limp. Stir in chrysanthemum leaves last.

6. Divide cooked vegetables into bowls with udon and top with slices of beef. Serve immediately with *shichimi togarashi* and pickled vegetables.

Udon in Miso Soup with Salmon

Miso soup should be made just before eating as the miso flavour fades if the soup is left standing or if it is reheated. Dissolve the miso in some dashi first before adding to the soup so that the miso dissolves quickly once it is in the pot. The salmon in this basic miso soup can be replaced with soft bean curd, chicken, pork or prawns. Chrysanthemum leaves can also be substituted with another quick-cooking vegetable.

COOKING TIME: 10 MINUTES

300 g (11 oz) udon/soba/*somen*

3 Tbsp white miso

1 litre (32 fl oz / 4 cups) dashi (page 45)

200 g (7 oz) salmon, thinly sliced

200 g (7 oz) chrysanthemum leaves

1 spring onion (scallion), chopped

1 tsp freshly grated ginger

CONDIMENTS
Shichimi togarashi (page 36)

1. Cook noodles in a pot of boiling water before making miso soup. Divide into serving bowls.

2. Mix miso with 250 ml (8 fl oz / 1 cup) dashi and set aside.

3. Bring remaining dashi to the boil. Add salmon and simmer for 1 minute or until salmon is nearly cooked.

4. Stir in chrysanthemum leaves and when soup returns to the boil, add diluted miso, stir well and remove from heat.

5. Ladle hot miso soup over noodles. Sprinkle spring onion and grated ginger into soup and serve immediately with *shichimi togarashi* on the side.

RINGING IN CHANGES IN FLAVOUR

For subtle changes in flavour, make miso soup with different stocks such as plain *konbu* or shiitake and experiment with different combinations of seafood, meat and vegetables. Some will taste better than others. Keep in mind that colour coordination is important in Japanese cuisine. Here are some suggestions:

- Prawns and shiso leaves
- Salmon and bean curd
- Fish cake (*kamaboko*) and leeks
- Crabstick and eggplant
- Soft bean curd and shiso leaves
- Stuffed soybean puffs and carrots
- Chrysanthemum leaves and chicken or pork
- Fresh mushrooms and prawns, salmon or chicken
- Fresh or dried mushrooms with assorted vegetables

Ladakhi Bow-Tie Noodles

CHHU TAGI

Ladakh was once a Himalayan kingdom but is now part of the Indian state of Jammu and Kashmir. Sitting on the edge of the Tibetan plateau, Ladakhi food and culture are similar to Tibet's. The original *chhu tagi* is a handmade wheat noodle shaped into a bow-tie and cooked in a simple vegetable stew. This recipe offers a dressed up dish.

COOKING TIME: 1 HOUR

3 Tbsp butter/ghee

2 onions, peeled and finely chopped

2 cloves garlic, peeled and thinly sliced

4 slices ginger, finely chopped

2 tsp chilli powder

1 tsp ground turmeric

200 g (7 oz) mutton/beef/chicken, cut into cubes

200 g (7 oz) potatoes, peeled and cut into cubes

1 1/2 tsp salt

1 litre (32 fl oz / 4 cups) water

250 g (9 oz) tomatoes, cut into quarters

100 g (3 1/2 oz) white radish, peeled and cut into cubes

6 leaves mustard cabbage/cabbage, cut into half or quarters, depending on size

600 g (1 lb 5 1/3 oz) bow-tie noodles (page 19)

4 Tbsp milk

1 bunch coriander leaves (cilantro), chopped

1. Heat butter/ghee in a saucepan and fry chopped onions, garlic and ginger until fragrant. Add chilli powder and ground turmeric, then quickly add meat. Stir-fry for 2 minutes.

2. Add potatoes, salt and enough water to stew meat until tender. Mutton or beef will require more water than chicken. There should be enough soup left to cook vegetables as well as form soup.

3. When meat is nearly tender, stir in tomatoes, radish and mustard cabbage, if using. Lower heat and simmer until mustard cabbage is tender. If using cabbage, add cabbage towards the end.

4. In a separate pot, boil bow-tie noodles for about 10 minutes until tender, then drain and add to vegetable stew. Alternatively, add bow-tie noodles to the stew and cook with other stew ingredients until tender.

5. Stir in milk and coriander leaves last. Divide into serving bowls and serve hot.

Bean and Other Noodles

The best known bean noodles are mung bean noodles, which are known in Korea and Laos as Chinese noodles. These noodles are made from the starch of the mung bean, one variety of which gives the ubiquitous bean sprouts used in numerous noodle dishes. Because they turn transparent when soaked in water, they are often also called glass or cellophane noodles. In Japan, mung bean noodles are known as *harusame* which translates into "spring rain noodles". Mung bean noodles are always sold dried and, depending on the manufacturer, some mung bean noodles look opaque and so are sometimes mistaken for rice vermicelli, especially if the labelling is vague. Some brands of mung bean noodles are clear and look like thin bits of plastic wire. Unlike rice vermicelli, mung bean noodles are pliable, tough and do not break easily. In fact, they have to be cut with scissors! Thus, some manufacturers make them in small bundles so that the required amount is easily taken out, doing away with the need to pull and cut the noodles which often results in the kitchen floor being littered with strands of noodles. Mung bean noodles also come as thin-cut flat ribbons which yield cooked noodles with a tasty, slippery mouthfeel.

Unlike most other types of noodles, mung bean noodles are also commonly found in dishes meant to be served with plain rice. They include the typical Straits Chinese mixed vegetable soup, *chap chye*; the Malay curry vegetable dish, *sayur lodeh*; the Thai dish of baked mung bean noodles with crabs or prawns; and Thai *yam woon sen*, a salad with mung bean noodles and seafood. The Chinese one-dish meal of mung bean noodles in fish ball soup is also often served as a soup to go with other dishes and rice; and in the Himalayan region, where mung bean noodles are called *feng*, they are usually cooked with assorted vegetables and served as part of *dhal bhaat*, the typical Himalayan meal of *dhal* on rice with assorted dishes.

Fried mung bean noodles keep well if cooked until fairly dry, although refrigerated cooked mung bean noodles turn wiry and need to be fluffed up by adding a spoonful of water when reheating. As mung bean noodles in any kind of soup or gravy will end up absorbing a lot of the liquid, it is best to prepare mung bean noodles in soup just before eating the dish. The soup can be cooked first and the noodles boiled in the soup just before it is served.

Although Chinese mung bean noodles were once noted for their keeping qualities, transparent look and tasty chew, these qualities are often missing in China-made mung bean noodles in recent years. I have even had Chinese mung bean noodles go mushy on me. Are the manufacturers using fillers? Look for Japanese mung bean noodles which cost more but have the traditional texture, appearance and keeping quality.

A relative newcomer to the bean noodle range is soybean noodles, sometimes labelled "bean noodles". Made from high-protein soybean flour, the noodles are usually flat, broad-cut and opaque-white in colour, unlike mung bean noodles which look transparent. It is easy to tell soybean noodles from mung bean noodles, as the former looks like Italian tagliatelle except for the whiteness of the noodle and the fact that they are packaged in long, coiled pieces or folded strands. Unlike other noodles, soybean noodles have a high protein content because of the flour. Soybean noodles also have a delicious al dente texture, and any fried leftovers retain their shape and much of their texture if not over-boiled. Soybean noodles are boiled straight from the packet for about 10 minutes before they are ready for frying. The boiled noodles can be left soaking in the pot for the few minutes before frying, and do not need to be drained in a colander. When ready, scoop the noodles directly from the pot to the wok.

In this category of "Other Noodles" are tapioca noodles which are eaten in Cambodia and Vietnam, and known as *my tho* noodles. Tapioca noodles were once common in Singapore during the 1942–1945 Japanese Occupation but cannot be found today. Their tough texture was much maligned! What can be found with some searching are sweet potato-potato starch noodles which are commonly eaten in northern China, Mongolia and Korea. Sweet potato-potato starch noodles look like grey-coloured mung bean noodles, as they are transparent and have a wiry texture. Depending on the manufacturer, the package may be labelled "potato glass noodles", with the ingredients listing potato starch and water. These noodles can substitute for mung bean noodles and vice versa, as the cooked noodles have a very similar texture if not the same appearance.

Bean noodles, tapioca noodles and sweet potato-potato starch noodles only come in a dried form and store very well. They do not attract weevils unlike dried wheat noodles.

BEAN AND OTHER NOODLES

Thai-Style Fried Mung Bean Noodles
PAD WOON SEN

As with other Indo-Chinese, the Thais often eat bean sprouts raw with noodles, as in this recipe. They also like sprinkling sugar, crushed peanuts and chilli flakes on their fried noodles.

COOKING TIME: 20 MINUTES

300 g (11 oz) mung bean noodles, softened in cold water

3 Tbsp cooking oil

1 Tbsp chopped garlic

50 g ($1^3/_4$ oz) pork/chicken, thinly sliced

100 g ($3^1/_2$ oz) prawns (shrimps), peeled and deveined

2 Tbsp fish sauce

2 eggs

1 small bunch Chinese celery, cut into finger-lengths

200 g (7 oz) bean sprouts, rinsed and drained

$^1/_2$ tsp salt

GARNISHING
Ground roasted peanuts

Toasted red chilli flakes (page 35)

Sugar

1. Bring a pot of water to the boil and boil noodles for 1–2 minutes. Drain well.

2. Heat 2 Tbsp oil in a wok and sauté garlic until golden brown. Add pork/chicken and stir-fry until meat is cooked.

3. Add prawns and sauté until they turn pink.

4. Add noodles and fish sauce and stir-fry for 1 minute.

5. Make a well in the centre of the wok, add remaining 1 Tbsp oil and when hot, crack eggs into hot oil. Let eggs set before stirring into noodles.

6. Mix well, adding a sprinkling of water if noodles stick to pan. Cover and cook for another minute.

7. Lastly, stir in Chinese celery, bean sprouts and salt. Mix well and turn off heat. The bean sprouts should still be raw.

8. Serve noodles with ground peanuts, chilli flakes and sugar on the side for guests to add according to taste.

Dressed Sweet Potato Noodles, Hamhung-Style

HAMHUNG NYAENG MYON

This dish is also called *bibim nyaeng myon*. Hamhung is in North Korea from where this dish is said to have originated. The dressing for the noodles serves one. Prepare more as needed.

COOKING TIME: 10 MINUTES

300 g (11 oz) sweet potato noodles, softened in cold water

200 g (7 oz) boiled beef brisket, thinly sliced

4 slices Korean pear

2 hard-boiled eggs, peeled and sliced

1 cucumber, cored and cut into slivers

$^1/_2$ cup kimchi (page 39)

Beef stock (page 44)

DRESSING (SERVES 1)

1 clove garlic, peeled and finely pounded

1 slice ginger, finely pounded

2 fresh red chillies, seeded

1 Tbsp sesame oil

2 tsp honey

1 Tbsp light soy sauce

1 Tbsp kimchi juice

CONDIMENTS

Korean sesame salt (page 38)

1. Prepare dressing. Pound garlic, ginger and chillies to a fine paste, then mix well with remaining dressing ingredients in a deep plate. Repeat for the number of servings.

2. Bring a pot of water to the boil and blanch noodles until tender but still al dente or about 3 minutes. Drain well and divide into serving bowls. Stir noodles into dressing, then twirl noodles into a heap in the centre of the plate.

3. Garnish with sliced beef, pear, egg, cucumber slivers and kimchi.

4. Serve with a small bowl of beef broth on the side if desired. The broth can also be emptied into the noodles.

Fried Mung Bean Noodles with Pork, Cantonese-Style

Despite the long list of ingredients, frying this dish takes very little time because all the essentials have been assembled ready for the wok.

COOKING TIME: 15 MINUTES

150 g (5$^{1}/_{3}$ oz) pork, cut into matchsticks

2 Tbsp peanut oil

1 tsp chopped garlic

3 slices ginger, finely shredded

300 g (11 oz) mung bean noodles, softened in cold water

1 spring onion (scallion), finely chopped

MARINADE

$^{1}/_{2}$ tsp dark soy sauce

2 tsp light soy sauce

1 tsp cornflour

1 tsp water

1 tsp sesame oil

A pinch of ground white pepper

SAUCE

250 ml (8 fl oz / 1 cup) chicken stock (page 44)

2 tsp Chinese rice wine

$^{1}/_{2}$ tsp salt

1 tsp sesame oil

2 Tbsp light soy sauce

1. Combine marinade in a bowl. Add pork and leave to stand for 10 minutes.

2. Prepare sauce. Stir all ingredients together and set aside.

3. Heat peanut oil in a wok and sauté garlic and ginger until fragrant.

4. Add marinated pork and fry for 1 minute before pouring in sauce mixture. Bring to the boil.

5. Add softened, drained noodles and simmer for 5 minutes or until sauce has been mostly absorbed into noodles. It should still be slightly moist.

6. Stir in chopped spring onion and serve hot.

Fried Chicken with Chinese Noodles, Laotian-Style

KHAO POON CHIN PAD HAENG

Mung bean noodles are known as Chinese noodles in Laos. This dish can be served with rice or as a meal on its own. If serving with rice, reduce the quantity of mung bean noodles and increase the amount of chicken.

COOKING TIME: 20 MINUTES

300 ml (10 fl oz / 1¼ cups) water

250 g (9 oz) grated coconut

4 Tbsp lard (page 45)

1 large onion, peeled and chopped

200 g (7 oz) chicken meat, cut into small pieces

6 kaffir lime leaves, crushed

3 Tbsp fish sauce

1 tsp ground white pepper

300 g (11 oz) mung bean noodles, softened in cold water

1 spring onion (scallion), chopped

SPICE PASTE

80 g (3 oz) shallots, peeled

1 Tbsp dried red chilli paste (page 33)

1 Tbsp water

1. Prepare spice paste. Combine ingredients in a blender and process until fine. Set aside.

2. Mix 4 Tbsp water with grated coconut and squeeze through a muslin bag or cloth-lined sieve to extract thick coconut milk. Set aside.

3. Add remaining water to squeezed grated coconut and extract second milk. Set aside.

4. Heat lard in a wok and sauté chopped onion until soft. Stir in spice paste and fry until fragrant.

5. Stir in chicken, kaffir lime leaves, fish sauce, pepper and second coconut milk. Simmer until chicken is cooked and there is still gravy in wok.

6. Stir in softened, drained noodles and thick coconut milk and simmer for 5 minutes until noodles are done. Garnish with spring onion and serve hot.

Fried Mung Bean Noodles with Dried Seafood

An aunt of mine would serve this dish whenever we visited her during the Chinese New Year.
It was a good way to use up the dried seafood that would be stored up in homes
as a preparation for the annual closing of the wet markets in Singapore for the
New Year festivities. The dish can be made more elaborate with the addition
of other types of dried seafood and even the extravagance of canned abalone.

COOKING TIME: 30 MINUTES

50 g (1³/₄ oz) dried squid

50 g (1³/₄ oz) dried scallops

50 g (1³/₄ oz) dried Chinese mushrooms

3 stalks leeks

4 Tbsp cooking oil

2 Tbsp chopped garlic

1 tsp salt

¹/₂ tsp ground white pepper

1 tsp dark soy sauce

2 Tbsp light soy sauce

300 g (11 oz) mung bean noodles, softened in cold water

1 spring onion (scallion), cut into finger-lengths

CONDIMENTS

Sambal belacan with lime juice (page 31)

1. Rinse dried squid, scallops and mushrooms clean, then soak each in 250 ml (8 fl oz / 1 cup) water. When seafood and mushrooms are soft, set 250 ml (8 fl oz / 1 cup) of combined soaking liquid aside for use when cooking noodles. Dried scallops take at least 1 hour to soften.

2. Slice softened squid very finely, unless it has been pre-sliced. Discard mushroom stems and slice mushrooms thinly. Shred softened scallops.

3. Clean leeks by cutting at the point where white turns to green. This is the part where grit collects. Rinse thoroughly. Cut into 1 cm (¹/₂ in) wide slices.

4. Heat oil in a wok and sauté garlic until fragrant. Add leeks, squid, scallops, mushrooms, salt, pepper and soy sauces and mix well.

5. Stir in drained noodles and reserved soaking liquid and bring to the boil. Stir-fry until noodles are tender but al dente. Stir in spring onion.

6. Dish out and serve hot with *sambal belacan* mixed with lime juice on the side.

Thai Baked Crab and Mung Bean Noodles

This dish can also be made with large prawns. Depending on the size of the prawns, provide three to four per person. Chop the feelers and tips of the head off the prawns, rinse clean and arrange the prawns on top of the mung bean noodles before baking.

COOKING TIME: 20 MINUTES

1 kg (2 lb 3 oz) crabs

3 bunches coriander leaves (cilantro) with roots

1 thumb-size knob ginger

2 tsp ground coriander

2 tsp ground white pepper

500 ml (16 fl oz / 2 cups) chicken stock (page 44)

3 Tbsp fish sauce

1 tsp dark soy sauce

1 tsp sugar

2 Tbsp garlic oil (page 30)

300 g (11 oz) mung bean noodles, softened in cold water

1. Scrub crabs clean, remove carapace and scrub inside as well. Remove spongy bits on either side of crab. Quarter or halve each crab, depending on size.

2. Cut roots from bunches of coriander, rinse clean and mash roots with the flat side of a cleaver. Chop coriander leaves and set aside.

3. Scrape ginger clean and bruise with the flat side of a large knife.

4. In a large ovenproof dish with a cover, except noodles, crab and coriander leaves, mix all ingredients together.

5. Stir in noodles and mix well. Top with crabs, cover and bake in a pre-heated oven at 180°C until crabs turn red. Do not overbake or crabs will be dry.

6. Before serving, mix noodles from bottom of dish with those on top, but leave crab arranged on top of noodles. Sprinkle with chopped coriander leaves and serve hot.

Fried Mung Bean Noodles with Crabmeat and Black Pepper

COOKING TIME: 15 MINUTES

4 Tbsp cooking oil

50 g (1³/₄ oz) shallots, peeled and thinly sliced

1 Tbsp chopped garlic

125 ml (4 fl oz / ¹/₂ cup) water

2 Tbsp light soy sauce

1 tsp dark soy sauce

¹/₂ tsp salt

300 g (11 oz) mung bean noodles, softened in cold water

400 g (14¹/₃ oz) crabmeat

1 tsp ground black pepper

1 bunch coriander leaves (cilantro), chopped

2 spring onions (scallions), chopped

1. Heat oil in a wok and sauté shallots until golden brown. Remove from wok and set aside.

2. Leave oil in wok and reheat. Add garlic and sauté until fragrant, then add water, soy sauces and salt. Stir well, then add mung bean noodles. Mix well.

3. Fry for about 3 minutes. If noodles dry out too quickly, add a bit more water.

4. Stir in crabmeat and pepper, then chopped coriander leaves and spring onions. Dish out and serve hot.

Fried Mung Bean Noodles, Filipino-Style

SOTANGHOON GUISADO

Squeezing lime juice on the noodles at the end of frying gives these mung bean noodles
a delicious piquancy that lifts the rich flavour of lard. Mung bean noodles
are known as *sotanghoon* in the Philippines.

COOKING TIME: 20 MINUTES

2 dried Chinese
mushrooms

125 ml (4 fl oz / $^1/_2$ cup)
chicken stock (page 44)

1 bay leaf, crushed

3 Tbsp lard (page 45)

2 Tbsp chopped onions

1 Tbsp chopped garlic

200 g (7 oz) chicken, thinly
sliced

3 Tbsp fish sauce

1 small carrot, peeled and
cut into matchsticks

2 stalks leeks, cut into
2.5-cm (1-in) lengths

300 g (11 oz) mung bean
noodles, softened in cold
water

2 Tbsp anatto oil
(page 29)

1 Tbsp lime juice

1. Rinse mushrooms clean, then soak in 4 Tbsp water until soft. Reserve soaking liquid. Discard stems and slice thinly.

2. Put mushroom soaking liquid, chicken stock and bay leaf into a pot and boil for 2 minutes. Discard bay leaf.

3. Heat lard in a wok and fry chopped onion and garlic until onion is soft. Stir in chicken, mushrooms, 1 Tbsp fish sauce and chicken stock mixture. Bring to the boil.

4. Add carrot and leeks and fry until leeks change colour.

5. Stir in noodles, anatto oil, remaining 2 Tbsp fish sauce and simmer for 3 minutes. The noodles should be moist rather than dry. Add a little more water if necessary.

6. Turn off heat and stir in lime juice. Dish out and serve hot.

Korean Sweet Potato Noodles with Beef and Mixed Vegetables

SOEGOGI CHAPCH'AE

This Korean dish is meant to be served with rice, but there is no reason why it cannot be eaten on its own. For a truly Korean flavour, stir in a tablespoon of raw chopped garlic or garlic slivers after the noodles are cooked. If sweet potato noodles are not available, substitute with mung bean noodles or even soybean noodles.

COOKING TIME: 20 MINUTES

300 g (11 oz) beef, cut into thin, narrow strips

300 g (11 oz) sweet potato noodles, softened in cold water

3 Tbsp cooking oil

1 large onion, peeled and thinly sliced

30 g (1 oz) dried Chinese mushrooms, softened in cold water, stems discarded and sliced

100 g (3^1/$_2$ oz) leeks, halved and slant-cut into 2.5-cm (1-in) lengths

100 g (3^1/$_2$ oz) carrots, peeled and cut into thin rounds

100 g (3^1/$_2$ oz) watercress, cut into 2.5-cm (1-in) lengths

^{1}/$_2$ tsp salt

250 ml (8 fl oz / 1 cup) chicken stock (page 44)

2 tsp sugar

MARINADE

A pinch of bicarbonate of soda

3 tsp sugar

1 Tbsp chopped garlic

1 Tbsp chopped spring onions (scallions)

1 Tbsp sesame oil

1 tsp dark soy sauce

1 Tbsp light soy sauce

^{1}/$_2$ tsp ground black pepper

DRESSING

1^1/$_2$ Tbsp light soy sauce

1 Tbsp Korean sesame salt (page 38)

1 Tbsp sesame oil

CONDIMENTS

Kimchi (page 39)

Peeled raw garlic bulbs

1. Combine marinade in a bowl and mix beef strips in to stand for 10 minutes.

2. Mix dressing for noodles in a large bowl.

3. Bring a pot of water to the boil and boil sweet potato noodles for 3 minutes. Drain well and place into bowl with dressing. Mix well and set aside.

4. Heat oil in a wok and sauté onion, mushrooms and leeks for 3 minutes before adding marinated beef. Fry for 1 minute.

5. Add carrots, watercress, noodles and salt and mix well. Fry for 2 minutes, then add chicken stock and continue frying until stock is absorbed into noodles.

6. Serve noodles on a large platter and kimchi and raw garlic as condiments on the side.

Fried Soybean Noodles
with Bean Curd and Leeks

Soybean noodles are high in protein and have a good bite. Leftover noodles keep well.

COOKING TIME: 30 MINUTES

300 g (11 oz) dried soybean noodles

4 Tbsp cooking oil

1 Tbsp chopped garlic

8 dried Chinese mushrooms, rinsed, softened in water, stems discarded and thinly sliced

50 g (1³/₄ oz) minced pork/chicken

100 g (3¹/₂ oz) prawns (shrimps), peeled and deveined

300 g (11 oz) leeks, thinly sliced

100 g (3¹/₂ oz) firm bean curd, cut into short, chunky strips

1 tsp dark soy sauce

2 Tbsp light soy sauce

125 ml (4 fl oz / ¹/₂ cup) chicken stock (page 44)/water

¹/₂ tsp salt

CONDIMENTS
Fresh red chillies with light soy sauce or *sambal belacan* with lime juice (page 31)

1. Prepare ingredients for frying before starting to boil noodles.

2. Bring a pot of water to the boil, then cook dried noodles using the boil-discard-add method (page 20) until noodles are al dente.

3. Heat oil in a wok and sauté garlic until fragrant.

4. Add mushrooms and pork/chicken and sauté for 1 minute.

5. Add prawns, leeks and bean curd and sauté until leeks are limp.

6. Add a few drops of dark soy sauce for colour and some light soy sauce for flavour.

7. Scoop out boiled noodles directly into wok, then mix in chicken stock/water, salt and remaining soy sauces. Fry until noodles are tender.

8. Dish out and serve hot with sliced red chillies in light soy sauce or *sambal belacan* with lime juice.

Mung Bean Noodles with Minced Pork

This is a quick noodle dish that can be prepared with whatever vegetables or meat that are on hand. You can even just add mushrooms and dried prawns. The *sambal belacan* and lime juice will give it plenty of zing.

COOKING TIME: 20 MINUTES

3 Tbsp cooking oil

1 Tbsp chopped garlic

1 Tbsp dried prawns (shrimps), cleaned and finely chopped

3 stalks leeks, thinly sliced

4 dried Chinese mushrooms, softened in cold water, stems discarded and sliced

100 g ($3^{1}/_{2}$ oz) minced pork/ chicken

300 g (11 oz) mung bean noodles, softened in cold water

250 ml (8 fl oz / 1 cup) chicken stock (page 44)/water

1 tsp dark soy sauce

2 Tbsp light soy sauce

$^{1}/_{2}$ tsp salt

CONDIMENTS
Fresh red chillies with light soy sauce or *sambal belacan* with lime juice (page 31)

1. Heat oil in a wok and sauté garlic until fragrant.

2. Add dried prawns and sauté for 1 minute, then add leeks, mushrooms and minced pork/chicken.

3. Stir in noodles, chicken stock/water, soy sauces and salt. Stir well and simmer over low heat for 3 minutes until noodles are tender.

4. Serve hot with sliced red chillies in light soy sauce or *sambal belacan* with lime juice on the side.

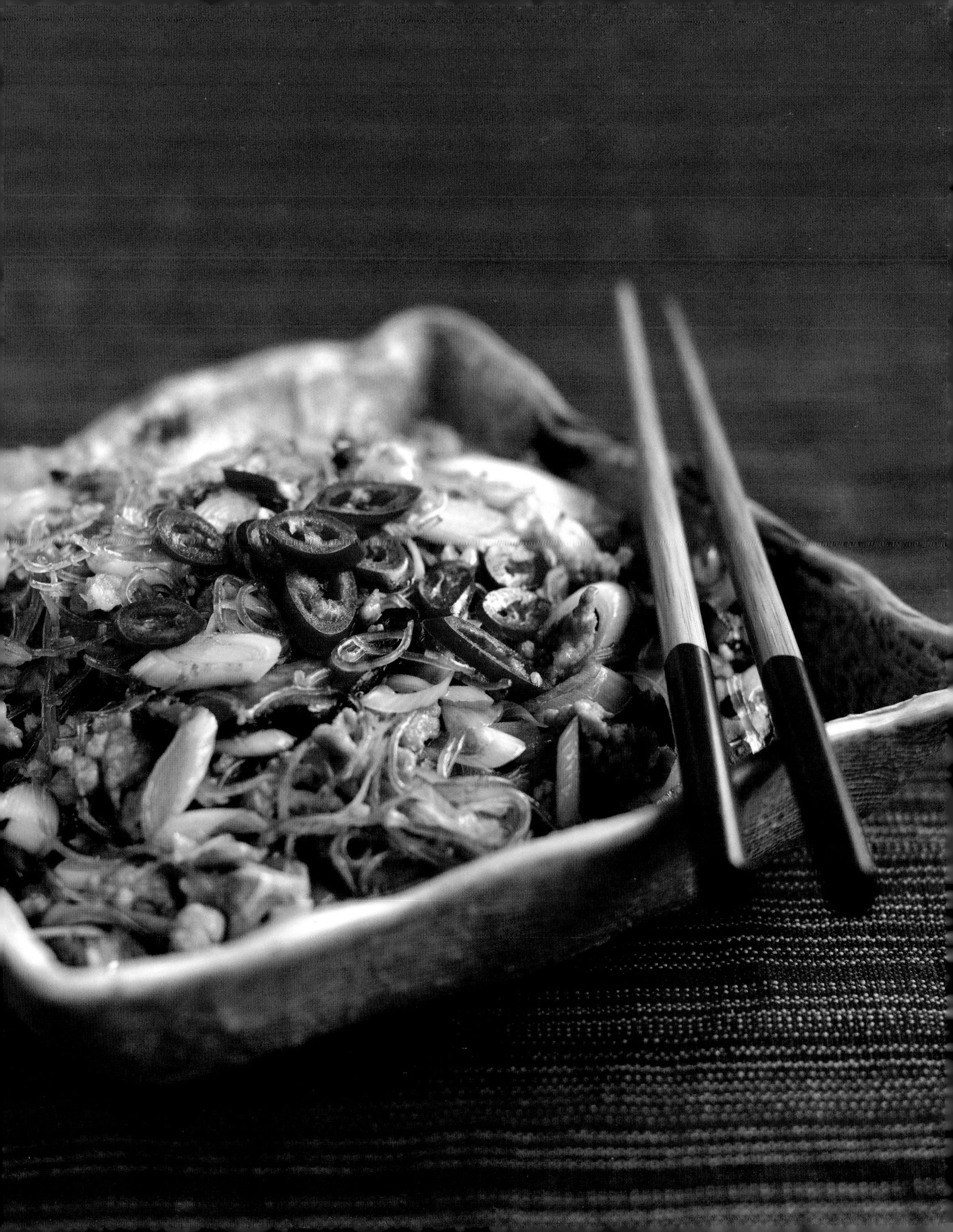

Cambodian-Style Stir-Fried Mung Bean Noodles with Prawns

UM UM XUA CHAR PAKON

This is a dish with contrasting flavours, from sweet to spicy and tangy from the mix of seasoning ingredients. This dish is rather Thai in character because of its spiciness, as Cambodian food is generally not so spicy.

COOKING TIME: 20 MINUTES

300 g (11 oz) coarse mung bean noodles, softened in cold water until pliable

4 Tbsp cooking oil

100 g (3¹/₂ oz) onion, peeled and thinly sliced

1 Tbsp chopped garlic

300 g (11 oz) prawns (shrimps), peeled and deveined

5 fresh red chillies, seeded and ground to a paste

1 canned 350 g (12 oz) bamboo shoots, drained and finely shredded

125 ml (4 fl oz / ¹/₂ cup) prawn stock (page 44)

200 g (7 oz) bean sprouts

1 spring onion (scallion), cut into finger-lengths

4 kaffir lime leaves, crushed

2 hard-boiled eggs, peeled and quartered

1 bunch coriander leaves (cilantro), chopped

SEASONING

4 Tbsp water

2 Tbsp tamarind paste

3 Tbsp fish sauce

1 Tbsp sugar

¹/₂ tsp salt

1 tsp dark soy sauce

¹/₂ tsp ground black pepper

1 Tbsp cornflour

CONDIMENTS

Tuk trey chu p'em (page 36)

1. Prepare seasoning. Mix water with tamarind paste. Strain liquid and discard solids. Add rest of ingredients to tamarind juice and stir well. Stir again just before adding to noodles.

2. Bring a pot of water to the boil and blanch noodles until al dente. Drain well and set aside.

3. Heat oil in a wok and fry onion and garlic until onion is soft and garlic fragrant. Stir in prawns and fry until they turn pink.

4. Add noodles, chilli paste, bamboo shoots and prawn stock and simmer until noodles are tender.

5. Stir in bean sprouts, spring onion and kaffir lime leaves. Add seasoning mixture and fry for 2 minutes.

6. Dish out onto a large serving platter and garnish with hard-boiled eggs and coriander leaves. Serve immediately with *tuk trey chu p'em* on the side.

Tapioca Noodles Fried with Mussels, Cambodian-Style

Noodles made from tapioca flour look like flat narrow-cut mung bean noodles. It is produced in Vietnam and most of it is exported to Cambodia, labelled as "*my tho* noodles". Tapioca noodles got a bad name in Singapore as a result of the Japanese Occupation between 1942 and 1945 when severe food shortages led to rice and wheat flour being substituted with tapioca flour which turned out chewy noodles and bread. Today, tapioca noodles are not easy to find in Singapore. Substitute with mung bean noodles, sweet potato noodles or coarse rice vermicelli if unavailable.

COOKING TIME: 20 MINUTES

1 kg (2 lb 3 oz) mussels

600 ml (19^1/$_3$ fl oz) water

300 g (11 oz) grated coconut

3 Tbsp cooking oil

1 onion, peeled and coarsely sliced

1 Tbsp chopped garlic

4 kaffir lime leaves, bruised

^{1}/$_2$ Tbsp sugar

3 Tbsp fish sauce

^{1}/$_2$ tsp salt

300 g (11 oz) tapioca noodles

SPICE PASTE

1 stalk lemongrass, finely sliced

1 thumb-size knob fresh turmeric, peeled

2 Tbsp water

1 Tbsp dried red chilli paste (page 33)

GARNISHING

1 cup *laksa* leaves, chopped

1 cucumber, cored and shredded

200 g (7 oz) bean sprouts, tailed and rinsed

CONDIMENTS

Tuk trey chu p'em (page 36)

1. Scrub mussels clean and place in a pot. Cover with 500 ml (16 fl oz / 2 cups) water and bring to the boil. Lower heat and simmer for about 2 minutes until mussels open. Shuck mussels, discarding any unopened ones. Let stock stand for 10 minutes, then strain and discard the last 1-cm (^{1}/$_2$-in) of liquid at the bottom of the pot. Set aside 300 ml (10 fl oz / 1^1/$_4$ cups) mussel stock.

2. Add remaining 100 ml (3^1/$_3$ fl oz) water to grated coconut and squeeze through a muslin bag or cloth-lined sieve to obtain thick coconut milk. Set aside.

3. Prepare spice paste. Combine lemongrass, turmeric and water in a blender and process to a fine paste. Mix in chilli paste and set aside. Heat oil in a wok and fry onion, garlic and spice paste until fragrant. Add kaffir lime leaves and mix well.

4. Stir in mussels, sugar, fish sauce and salt. Mix well, add reserved mussel stock and bring to the boil. Add coconut milk and return to the boil. Set aside.

5. Bring a pot of water to the boil and cook noodles until tender but still chewy. Drain well and add to sauce in pot. Stir noodles into sauce and mix well.

6. Divide sprouts and shredded cucumber into deep-dish plates. Divide noodles and sauce into prepared serving plates on top of vegetables. Garnish with *laksa* leaves and serve with *tuk trey chu p'em* on the side.

Sweet Potato Noodles in Black Bean Sauce

CHAJANG MYON

Chajang myon is a Chinese-Korean fusion dish found in Chinese restaurants in Korea.
It pairs Chinese salted black beans with Korean sweet potato noodles. It was probably inspired
by *cha jiang mian*, a common Northern Chinese noodle dish (page 142). Chinese salted
black beans are found in most Asian stores around the world. Sweet potato noodles
should be eaten soon after cooking, as they become a gluey lump once cool.

COOKING TIME: 20 MINUTES

4 Tbsp cooking oil

1 Tbsp sesame oil

1 Tbsp chopped garlic

1 Tbsp salted black beans, finely mashed

200 g (7 oz) Tientsin cabbage, coarsely shredded

4 Tbsp chicken stock/water

300 g (11 oz) sweet potato noodles, softened in cold water

200 g (7 oz) minced beef/ pork

2 Tbsp sugar

1^1/$_2$ Tbsp light soy sauce

1 Tbsp dark soy sauce

1 spring onion (scallion), chopped

1 bunch coriander leaves (cilantro), chopped

THICKENER
125 ml (4 fl oz / ^{1}/$_2$ cup) chicken stock (page 44)

2 Tbsp cornflour

^{1}/$_2$ tsp ground black pepper

CONDIMENTS
Kimchi (page 34)

Chinese chilli oil (page 35)

Korean sesame salt (page 38)

1. Combine ingredients for thickener in a bowl and stir well again just before adding to wok.

2. Combine cooking oil and sesame oil in a wok and heat. When hot, fry garlic and black beans until fragrant.

3. Stir in Tientsin cabbage and chicken stock/water. Fry until Tientsin cabbage softens.

4. Meanwhile, bring a pot of water to the boil and blanch sweet potato noodles for 3 minutes. Drain and place noodles directly into wok.

5. Add minced beef/pork, sugar and soy sauces and fry for 1 minute. Add boiled noodles and fry for 2 minutes.

6. Stir in thickener and bring to the boil.

7. Dish out and garnish with spring onion and coriander leaves. Serve immediately with kimchi, chilli oil and Korean sesame salt on the side.

Filipino Mung Bean Noodles in Soup

LANG LANG

Mung bean noodles in soup, together with fish balls, minced meat and greens like chopped spring onion and coriander leaves, is common all over South East Asia wherever mung bean noodles are found. This is from the Philippines.

COOKING TIME: 30 MINUTES

4 dried Chinese mushrooms

500 g (1 lb 1^1/$_2$ oz) chicken

1 litre (32 fl oz / 4 cups) chicken stock (page 44)/ water

1 small onion, peeled and chopped

1 Tbsp fried garlic (page 30)

3 Tbsp fish sauce

^{1}/$_4$ tsp ground black pepper

300 g (11 oz) mung bean noodles, softened in cold water

100 g (3^1/$_2$ oz) prawns (shrimps), peeled and deveined

2 Tbsp garlic oil (page 30)

1 spring onion (scallion), chopped

1. Rinse mushrooms and soften in some water. Remove and discard stems and slice mushrooms. Reserve soaking liquid.

2. Place chicken into a pot with chicken stock/water and bring to the boil. Lower heat and simmer gently until chicken is well cooked.

3. Remove chicken and shred meat. Set meat aside and return bones to pot. Simmer stock for another 10 minutes, then strain stock and discard solids.

4. Add mushrooms, reserved soaking liquid, onion, half the fried garlic, fish sauce and pepper to pot and simmer for 10 minutes.

5. Add mung bean noodles and prawns and simmer for another 3 minutes.

6. Heat garlic oil in a pan and fry shredded chicken to reheat.

7. Divide noodles and soup into serving bowls and garnish with chopped spring onion and remainder of fried garlic. Top with shredded chicken and serve hot.

Glossary of Ingredients

Alkali salts
Alkali salts give Chinese noodles their springy texture and may be either potassium bicarbonate (KHCO3) and sodium bicarbonate (NaHCO3) also called bicarbonate of soda or baking soda, or a combination of both. Usually sold as orange or pale yellow crystals, the salts are sometimes also available dissolved in water, labelled as "potassium water", "alkali water" or "lye". Use bicarbonate of soda if unavailable.

Anchovies, dried *(Fam. Engraulidae stolephorus indicus) (Van Hasselt)*
Better known in South East Asia as *ikan bilis* (Malay), this tiny dried fish is used to flavour stocks, or fried to a crisp as a snack. Japanese dried anchovies are similar in appearance and taste but cost more.

Anatto seeds *(Bixa orellana)*
Also *achuete* or *asuete*, anatto seeds are used mainly to colour food an orange-red. A central and South America native, the plant was introduced to the Philippines by the Spanish and continues to be used in Filipino and South American cooking today. To extract the best colour, heat the seeds in oil, although soaking them in water will also release some of the colour. Once the colour is extracted, the seeds are discarded. Anatto is available whole or in powdered form.

Banana *(Musa x paradisiaca)*
There are several hundred varieties of bananas, with some better eaten as a fruit and others cooked as a vegetable. Almost all parts of the banana plant may be used, from the trunk and flower, to the fruit and leaves. The tender inner part of the trunk is used in different parts of Indo-China as a vegetable, as is the inflorescence at the end of a bunch of bananas. The banana stem on which the bananas hang is essential in the Burmese national dish of *mohinga*. It is what gives the dish its characteristic grey colour.

Bean sprouts *(Vigna radiata)*
The bean sprouts most commonly used in Asian noodle dishes are mung bean sprouts. The sprouts sometimes come soaked in water or packaged with water. To keep such bean sprouts for later use, dry them out by wrapping in newspaper or paper towels and store in the vegetable compartment of the fridge. Do not store for more than a couple of days. It is preferable to cook them on the day of purchase. On the other hand, bean sprouts that are sold "dry", without a water bath, can keep for nearly a week if the bean sprouts are very fresh. Store wrapped in newspaper and rinse only when ready to use. Substitute with soybeans sprouts if unavailable, or sprout mung beans. Soak mung beans overnight, then spread out on a piece of sacking soaked in water. Keep moist and leave in a warm dark spot for 3–4 days.

Belly pork

This cut of pork has layers of fat and lean, giving a moist and flavourful combination which makes the cut popular in dressing noodle dishes in Asia. Belly pork is usually sold in strips complete with skin. Because belly pork is a little tough, the boiled meat is usually sliced thinly or stewed long enough to soften the meat. When used in fried noodles, the meat is always pre-boiled, then sliced. The water used for boiling the meat is turned into a simple soup to go with the fried noodles or used in cooking the noodles.

Black prawn (shrimp) paste (haeko)

This paste must not be confused with dried prawn paste (*belacan*). Black prawn paste is literally black in colour and comes in a jar. This thick paste is a specialty of Penang, Malaysia. It makes an excellent dip for vegetable sticks such as cucumber and is often diluted with hot water to make a sauce. *See also* dried prawn paste (*belacan*).

Candlenuts *(Aleurites moluccana)*

A native of Maluku in Indonesia, Malaysia and the South Pacific, candlenuts or *buah keras* as they are known in Malaysia and Singapore, and *kemiri* in Indonesia, are oily nuts that are ground and used as a thickener in curry pastes. Their name came from the fact that oil from the nuts used to be made into lamp oil. Substitute with macadamia nuts.

Chickpea *(Cicer arietinum)* flour

Made by grinding dried chickpeas into a heavy flour and often called by its Indian name of *besan*, it is easily found in stores that sell Indian foodstuffs. Chickpeas are also known as garbanzo beans, channa *dhal* and *kachang kuda* in Malay. Grinding dried chickpeas into flour at home is practically impossible because they are very hard. Chickpea flour is used as a thickener and as a flavouring in Burmese noodle dishes. Substitute with gram *dhal* flour or soak a handful of chickpeas overnight, boil until soft, then blend to a fine paste.

Chillies *(Capsicum frutescens)*

Sometimes called chilli peppers or red peppers to distinguish them from pepper (*Piper nigrum*), the range of this Mexican and Central American native is huge with an equally wide variation of flavours from sweet to explosive. The hottest chillies are said to be the habanero peppers sometimes called the Scotch bonnet, but the tiny Thai *prik kee nu* (not bird's eye chillies) has to be a very close second. The heat comes from capsaicin which is found especially around the seeds; hence the instruction is often to seed the chillies to reduce the heat while retaining the bulk. Another reason to seed the chillies is that the seeds do not process well in the modern blender. Chillies come fresh red or green, but the two are not interchangeable as there is a difference in the flavour and usually one or the other is the desired taste.

Chillies also come dried and these can now be found all over the world, especially where there are large communities of Mexicans. Dried chillies range from the small cayenne to the very mild ancho. Note that some Mexican dried chillies are smoked and so are not suitable for any of the recipes in this book. To get the right combination of bulk and heat, mix mild chillies such as *guajillo* with bird's eye chillies.

Dried chillies and fresh red chillies are mutually exclusive in all the recipes in this book and to get the right flavour, one should not be substituted for the other. Prepared chillies come as ready-to-dip sauces, pastes, powders and toasted flakes. Chilli sauces keep well in the fridge and homemade pastes in the freezer. So when chillies are in season in countries with seasons, it is a good idea to make more fresh chilli paste and store it in the freezer. Although dried chillies are available all year round, advance preparation of chilli pastes using dried chillies will speed up preparation times. Condiments of one preparation or another of chillies are almost de rigueur in many of the recipes in this book. However, not all can be prepared in advance nor are their flavours interchangeable. Where alternatives do not compromise the ethnic flavour, they have been indicated.

Wear rubber gloves when preparing fresh or dried chillies to minimise contact with bare hands. Chillies leave a sting on the skin which can be passed on to other parts of the body by mere contact. Take care not to rub your eyes or face if you have recently handled chillies.

Chinese celery *(Apium graveolens)*

Chinese celery is a relative of western celery but has a much stronger flavour that resembles that of Italian (flat-leaf) parsley. It is sometimes called Chinese parsley. In China and South East Asia, it is used as a herb and a sprinkling of chopped leaves does wonders for soups, hence its Malay name, *daun sop* (soup leaves). Its strong flavour is particularly desired in Chinese fish soups and beef soups. In parts of the Himalayan region such as Sikkim and Nepal, the stems are stir-fried with slices of meat such as water buffalo. Substitute with western celery or Italian parsley.

Chinese Mushrooms *see* Shiitake Mushrooms

Chives *(Allium tuberosum)*

Sometimes called garlic chives or flat chives, they are available in South East Asian markets as young edible leaves or mature stems and flowers. The latter is usually prepared as a vegetable while the young leaves are used as a herb. Chives also come in a pale yellow colour, the result of growing them deeply shaded. The flavour of yellow chives is milder than the dark green variety. Chives are more strongly-flavoured and have larger leaves than temperate-climate chives. To prepare chives, rinse well, remove any brown bits and cut into small pieces. Substitute with temperate-climate chives or garlic leaves.

Choy sum *(Brassica chinensis var. parachinensis)*

Also known as Chinese flowering cabbage or *cai xin*, this member of the cabbage family is commonly used in noodle dishes in Singapore and Malaysia. When mature, the vegetable has pretty tiny yellow flowers. All parts of the vegetable can be eaten although the tougher outer skin of the stem nearest the roots may have to be peeled off. To prepare the vegetable, rinse well and cut into finger-lengths. The vegetable is either stir-fried with other raw ingredients or blanched before serving with dressed noodles. A good substitute is one of the huge variety of bok choy (*Brassica rapa chinensis*), the common western name taken from the Cantonese *pak choy* (white vegetable). Baby bok choy has the mild flavour of *cai xin* and is commonly found in many parts of the world. One variety of *Brassica rapa chinensis* with bright or dark green leaves and thick white stems, is fairly mild and can substitute for *choy sum*.

Chrysanthemum leaves (*Chrysanthemum coronarium*)

The leaves of a variety of chrysanthemum, this is eaten in East Asia and by Chinese elsewhere. Also called garland chrysanthemum, the leaves are popped into soups or stir-fried like any green vegetable. They are also delicious blanched and served with dry noodles. Chrysanthemum leaves do not store well and should be eaten the day of purchase.

Cockles (*Fam. Arcidae Anadara granosa (Linnaeus); Arca granosa*)

Also known as arkshell, chest clam, blood clam or bloody clams, and as *kerang* in Malay and *haam* in Hokkien, this shellfish exudes a blood-red juice that some find off-putting. Cockles are regarded by some as an essential ingredient in Singapore *laksa* and Singapore *char kuay tiao*. The cockles are briefly dunked in boiling water, then shelled before they are added to fried noodles or *laksa*.

Coriander leaves (cilantro) (*Coriandrum sativum*)

This herb is indispensable in many parts of the world from Asia to South America. The seeds are an essential ingredient in Indian and South East Asian curry powders as well as used on their own in various dishes such as Thai baked crabs with mung bean noodles. The leaves are chopped and sprinkled in soups, used in dumplings, added to minced meats and eaten raw. Thai cooks clean and pound up the roots for added flavour in their dishes. If coriander leaves are sold without the roots, substitute with the stems. To prepare, rinse well to get rid of any

sand or soil, then chop. Whole stalks complete with leaves are often used as a garnish.

Curry leaves (*Murraya koenigii*)

The fresh leaves are used in South Asian, Sri Lankan and Burmese cooking. Many homes in these countries and where there are large Indian communities such as Singapore and Malaysia will have a *karupillay* plant among their herbs. Fresh and dried leaves may be available in Asian stores selling Indian foodstuffs. The fresh leaves can be dried in a dehydrator, microwave oven or a warm convection oven for later use.

Curry powder

This is a blend of spices mixed for use with meat, seafood or vegetables. The label should indicate its use. Curry powders are not all alike; different powders produce different flavours. Avoid commercial curry powders that look very yellow as this indicates a large amount of turmeric. Turmeric is never the main ingredient in good curry powders. To prepare a curry powder for cooking, mix it first with a little water into a thick paste. Curry powder should never be fried dry as it burns easily in hot oil.

Daikon *see* Radish, white

Daun kesom *see* Laksa leaf

Devil's tongue (*Amorphophallus konjack*)

In Japan, this yam is turned into slabs of grey or black jelly known as *konnyaku*. In China, its Chinese name means "devil's taro". *Konnyaku* is added to Japanese soups and stews. It is also made into noodles of various thickness, one of which is called *shirataki* (white waterfall) and is a traditional ingredient in classic *sukiyaki*. *Konnyaku* noodles are added to dishes to give textural interest rather than as the main star.

Dried prawn paste (*belacan*)

This is made from tiny prawns and salt, and dried into a block. Known as *belacan* in Singapore, Malaysia and Indonesia, it is an essential ingredient in South East Asian curries and

practically all of South East Asia has a version of *belacan*. Outside of South East Asia, dried prawn paste can be found in Asian stores and the best known is by Lee Kum Kee (a Hong Kong brand) in which the *belacan* has been blended with water into a thick sauce. It is an acceptable substitute for South East Asian dried prawn paste. *Belacan* should not be confused with *sambal belacan* which is a condiment made from pounding together fresh red chillies and toasted *belacan*. See also Black prawns (shrimp) paste (*haeko*).

Dried sour fruit (*Asam Gelugor*) (*Garcinia astroviridis*)

The fruit of a medium-size tree native to Malaysia, this is used as a souring agent. The sliced and dried unripe fruit is sold in small amounts and used in several South East Asian dishes, in particular with fish or prawns. It is essential in classic Penang *laksa*. *Asam gelugor* is more sour than tamarind and a little goes a long way. To prepare, rinse under running water, then place into the stock or soup for boiling. The pieces of *asam gelugor* can be eaten although it is normally discarded after cooking.

Fish sauce

This sauce is an essential ingredient in Burmese, Indo-Chinese and Filipino cooking. A Chinese dialect group that uses fish sauce in its dishes is the Teochew community noted for their fish preparations and seafood products. Fish sauce is made by fermenting fish and salt, then draining off the light brown fishy-smelling liquid. The ancient Romans produced fish sauce using a similar method. In northern Thailand and Laos, there is a variety known as *padek* which contains pieces of the fish as well. A good substitute for *padek* is fish pickled in salt such as canned anchovies or fermented fish from the Philippines. In Cambodia, fermented fish is known as *prahok*. Ordinary fish sauce is now available in any good Asian store around the world, but note that the salt content varies from brand to brand. Fish sauce is known as *nuoc nam* in Vietnam, *nam pla* in Thailand, *tuk trey* in Cambodia, *ngan pya ye* in Burma, *nam pa* in Laos and *patis* in the Philippines. In Indo-Chinese cooking, fish sauce is always used in lieu of salt or in combination with salt, giving Indo-Chinese food its special flavour.

Five-Spice powder
This is a blend of spices, principally star anise, cinnamon, cloves, fennel, licorice root and anise seeds. The blend varies according to the manufacturer and may be more or less than five.

Galangal, greater *(Languas galanga or Alpinia galanga (greater))*
Known also as *khaa* in Thailand, *lengkuas* in Singapore and Malaysia, and *laos* in Indonesia, this is an essential ingredient in South East Asian cooking and the one used in most South East Asian spice pastes. It is a large, tough, fibrous rhizome with an orange-red skin. Young rhizomes are paler, more tender but also less strongly flavoured. The root is used whole or ground in spice pastes.

Galangal, lesser *(Languas officinarum/Alpinia officinarum (lesser))*
Known as *kencur* in Indonesia and *chekok* in Malaysia, both the roots and leaves of this small herb-like plant, which is a ginger member, can be used. The finely sliced leaves go into salads such as Malay and Straits Chinese *nasi ulam* (rice salad) while the root is a must in Indonesian *opor ayam*.

Garam masala
In South Asian cooking, this is a spice blend that is shaken over a freshly cooked dish to maximise the fragrance of spices. The ideal is to blend the garam masala on the spot from freshly ground spices but few modern cooks have the time. The usual practice is to mix a batch and store the bottle in the fridge to extend its shelf life. Mix your own rather than buy a commercially-blended garam masala (page 37).

Ginger *(Zingiber officinale)*
This best-known member of the ginger family can now be found in supermarkets all over the world. It is an essential ingredient in the cooking of almost every part of Asia where the fresh root is used and dried powdered ginger unheard of. This versatile root

herb can be used in both sweet and savoury preparations. Ginger is sold as old or young ginger, the latter having a very mild flavour, pale yellow-pink rhizomes and very thin skin. Old ginger has a pronounced brown-beige skin, a stronger, spicier flavour and is more fibrous than young ginger, which is often pickled and used as a condiment. In Chinese cooking, ginger is usually chopped, slivered, sliced finely or used whole. In South East Asian cooking, it is often ground into the spice paste.

Herbs
A variety of fresh herbs are essential in South East Asian noodle dishes and for which there are no substitutes. Indo-Chinese noodle dishes are particularly rich in fresh herbs which are eaten raw in garnishes or chopped or crushed and added at the end of cooking. Look for them in Asian stores that are patronised by South East Asian communities. Some such as basil, *laksa* leaf, mint and Chinese celery are easy to re-sprout. For Chinese celery, keep the root stock and part of the stem above. Stand in a fresh change of water daily until young leaves appear, then plant in a tall pot set in a warm, fairly sunny spot. Cut off the older leaves for use. To re-sprout *laksa* leaves, mint or basil, stand older stalks of the herb in a jar of water that is changed daily until roots appear on the stem nodes. Plant in a pot and set in a sunny spot.

Mint *(Mentha piperita)*
There are several varieties of mint, the most popular of which are spearmint and peppermint. Fresh mint is essential in several South East Asian noodle dishes but happily, it is also easy to find in many supermarkets around the world. It grows easily from stem cuttings.

Kaffir lime *(Citrus hystric D.C.)*
Known also as *makrut* lime or *limau perut* in Malay and "leprous lime" in Chinese (because of the knobbly fruit), the peel of its fruit and leaves are used for their incredible fragrance. Found and used all over South East Asia but particularly in Thailand, Cambodia, Indonesia, Singapore and Malaysia, the leaves are crushed, the rind of the knobbly fruit chopped finely, and added to curries. The fruit itself has

almost no juice and only the peel is used. Lime or lemon leaves are poor substitutes.

Kimchi
The Korean national dish, kimchi is a fermented vegetable relish made with Tientsin cabbage. Fermentation gives the pickle its sourness, and chillies, garlic and ginger add zing. Kimchi goes particularly well with Korean and Japanese noodles. The strongly-flavoured, spicy red kimchi exported all over the world is winter kimchi. It is traditionally pickled at the start of autumn in September for consumption during the winter months. Summer kimchi is not fermented and is more like a light vinegared salad.

Konbu *(Laminaria japonica)*
Known also as kelp, this thick-fleshed dried seaweed is essential in making the Japanese stock, dashi. The thicker the seaweed, the better the quality. Konbu should not be rinsed in water but wiped clean before cooking. It is rich in glutamic acid which is what gives seaweed stock its flavour. Ubiquitous monosodium glutamate was first extracted from konbu.

Krachai *(Boesenbergia pandurata, B. rotunda, Kaempferia pandurata)*
Also known as Chinese keys and often mistaken for lesser galangal, this member of the ginger family is characterised by its many fingers growing out of a small rhizome. The fingers are thin and pale brown while the mother rhizome is dark and round, resembling the lesser galangal. Although members of the same ginger family, the two herb roots are different and have a different flavour. *Krachai* is widely used in Thai cooking, often with seafood. Look for it in Asian stores with strong Indo-Chinese patronage where the root may be found pickled in brine or dried. They could be labelled *kachai* or (wrongly) as lesser galangal.

Laksa leaf *(Pericaria odorata, syn. Polygonum odoratum)*
This herb is so associated with *laksa* that it is known in Malaysia and Singapore as *laksa* leaf. It is also used in Indo-Chinese cooking where it is known as Vietnamese mint, Cambodian mint and hot mint. However, it is not part of the mint

However, it is not part of the mint family. The herb is eaten raw in salads and noodle dishes and also cooked in the gravies of Penang and Singapore *laksa*. It is known as *daun kesom* in Malay.

Laver *(Nori) (Pophyra tenera, P. umbilicalis)*

Known also as nori in Japan and *keem* in Korea, this paper-thin toasted seaweed is used in Korean and Japanese cooking. It is sold in various forms, from powder as a condiment, to strips for adding to soups and large sheets for sushi-making. Prepared nori sheets are oiled and toasted and may taste rancid if not fresh. If available, buy unprepared nori sheets and toast when needed. Simply brush each sheet lightly with sesame oil and toast under a hot grill.

Lemongrass *(Cymbopogon citratus)*

This tropical grass is an essential root herb in South East Asian cuisines. The most fragrant and edible part is the thick bulbous base near the woody root. Known as *serai* in Malay and *sereh* in Indonesian, lemongrass is increasingly available fresh in western supermarkets as well as Asian stores in areas where there are large communities of South East Asians. Lemongrass can also be found in powdered dried form although there is nothing like fresh lemongrass. Ground fresh lemongrass freezes well. So if fresh lemongrass appears at farmers' markets near you, buy them up, grind to a paste and freeze. Whole lemongrass can also be frozen in a plastic bag. To prepare lemongrass, discard all but the 12-cm (5-in) from the woody root. Using a sharp knife, slice the bulb thinly before blending with other ingredients in a blender. Lemongrass must be sliced thinly before processing as the fine hair-like fibres are not easy to grind up. Lemongrass is sometimes used whole, in which case, the bulbous end is bruised first to release its fragrance.

Lettuce *(Lactuca sativa)*

The kind of lettuce used in noodle dishes in South East Asia is a frilly loose-leaf variety that has very little crispness or flavour. It is used as a garnish in noodle soups as well as dry noodles. Substitute with iceberg or romaine lettuce.

Limes

The limes referred to in these recipes are calamansi *(Citrus mitis var. microcarpa)*, a native of the Philippines but now found all over South East Asia. Also known as musk lime, *limau kasturi* in Malay, and *ma nao wan* in Thai, calamansi are small, thin-skinned, juicy and very sour even when ripe. These limes are a standard garnish in numerous South East Asian noodle dishes from fried to soupy ones.

Another lime found in South East Asian wet markets is the larger green lime *(Citrus aurantifolia)*. It has a thick skin and white pulp and can sometimes be rather dry, but the peel and juice have a distinctive fragrance. It is often used in Thai salads because of the fragrance. It is also called *limau nipis* or *limau asam* in Malay. Substitute with yellow lemons if limes are not available.

Mirin

Usually labelled as "sweet cooking rice wine", mirin is an essential ingredient in many Japanese noodle dishes. If mirin cannot be found, look for Japanese sake and dilute it with sugar syrup and water to get an approximation of mirin.

Miso *see* Soybeans

Monosodium glutamate

This is an artificial protein salt that is used by many hawkers and Asian restaurants because a little pinch does wonders for the flavour of the dish. Also known as gourmet powder, MSG, and sometimes by brand names such as Aji-no-moto or Ve-tsin, this flavour enhancer is almost always over-used commercially. In the home kitchen, it can help lift the flavour of soups and stocks particularly if the stock is not rich enough. Rich stocks do not need MSG as they are already full of glutamic acid, the natural protein salt, from the bones and meat. Note that the operative ingredient in stock cubes is actually MSG.

Sugar is sometimes used as a substitute for MSG, but its sweetness is not the same as the meatiness of MSG. In fact, the Japanese insist that MSG is a taste all its own and have given it a special word—umami. In Japan, and some parts of South East Asia, it was once the custom to put

out a small dish of MSG crystals as a condiment much like salt or sugar.

In some people, MSG gives rise to a range of alarming symptoms collectively known as Chinese Restaurant Syndrome, consisting of headaches, heart palpitations, dizziness, tightness in the throat, thirst and several other allergic reactions. A common way to alleviate some of the symptoms is to down a caffeinated drink such as a cup of coffee, or avoid the restaurant altogether.

Mussels *(Fam. Mytilidae Perna viridis (Linnaeus); Mytilus smaragdinus; Mytilus viridis)*

Known as *kupang* in Malay and *tahong* or *amahong* in the Philippines, these mussels have a greenish-black shell and are a very popular seafood in South East Asia.

Mustard cabbage *(Brassica juncea var. rugosa)*

This particular mustard green has thick stems, relatively little leaf and is bitter. Sometimes just the stems are sold. The stems and leaves, if any, are usually blanched in boiling water before frying.

Oils

Lard is the traditional oil used in many Chinese and South East Asian noodle dishes because it is so flavourful. However, vegetable oils are increasingly replacing lard even in hawker noodle dishes, mainly because of the general international decline in the consumption of saturated fats such as lard in the developed world. When the recipes call for "cooking oil", it refers to the bland vegetable oils such as soy, corn, canola and safflower, but not peanut oil, unless specified. Olive oil is never used in Asian noodle dishes. Where the traditional flavour calls for lard, this particular oil has been specified. However, lard can be substituted with one of the bland vegetable oils. See page 45 for rendering lard.

Palm sugar

This is sugar from the sap of a variety of palm trees. The sap is boiled down to a moist heavy dark brown sugar that has a fragrance all its own. It is commonly used in South East and South Asian desserts and may be sold in cakes wrapped in palm leaves or in rolls of various sizes. In

Malaysia and Singapore, palm sugar is known as *gula melaka* because the best was supposed to come from this ancient town on the west coast of West Malaysia. Note that Indo-Chinese palm sugar is a pale gold colour.

Pork belly *see* Belly pork

Pork crackling

In the parts of Asia where the non-Muslim population is dominant, ready-fried pork crackling can be found easily. This crackling is either pounded fine or chopped and used as a garnish with noodle dishes.

Prawns (shrimps), dried

These are small whole prawns that have been salted and dried. They are usually shelled first but often bits of shells remain on the prawns. Dried prawns have to be soaked in water first to get rid of the salt and the bits of shells picked off. They are fairly easy to find in big Asian food stores. The flavour is strong and a little goes a long way.

Prawns (shrimps), fresh

Prawns are an important garnish in many Asian noodle dishes whether boiled or fried with the noodles. In South East Asia, prawns are usually sold whole in their shells complete with their heads. Select prawns that have their heads firmly attached to the body and without any pink discolouration in the head, which is usually a sign that the prawns are going off. Unshelled prawns freeze well. Outside Asia, look for whole prawns in the freezer section of big Asian stores.

Radish, white *(Raphanus sativus)*

The Chinese sometimes call white radish or daikon "white carrot" to distinguish it from the common "red" carrot. Chinese carrot cake (the one found in Singapore food centres as a savoury pan-fried dish) contains white radish, as does Singapore Chinese New Year raw fish salad, *yu sheng*, when the radish is eaten often in three ways: raw, sugared and pickled. There is a green variety that has a milder flavour. Radish makes good pickle. The Japanese eat it grated and raw as a condiment.

Rice flour

There are two kinds of rice flour, one ground from long grain rice, the other from glutinous rice. Long grain rice flour is the kind used in making rice noodles while glutinous rice flour is more often turned into sweets and desserts. Glutinous rice is also labelled as "sweet rice". The two flours are not interchangeable. Making rice flour is a tedious but not impossible task. Rice is soaked overnight, then ground with water to a very fine paste. The paste is then dried to obtain the flour.
In several parts of South East Asia, from the Philippines to Myanmar, roasted rice flour is used as a thickener for soups and stews. Rice is first dry-fried to a beige colour before it is pounded or ground to powder and mixed with water for use as a thickener. Packets of ready-fried rice flour can be found in stores selling Burmese, Indo-Chinese and Filipino food products. The flour has a pale beige tint and is a little more coarse than ordinary untoasted rice flour.

Pandan (Screwpine leaf) *(Pandunus latifolius, P. amaryllifolius)*

This leaf is used in savoury food as well as in desserts. The juice of the leaves is extracted to colour and flavour desserts, and *nasi lemak*, a Malay rice dish, is not the same without the fragrance of these leaves. *Pandan* leaves may sometimes be found in the freezer section of Asian stores specialising in South East Asian foodstuffs.

Sawtooth coriander (eryngo) *(Eryngium foetidum)*

Common in Indo-Chinese cooking, this herb is also known as sawtooth coriander because of the tiny barbs on the edge of the leaves. In Thailand, it is known as *pak chee farang* (foreign cilantro) and in Vietnam as *ngo gai*. It is also called Mexican cilantro or culantro. It is used both raw and cooked and in Vietnamese cooking is often one of the several herbs served up with noodle dishes among others.

Sesame *(Sesamum indicum)*

Sesame seeds come either black or white but white is more commonly used as black sesame seeds are mildly bitter when toasted. Sesame oil made from the seeds also come as either black sesame seed oil or white sesame seed oil with subtle differences in the fragrance. Sesame seeds and sesame oil are often essential ingredients in East Asian cooking. Sesame salt is a standard Korean and Japanese condiment for many dishes while sesame seeds are essential in the Japanese noodle condiment of *shichimi togarashi* (seven-flavour chilli).

Chinese sesame paste, which is made from toasted sesame seeds ground with sesame oil, cannot be substituted with tahini, the Middle Eastern sesame paste, as the taste is different. Chinese sesame paste also comes in either black or white and sometimes with chilli oil added. Large markets in cities in China have stalls where freshly-prepared sesame paste is sold. If unavailable, substitute with reconstituted sesame seed powder stirred together with sesame oil in the ratio 1:1. Sesame seed powder also comes in black or white. Alternatively, stir sesame oil into creamy peanut butter to get an approximate flavour and texture of sesame paste.

Shallots *(Allium ascalonicum)*

Similar in flavour to onions, shallots are smaller and ovoid rather than round and may come clustered together like garlic heads. Shallots are less juicy than onions and are easier to pound. They may also be sliced and fried for use as a garnish or to get shallot oil. Onions may substitute for shallots by weight in spice pastes. If onions are thinly sliced and browned in oil, the results will be close enough in flavour to fried shallots and shallot oil.

Shiitake mushrooms *(Lentinus edodes)*

When dried, shiitake mushrooms are more commonly known as dried Chinese mushrooms. With the dried variety, the woody stem is usually discarded and only the caps used. Fresh shiitake can sometimes replace dried shiitake although the flavour of dried shiitake is more intense. When making shiitake dashi however, only dried shiitake should be used. Dried shiitake comes in different sizes. The thicker, fleshier whole mushrooms are more expensive than the thinner, torn mushrooms. Shiitake mushrooms are widely used in East Asian cooking.

Soybeans *(Glycine max)*

Cultivated in China for thousands of years, soybeans are made into numerous ingredients that feature prominently in the cooking of Asia. Here is a list of some soybean products that an Asian noodle cook needs to know about.

• Soy sauce

Soy sauce is made by fermenting soybeans. There are two main kinds of soy sauces used in Asia—light and dark. Light soy sauce is the saltier of the two while dark soy sauce has caramel added to turn it black. Light soy sauce is used not only for its flavour but also in place of salt, while dark is used as a flavouring by itself as well as to colour food. Thus, only a small amount of dark soy sauce is used. The soy sauce sold in western supermarkets tends to be a blend of both dark and light. It is worth searching for light and dark soy sauce as they make a big difference to the flavours in many recipes. Japanese and Korean soy sauces also come in light and dark with basically the same flavours, although the salt content may vary.

Soy sauce may be flavoured with various ingredients so read ingredient labels before buying. The Chinese have a mushroom-flavoured soy sauce while the Japanese have *ponzu* which is soy sauce flavoured with lime or lemon juice. Some Japanese soy sauces are combined with mirin or other flavours. The Indonesians have *kicap manis* which is a heavily sugared dark soy sauce. A similar product is Chinese dark sweet sauce used in Singapore fried broad rice noodles (*char kuay tiao*). There is also a lighter coloured sweet soy sauce that is used as a dip for many fried foods as well as in the spring rolls sold in Singapore food centres.

• Bean curd

They come either firm or soft, the former used in braised dishes or deep-fried as a garnish, the latter put into soups.

• Bean curd skin

These are thin sheets of salted dried soybean milk skin used for wrapping rolls of meat and seafood or for turning into vegetarian delicacies such as "roast goose" or "roast duck".

• Bean curd sticks

These are unsalted sticks of dried thick soybean milk skin. They do not export well, as they require more care in handling to prevent them from crumbling to bits. The sticks are soaked in cold water and cut into half finger-lengths, then braised or put into soup. Being bland, they take on the flavours of the braising liquid while retaining much of their texture.

• Sweet bean curd

These are rectangular slices of sweetened dried bean curd. Unlike dried bean curd sticks, they should not be over-boiled as they break up. Sweet bean curd that still has its slightly chewy texture will also sometimes have a vague smoked flavour. It is usually cut into strips and deep-fried as a garnish or added to mixed vegetable dishes.

• Fermented soybeans

There are different kinds of fermented soybeans. Chinese fermented soybeans is known as *taucheo* (bean sauce) which comes as whole beans. Japanese fermented soybeans is known as miso which is available in different stages of fermentation from pale blonde to dark brown and mashed to a smooth paste. The darker the colour, the stronger the flavour and the more salty the miso. Medium-brown miso is practically identical in flavour to Chinese *taucheo* and one can substitute for the other. Because *taucheo* is whole beans, the beans need to be rinsed quickly and mashed before cooking. Bottled Chinese fermented soybeans keep for years without refrigeration, unlike miso which should be refrigerated after opening, but keeps well in the fridge. Korean fermented soybeans known as *toenjang* is made from the soybeans fermented for making soy sauce. The beans are then mashed with dried red chilli seeds and salt to a paste. It keeps well in the fridge. Substitute *toenjang* with Chinese chilli bean sauce or *taucheo* mashed with some chilli powder. Chinese *taucheo* is used in a number of Asian noodle dishes. Northern Chinese cooking uses chilli bean sauce that is spiced with chilli powder, rather like Korean *toenjang*.

In the highlands of Myanmar, fermented soybeans, *ponyegyi*, are dried and ground to powder, then used as a thickener and flavouring agent in various dishes. Outside of Myanmar, look for this powder in stores that specialise in Burmese food products. Substitute with finely mashed medium-aged Indonesian *tempeh*. In Indonesia, fermented soybeans is known as *tempeh* which also comes in various stages of fermentation. The longer the fermentation, the softer and more strong-smelling the *tempeh*. *Tempeh* is usually eaten deep-fried or in curries. Deep-fried *tempeh* makes a good garnish.

• Soybean puffs

These fried puffs may be sold on their own or stuffed with fish paste. They are often cooked in soups and curries to go with noodles.

Spring onion (scallion) *(Allium fistulosum)*

Also known as scallions, green onions or Welsh onions, this is probably the most common herb used in many parts of Asia, as a garnish in all sorts of dishes. Sold in bundles, spring onions are usually eaten raw although they are also tasty when fried as a vegetable with prawns and bean curd. In Thailand, fried rice and noodles often come served with raw spring onion. The Vietnamese make green onion oil by frying chopped green onions till fragrant. It is a mild version of shallot oil.

Starches

Cornflour (*Zea mays*) is the most common starch used for thickening in Chinese cooking. It mixes easily with water and thickens without lumps. However, it should be added right at the end of cooking and not be reheated or over-boiled as it breaks down easily. Cornflour is also called cornstarch or maize flour but note that Mexican maize flour (masa) is not the same as cornflour.

Other starches that may be found in a good Asian store are starches from water chestnut (*Eleocharis dulcis*), tapioca (*Manihot esculenta*), sweet potato (*Ipomoea batatas*), arrowroot (*Maranta arundinacea*) and kudzu (*Pueraria thunbergiana*). They range from cheap to expensive and vary in their binding properties and stability. Experiment. Tapioca starch is made into noodles that resemble mung bean noodles.

Sweet potato *(Ipomoea batatas)*
Sometimes called yams in the United States, boiled sweet potatoes are used as a thickener in Malay *mee rebus*. Sweet potato starch is made into a springy noodle that resembles mung bean noodles in texture but not appearance, sweet potato noodles being a translucent grey. Sweet potato starch can be used as a thickener in place of cornflour.

Tamarind *(Tamarindus Indica)*
Called *asam jawa* or just *asam*, the fleshy fruit of the tamarind tree can commonly be found packed for sale without their pods. Tamarind pulp turns darker with age but remains edible. It stores well without refrigeration.

To prepare, soak the pulp in water, then strain and use the liquid. Discard the bottom 1 cm ($^1/_2$ in) of liquid as there may be grit in the pulp. Tamarind juice is used in many South East Asian curries as both a souring agent and thickener. It is milder than dried sour fruit *(asam gelugor)*. If a more sour flavour is desired, add a few slices of dried sour fruit.

Taucheo *see* **Soybeans, fermented soybeans**

Tientsin cabbage *(Brassica Pekinensis var. cylindrica)*
A north Asian native, Tientsin cabbage is also known as Peking cabbage, celery cabbage and long white cabbage. It is widely used in northern Asia. In Korea, Tientsin cabbage is made into winter kimchi. The chopped leafy portions are also pickled in salt and sold as *tang chye* (Hokkien). *Tang chye* is a traditional garnish for Chinese noodle soups.

Torch ginger bud *(Zingiberaceae Phaeomeria speciosa Koord/ Nicolaia speciosa)*
Also known as *bunga kantan* or *bunga siantan* in Malay, this bud of the torch ginger grows out from the base of the tall herbaceous perennial plant. The flower buds, fruit and leaves are all edible. The chopped flower bud goes into salads and soups.

Turmeric *(Curcuma longa)*
A member of the ginger family, turmeric is a common root herb in South and South East Asia and the Himalayan regions. The Singapore Chinese call it "yellow ginger"; and to the Malays, it is simply *"kunyit"* meaning yellow, an indication of its strong yellow colour and its possible use as a dye. Turmeric comes whole, fresh or dried, as well as in powdered form. In parts of South East Asia, the leaves are also used as a herb. Dried turmeric is an ingredient in curry powders, while fresh turmeric is an important ingredient in many South East Asian curry pastes. When using fresh turmeric, pick old rhizomes—those with a darker brown-biege skin—because they have the best colour.

Note that ground turmeric is not a cheap substitute for saffron because turmeric does not have saffron's somewhat "iron-y" taste. While there are differences in the flavour of fresh and dried turmeric, it is not strong enough to justify going out in search of fresh turmeric if none is easily available. Ground turmeric will do. To prepare fresh turmeric, scrape the skin off with a sharp knife. Handle with gloves to avoid staining your hands. Turmeric stains do not burn but they do last for days. Hence take care with clothing, as turmeric stains are removable only with strong bleach.

Vinegar
Vinegar as a souring agent is more common in East Asia than in South East Asia where limes are plentiful and tamarind more widely used. Vinegar is made from all kinds of grains and fruit but the two kinds used in these recipes are either white or black rice vinegar. The preferred vinegar for noodle dishes needing black vinegar is Chinkiang vinegar from Zhejiang on the northern coast of China. Chinkiang vinegar is made from glutinous rice and malt. Some Chinese black vinegars, as with Japanese "seasoned vinegar", have sugar added. Chinese white rice vinegar, however, usually comes plain.

Wasabi *(Wasabia japonica, Eutrema japonica)*
Wasabi is a rhizome with a brown-yellow skin, green-yellow flesh and a fragrance and heat that combines well with seafood. It is usually grated just before use to retain its volatile fragrance and flavour. The plant is difficult to grow, making wasabi a very expensive ingredient. What is sold as wasabi paste or powder is actually horseradish that has been coloured to mimic true wasabi's greenish tint. Mustard is sometimes added to reproduce wasabi's complex spiciness.

Water Convolvulus *(Ipomoea aquatica)*
This iron-rich vegetable is also called water morning glory, water spinach, swamp cabbage or *kang kong* in Singapore and Malaysia. It is a member of the same family as the climbing morning glory found in most parts of South East Asia. Two types of water convolvulus are found in South East Asian markets. One has larger leaves and thicker stems while the other is a smaller, shorter plant with slender stems and leaves. The latter is more tender and easier to prepare.

Water convolvulus does not store well in the fridge and should be used the day of purchase or not more than a couple of days after.

Watercress *(Rorippa nasturtium aquaticum)*
Originally a native of Europe, peppery watercress is usually added to Chinese soups and is one of the ingredients of Korean kimchi. Watercress does not keep well and should be used the day of purchase. The lower stems are tough. Use the leaves and tender upper stems.

Yamaimo *(Dioscorea batatas, dioscorea opposita)*
This is a range of various East Asian yams with a similar texture and flavour but different shapes. One type is a long, tubular root that either comes brown or beige-coloured. Another is flattish and irregularly shaped. All have tiny dark brown spots and scattered hairs on the skin. The Chinese use the yams for medicinal purposes while the Japanese eat it either raw or cooked. Eating raw yam can cause severe allergic reactions due to the calcium oxalate crystals in the tuber. The stickiness of mountain yam makes it an essential ingredient in Japanese buckwheat noodles.

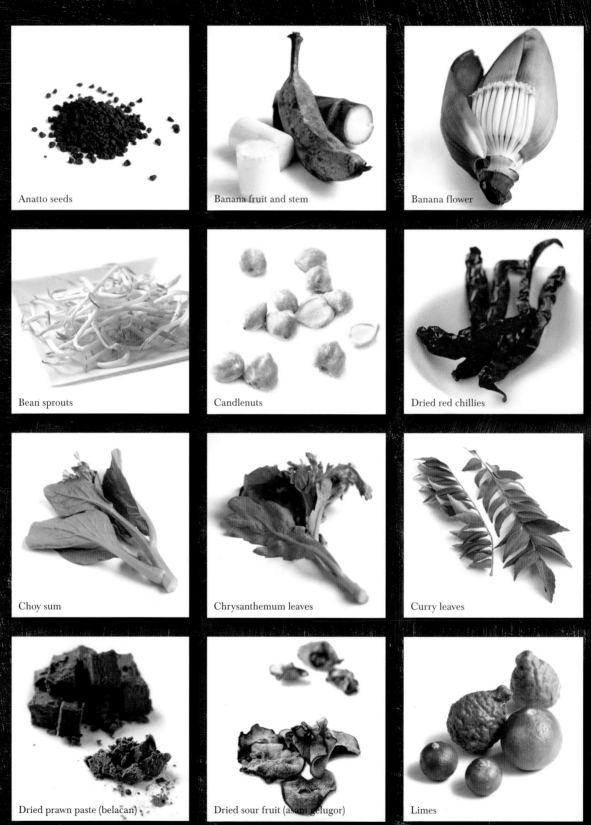

Anatto seeds

Banana fruit and stem

Banana flower

Bean sprouts

Candlenuts

Dried red chillies

Choy sum

Chrysanthemum leaves

Curry leaves

Dried prawn paste (belacan)

Dried sour fruit (asam gelugor)

Limes

Galangal, lesser

Laska leaves

Lemongrass

Palm sugar

Prawns (shrimps), dried

Pandan leaves

Sawtooth coriander

Tamarind paste

Tientsin cabbage, salted

Torch ginger bud

Turmeric

Yamaimo

Noodle Recipes by Country

Bibliography

Alejandro, Reynaldo. *The Philippine Cookbook*. New York, Coward-McCann, 1982.

Andoh, Elizabeth. *At Home with Japanese Cooking*. New York, Alfred A. Knopf, 1980.

Burum, Linda. *Asian Pasta*. Berkeley, CA, Aris Books, 1985.

Davidson, Alan. *Seafood of South-east Asia*. Singapore, Federal Publications, 1976.

Dayrit, Pat Limjuco. *Favorite Filipino Recipes*. Manila, Tradewinds, 1975.

Dekura, Hideo. *The Fine Art of Japanese Cooking*. Sydney, Bay Books, [c.1974?]

Fu Pei-Mei. *Pei-Mei's Chinese Cook Book*. [Taipei, ?, ?]

Handy, Ellice. *My Favourite Recipes*. 2nd ed. Singapore, M.P.H., 1960.

Hom, Ken. *Fragrant Harbour Taste: The New Chinese Cooking of Hong Kong*. London, Bantam Press, 1991.

Homma, Gaku. *The Folk Art of Japanese Country Cooking: A Traditional Diet For Today's World*. Berkeley, CA, North Atlantic Books, 1991.

Hutton, Wendy. *Thai Food*. Singapore, Landmark Books, 1991.

Jacquat, Christiane. *Plants From the Markets of Thailand*. Bangkok, Editions Duang Kamol, 1990.

Kongpan, Sisamon. *The Best of Thai Cuisine*. Bangkok, Sangdad, 1988.

Kittakara, M.L. Taw, and Amranand, M.R. Pimsai. *Modern Thai Cooking*. Bangkok, Editions Duang Kamol, 1977.

Lee Chin Koon, Mrs. *Mrs Lee's Cookbook*. Singapore, self-published, 1974.

Majupuria, Indra. *Joys of Nepalese Cooking*. Lashkar, S. Devi, 1988.

Mi Mi Khaing. *Cook and Entertain the Burmese Way*. [Yangon, ?, ?]

Miller, Jill Nhu Huong. *Vietnamese Cookery*. Rutland, VT., Charles E. Tuttle, 1968.

Noh Chin-hwa. *Practical Korean Cooking*. Elizabeth, NJ, Hollym International Corp., 1985.

Noh Chin-hwa. *Traditional Korean Cooking*. Elizabeth, NJ, Hollym International Corp., 1985.

Nguyen, Andre and Moriyama, Yukiko. *Vietnamese Home Cooking For Everyone*. Tokyo, Joie., 2001.

Singapore. Primary Production Dept./Marine Fisheries Research Dept. *A Colour Guide to the Fishes of the South China Sea and the Andaman Sea*. Singapore, 1982.

Our Favourite Recipes: Meals From Asian Kitchens. Published in celebration of the centenary of the Methodist Girls's School. Singapore, Landmark Books, 1987.

Phia Sing. *Traditional Recipes of Laos*. Translated by Phouangphet Vannithone and Boon Song Klausner and edited by Alan and Jennifer Davidson. London, Prospect Books, 1981.

Reifenberg, Gabriele. *Ladakhi Kitchen*. Leh, Melong Publications of Ladakh, 1998.

Solomon, Charmaine. *Encyclopaedia of Asian Food*. Singapore, Periplus Editions (HK), 1998.

Tan, Cecilia. *Penang Nonya Cooking*. Petaling Jaya, Eastern Universities Press, 1983.

Tannahill, Reay. *Food in History*. New York, Stein and Day, 1973.

Tham Yu Kai. *Cookery by Tham Yu Kai*. [Singapore, Tham Yu Kai, 1973]

Wandee Na Songkhla. *Royal Thai Cuisne* (sic) *Book 1*. From *Karb Hea Chom Kreaung Kaow Wan of King Rama the Second* (The Royal Poems Praising Foods and Desserts Written by King Rama the Second). [Bangkok, ?, ?]

Win, Daw Ena. *Myanmar Cook Book*. [Yangon], U. Tin Ong, 1999.

Winodan, Dershini Govin. *Indian Food Today*. Singapore, Landmark Books, 1990.

Tropical Vegetables of Malaysia & Singapore. Text and recipes by Wendy Hutton. (Singapore), Periplus Editions (HK), 1996.

Yeap Joo Kim. *The Penang Palate*. Penang, self-published, 1990.

Yew, Betty. *Asian Delights*. Singapore, Times Books International, 1989.

http://www.khmerkromrecipes.com